LAW DOGS

GREAT COPS IN AMERICAN HISTORY

LT. DAN MARCOU

T0159385

Thunder Bay Press

Law Dogs
by Lt. Daniel Marcou

© 2015 Lt. Daniel Marcou
All rights reserved.

Thunder Bay Press, Holt, MI 48842
www.thunderbaypressmi.com

First Printing, September 2015

20   19   18   17   2   3   4   5

ISBN: 978-1-933272-52-8
Library of Congress Control Number: 2015930377

Book and cover design by Julie Taylor.

Printed in the United States of America.

Dedicated to the 100,000 men and women whose names are etched upon the wall of the Law Enforcement Memorial.

They wore their uniform with pride, and in that uniform they died.

TABLE OF CONTENTS

PREFACE

In the pages that follow you will find stories as true as possible considering some of these law officers' lives have been lionized and their stories have been distorted to such a degree that it is difficult to know what is truth and what is fiction. I have tried to distinguish the difference and let readers know an imperfect, but credible, version of the truth.

One thing I noticed while researching this book was the dizzying variety of ways one person's name could be spelled in a lifetime. For example, Wild Bill Hickok was Jim Hickok, James Butler Hickok, "Duckbill" Hickok, "Wild Bill" Hickok, and even Haycock at varying times during his life.

This story contains individuals whose names were spelled differently throughout their lives due to personal preference, illiteracy, and even the misspelling of storytellers and newspapers. Sometimes individuals changed names deliberately to establish an alias, to start a new life, or to conceal the mistakes of an old life. Therefore, I have tried to arrive at the most common spelling of many of these early heroes and villains, realizing other spellings may exist.

In choosing which stories to relate, I needed to include those famed lawmen whose legacies have been told many times. Therefore, you will have the opportunity to read about "Wild Bill" Hickok and the Earps. Their stories continue to be interesting, but in reading them you will note that their accomplishments pale in comparison to the careers of less famous law officers such as Frank Hamer and Bill Tilghman.

Discover why the Texas Rangers are so proud of their heritage. The Texas Rangers have the distinction of being the only law enforcement agency in the country that has served not only in a law enforcement role but also in war as a crack military unit. In both arenas they excelled and have been universally feared and respected by their foes.

Decide for yourself whether Bass Reeves, a former slave, was the inspiration for the story of the Lone Ranger. It is speculation to conclude that he was, but it is an absolute fact that his real life makes a better story than the Lone Ranger's fictional life. Reeves put over 3,000 of the most dangerous criminals behind bars. He was a legend in his own time.

Learn why the modern FBI was born in 1934 and discover what a truly painful birth it was. It was year filled with careening cars and chattering "Tommy Guns." These early agents experienced great triumphs but also suffered nearly unbearable tragedies.

Each chapter is a stand-alone read about a particular officer or group of officers. Some earned their place in this book because of an outstanding career, others due to their decisiveness during one incredible moment.

Women did not break into law enforcement until recent history, so there are only two stories about women law officers told here, but oh what stories they are!

There are even some chapters about citizens who quite famously came to the aid of law enforcement.

Now, I would like to introduce you to some of my heroes...
The Law Dogs!

ACKNOWLEDGMENTS

I would like to acknowledge the assistance I received from Professor Art Burton, Marcus Young, Stacy Lim, John Dodson, the family of Brian Terry, Dan Brooks, Frank Pobjecky, Justin Garner, The Texas Ranger Museum, the La Crosse County Historical Society, the Kansas State Historical Society, and the Oklahoma State Historical Society.

I would also like to thank my editor, Julie Taylor, who quite simply makes me a better writer, and Doug Wyllie and the readers of policeone.com, who have encouraged me to continue writing by reading my sincere scribblings.

PART ONE

THE WILD WEST

CHAPTER 1

JOHN "JACK" COFFEE HAYS, TEXAS RANGER

John "Jack" Coffee Hays was born on January 28, 1817, at Little Cedar Lick within Wilson County, Tennessee. He was the son of Elizabeth (Cage) Hays and Harmon Hays. Harmon Hays saw action serving with Andrew Jackson and Sam Houston while fighting the British during the War of 1812. Harmon named his son after his life-long friend, Colonel John Coffee.

In 1836 "Jack," at the age of nineteen, traveled to Texas to join its fight for independence against Mexico. Jack carried a letter of recommendation from his uncle, President Andrew Jackson. Sam Houston, who knew Jack's father well, assigned him with a group of Texas Rangers under the command of Erastus "Deaf" Smith.

Jack was immediately immersed in the horrors of war when his unit was tasked with burying the dead of Goliad. These Texans, after being cut-off and out-numbered, attempted to avoid the fate of the Alamo defenders by offering up their surrender.

Hays heard the story their death as well as their commander, Colonel James Fannin. Colonel Fannin was wounded in battle and eventually surrendered himself and his men to the mercy of Santa Anna.

Santa Anna was incapable of such mercy. Fannin was made to stand by and bear witness as each man in his command was executed. Colonel Fannin was executed last. Due to the severity of his wounds, he was carried before the firing squad in a chair. His last requests were:

1. To have a letter and his personal affects be sent to his wife.
2. To be shot in the heart.
3. To be given a Christian burial by his Christian enemies.

Instead, Fannin was shot in the face and his body was looted. With these indignities completed, his remains were ignominiously thrown onto the heap of his murdered soldiers, and all were set on fire. No words or blessing were said over their bodies.

This event convinced Jack Hays that the Republic he had traveled so far to help create would have something better to offer than the harsh brutality of Santa Anna's dictatorship.

When Jack's command won a sharp skirmish against the Mexicans, he personally captured the Mexican Commander Juan Sanchez who had been at the Alamo and Goliad. Instead of exacting revenge against Sanchez for the merciless killings of surrendered soldiers, Sergeant Hays treated Sanchez with the dignity and respect of a prisoner of war.

John Coffee Hays Texas Ranger

After Texas earned its freedom by defeating Santa Anna at the battle of San Jacinto, John "Jack" Coffee Hays joined the Texas Rangers. He intended to help tame the lawless land they had just won so that others might be able to live in peace in this new country called The Republic of Texas.

As he formed his new nation, Sam Houston realized the Texas Rangers were an inexpensive and efficient way to protect the frontier of his blossoming new nation. He officially formed them in 1841, and Hays was appointed a Captain. Hays promptly began forming and training his company.

Hays was a born leader. In a time filled with tough and courageous men, Hays became someone others wanted to follow and emulate. Hays rode and shot with the best of them and was always cool under fire. He also had a knack for training his men.

Early in his leadership role, Captain Hays showed foresight by recognizing the advantage of having superior firepower over opponents. In a truly historic move, Captain Hays arranged for each of the Rangers in his command to replace their heavy single-shot horse pistols with two fast firing, .36 caliber Colt Paterson #5 revolvers. These weapons fired five rounds each before needing to be reloaded.

Hays took the time to train his Rangers so they could hit with every shot they fired while on horseback. The Rangers came to handle these weapons like they were an extension of themselves. Although the weapons showed promise during training, they had yet to be tested in an actual combat situation against one of the most skilled light cavalry in the world, the Comanche Warriors.

Battle of Walker Creek

By the time Hays and his troop hit the trail, pursuing the warring Comanche in 1844, they could ride, shoot, and fight as one cohesive unit. The Comanche they were following were raiding and killing throughout what was called the Texas Comancheria.

Hot on the trail of the Comanche, Hays made camp next to Walker's Creek. On June 8, 1844, one of Hays' Rangers climbed a tree to get some honey from a beehive. The higher vantage point provided a view of impending danger. He spotted about eighty Comanche warriors riding hard and fast toward their camp. With honey bucket still in hand, this Ranger shouted a timely warning and spoiled their surprise. He loudly declared, "Captain! Yonder comes a thousand Indians." In a company of sixteen Rangers, eighty Comanche must have looked like "a thousand."

Captain Hays formed a plan instantly. He realized the Comanche were charging to trigger and absorb a one-shot volley, then overwhelm and kill every one of the Rangers before they could reload. Captain Hays had a surprise of his own prepared for the Comanche.

Hays had his men mount and form up as he gave them their orders. "They're fixin' to charge us, boys, and we must charge them first." He added, "Don't fire until we're among them."

After those simple instructions, he shouted, "Charge!" Hays' voice thundered sparking a lightning bolt of courage through the spine of every Ranger as they made their advance. Not one of them faltered. As the Rangers neared their adversaries, Captain Hays fiercely growled out one last directive, "Crowd them! Powder-burn them, boys!"

Captain Hays' and his men cut into the surprised Comanche and leveled deadly fire nearly point blank into the faces of the Comanche. It seemed as if one Comanche fell off a horse for each shot that was fired. One of the Comanche survivors later described the reason for their decisive loss that day. He said each Ranger "had a shot for every finger on the hand."

The Rangers' fire appeared unending to the Comanche because the Rangers had practiced quickly exchanging their expended cylinders with extra pre-loaded cylinders while on horseback. The shocked Comanche turned to flee from the withering fire, but the Rangers would not let up. They pressed forward until all the Comanche ran, then pursued them relentlessly. The Comanche ranks gradually melted away in the heat of the .36 caliber inferno.

Their courageous leader, Chief Yellow Wolf, would not abide such a rout. In desperation he tried to rally his fleeing band of raiders for a counterattack, but Hays' keen eye spotted Yellow Wolf. Hays was in the midst of a reload, so he shouted, "Any man with a load left, kill that chief!"

Texas Ranger Robert Gillespie heard the command and answered it with an unintelligible growl. Gritting his teeth, he spurred his mount forward. While on the run he took careful aim at Chief Yellow Wolf and fired. Gillespie's bullet found its mark. Yellow Wolf's limp body slid from his pony. He died as he would have wished, a warrior bravely fighting to hold on to a way of life.

In spite of being outnumbered four to one, the Rangers handed these skilled warriors a decisive defeat. Not long after the Battle of Walker's Creek, the Colt Revolver became known as "The Great Equalizer."

Colt Revolvers may have made the Rangers equal to the Comanches that day, but having Captain Jack Coffee Hays leading these Rangers made them indomitable. Jack Hays was the first to see the value of arming fighting men with this weapon.

The War with Mexico

The Texas Rangers are the only "civilian" law enforcement agency which also has a rich and colorful military tradition.

During the Mexican-American War, Colonel Jack Hays commanded the First Regiment, Texas Mounted Riflemen, which served with General Zachary Taylor. It was during this time that Hays breathed a tradition of excellence into the Rangers which still exists to this day. Hays led his men into battle at Veracruz, Palo Alto, Resaca de la Palma, and Buena Vista.

During this war Hays and his Rangers waged a relentless war against the Mexican Guerillas. Out of fear, respect, and hatred, the Guerillas called the Rangers "Los Diablos Tejanos," the Texan Devils.

At the war's end, Hays and his beloved Texas Rangers were legends nation-wide. From their ranks rose some of the most famous Texas Rangers ever: Sam Walker (see chapter two), Captains Ben and Henry McCulloch, W. A. A. "Big Foot" Wallace, and Robert Addison "Ad" Gillespie.

Sheriff Hays

In 1850 Hays left the Rangers and moved to San Francisco to become the first elected sheriff in this lawless town. It was not uncommon for a man to leave a home in the East bound for San Francisco and never be heard from again. San Francisco was a wild, lawless city filled with danger and corruption.

Upon his arrival, Sheriff Hays discovered that the good citizens had formed a Committee of Vigilance because they felt the criminal element was so out of control in their city. These vigilantes were taking part in extra-judicial hangings.

Hays sought to establish the sheriff's department as the law and immediately began building a new jail. In a surprise move, he also raided the headquarters of the Committee of Vigilance rescuing two ruthless killers, Robert McKenzie and Samuel Whittaker, from the noose. He placed them in his jail to await a legal trial.

Even though it was quite possible Hays had only changed the location of their demise, Hays believed he had succeeded in insuring the criminal justice system would administer justice. Now that he was Sheriff, there would be rule of law rather than mob rule. He felt this raid was a critical step toward making San Francisco a safe place to raise a family.

As it turns out, Hays counted his criminals before they were hanged.

Four days after the raid, Hays was lured away from the jail to watch a bull fight. While Hays was away, the Committee of Vigilance raided the jail, acquired the prisoners, and summarily lynched them.

On one hand, Sheriff Hays was outraged. On the other, he was keenly aware that this situation existed because there had been an absence of justice. He surmised that the good citizens of San Francisco had to be served an example of the triumph of justice before they would trust him. Hays prioritized the completion of the new sheriff's department and jail.

Once the jail was completed, it served as tangible evidence of the criminal justice system. Now all they needed was an example of that system working.

After a high profile trial in December of 1852, Jose Fomer was convicted of murder and sentenced to hang by the neck until dead.

As usual during these days, a large crowd gathered on the appointed execution day. As the clock ticked down toward Fomer's hour of judgment, Sheriff Hays stood on the scaffold he had helped build. Hays read the order for execution. He placed the noose around the convicted killer's neck. Then he picked up an ax and personally cut the rope, releasing the hatch, which dropped the thirty-two-year-old Jose Fomer to either his eternal punishment or reward.

A sudden hush came over the crowd. After a time they slowly walked away, having finally witnessed tangible proof that the law had come to San Francisco. Here was a murderer caught and effectively held by the sheriff and tried by a functioning court of law. This sheriff was susceptible to neither bribery nor intimidation.

In the end Hays instilled the belief that not only had the law arrived in San Francisco, but the law was here to stay.

Hays Last Battle

With the sheriff's department built and the rule of law established in San Francisco, Hays took a job as a surveyor. Unknown to most, being a lawman was not Hays' life ambition. He was a trained and highly skilled surveyor. What had continually kept him from his chosen profession was the indisputable fact that the nation's lands, which needed to be surveyed, first had to be tamed, and Hays had the skills to tame them.

After serving his term as surveyor, Hays went into Real Estate and became one of the principal founders of Oakland, California. It was his intent to live the rest of his life peacefully in Oakland; however, this was not to be. Hays would be needed again.

The Battle of Pyramid Lake

In May of 1860, Williams Station, a combination Stagecoach Station, Saloon, and General Store, was raided by Paiutes. This raid, which the Paiutes claim was retaliatory, took three lives. One potential victim escaped and spread word of the raid.

A volunteer militia consisting of 105 men was formed, and was commanded by Major William Ormsby. This angry armed mob set off, intent on apprehending the perpetrators of the raid.

As the contingent arrived at Pyramid Lake, they were met by a small band of well-fortified Paiutes who fired on the militia. After a brief exchange, the Indians fled, and the untrained militia pursued them. The small group of decoy Paiutes led the militia into a ravine where an estimated 200-300 Paiutes were strategically placed and waiting. As Ormsby's men entered the ravine, the Paiutes closed a trap on them.

The Paiute warriors led by Chief Numaga killed seventy-six militia members and wounded many others. Survivors of the battle barely escaped with their lives. They revealed their breathlessly-told tale to anyone who would listen that the Paiutes pursued them for twenty miles after they fled the battlefield. Paiute casualties were not counted but said to be minimal.

John Coffee Hays was famous for his exploits and was undoubtedly the most experienced "Indian Fighter" in California. He was asked to command a force that would re-engage the Paiutes. He could hardly say no to his friends and neighbors. He was needed.

Hays raised and organized the Washoe regiment, a group of American Regulars combined with citizen soldiers. Hays' presence made the regiment supremely confident in their ability to confront the warring Paiutes. He insisted on training them before the met the Paiutes again.

In late June Hays and his regiment moved into the Pyramid Lake region. Here they also met Chief Numaga in battle. Clearly, Hays was not Ormsby. The Paiute Chief Numaga was soundly defeated. It is estimated that 160 of his Paiute Warriors died in the fight while the Washoe Regiment lost four of their own.

Hays would be called upon to serve yet one more time.

The Civil War

Less than a year after the Second Battle of Pyramid Lake, the United States of America divided as never before, or since. It was at war with itself.

As hostilities broke out, both the North and the South were looking for experienced leaders. Many men who had served as lieutenants in the War with Mexico would serve as generals in the War Between the States.

Captain Hays, a well-known hero in both the North and South, was offered a command by the Union and the Confederacy. Hays had a problem. He had raised his hand and sworn an oath of allegiance to the Republic of Texas and the United States of America. It seemed that he would have to violate one of these oaths to take up arms in this conflict.

His beloved Texas had seceded from the Union, and many of his Texas Rangers would be fighting for the South. He concluded he could never bear arms against Texans wearing the Lone Star.

He also had also fought and bled for the Stars and Stripes, and he could not in good conscience fire upon a soldier carrying the flag he loved so dearly and would still die for.

Hays, as decisive as ever, declared that they were all his countrymen. He reckoned the two sides could decide the issue without him. They did, but not before 600,000 Americans died in the heated discussion that followed.

Hays chose to stay in California and help give birth to a new state, for the second time in his life. After Pyramid Lake, Hays never again wore a star or fired a gun in combat again.

The Curtain Closes

In times of need, this country has given birth to leaders who manage to combine innovation and inspiration to achieve great things. John Coffee Hays, without formal training, developed tactical combat concepts that are still used today. Hays' philosophy of giving men superior weapons, training them well, and utilizing speed and audacity on the battlefield would be adopted later by another Californian, George Patton.

Hays' legacy is felt today in Texas as well as California. Hays' impact on this nation's history is incalculable. He triumphed as a soldier, a peace officer, a leader of men, and, in quite a remarkable contrast, as a city planner.

John "Jack" Coffee Hays set out as a young man intent on surveying the West, and he ended up being one of the most memorable men who tamed it. Hays died peacefully in his estate in Oakland Hills, California, in 1883.

Hays succeeded in so many things in life, but history shall forever remember him wearing his hat with one brim folded up on the left side, a star on his chest, a pistol in each hand, and reins in his teeth galloping outnumbered into a murderous horde with guns blazing.

He will always be remembered as the audacious Captain John "Jack" Coffee Hays, Texas Ranger.

CHAPTER 2

SAMUEL WALKER, THE REAL WALKER TEXAS RANGER

One can hardly discuss the importance of John "Jack" Coffee Hays to the Texas Rangers without mentioning Samuel Walker. Hays was Walker's commander, and they shared many trails and faced many adversaries together. Each became legends in their own time, on their own terms, in their own way.

Samuel Walker was an intellectual and a brilliant military leader. He was an innovative armorer. He helped give the Texas Rangers their mystique.

Maybe he had to do so much so quickly because he sensed that he was not destined to live a long life. Clairvoyance wasn't needed to come to this conclusion. It was ever in his nature to be at the front of every charge and in the middle of every fight. This trait would define his life as well as end it.

Sam Walker's Early Years

Walker's early life is a bit of a mystery. He was born in either 1815 or 1817 in Prince George's County, Maryland. He had a well-educated bearing, most probably from his time in Washington where he spent four years in his late teens. Then Sam enlisted in the army to fight against the Seminoles.

Sam Walker excelled in combat under the command of Zachary Taylor while fighting Chief Osceola in the unforgiving everglades of Florida. Walker was promoted to Corporal after the Battle of Hatchee-Lustee, in January 1837, by showing "exceptional courage" in the uniquely deadly conditions of that war.

In 1838 Sam mustered out of the army and worked railroad construction for several years throughout the South. Building railroads was satisfying work, but Sam Walker had tasted a more exciting life and longed for it once again. The restless young man traveled to Texas.

Texas Rangers

In January 1842 Walker joined the Texas Rangers. He served in the company of Captain John "Jack" Coffee Hays (see chapter one). During the days after the Texas Revolution, peacekeeping for the Rangers looked more like a military operation then a modern law enforcement endeavor. The Texas Rangers were indeed "rangers." They ranged across wide swaths of territory and fought with raiding Mexican Bandits, Texas Bandits, and Mexican Soldiers. They also fought with the Comanche, who were fighting against the encroachment of Texans and Mexicans alike.

The border between Mexico and Texas was in dispute from day one of the life of the Republic of Texas. In 1842, the smoldering conflict between the antagonistic neighbors boiled over.

Santa Anna was never satisfied that he had been forced to give up so much territory under duress after the battle of San Jacinto. In March 1842 he authorized Rafael Vasquez to invade Texas. Vasquez raided San Antonio, plundered it, and almost immediately returned to Mexico unmolested.

President Sam Houston's leadership was all that kept an all-out war from breaking out after the incursion. Houston did not want another war. President Houston calmed the citizens of Texas and convinced his fellow Texans to forgive, but remember.

Texans did not have to remember long. In September of 1842, a Frenchman named Adrian Woll led another Mexican Army into Texas. He attacked and occupied San Antonio for ten days. Sam Houston called upon Texas volunteers who came forward to answer this outrage. Houston placed Alexander Somervell at the head of this quickly-formed Texan Army.

The Texas Rangers, including Sam Walker and Jack Coffee Hays, were blended into Somervell's army. The army fought repeated skirmishes as it forced Woll's men back into Mexico. Somervell perceived that the cork was back in the bottle with the invaders back on their own side of the border. On December 18, 1842, Somervell declared the fighting successful and over. He refused to pursue the invaders across the border.

This did not set well with everyone in his command. One hundred eighty-nine of his Texans were tired of the deadly incursions and wished to continue the pursuit into Mexico. These angry men elected William Fisher their commander, and Sam Walker joined them. Somervell warned these Texans against taking any foolhardy actions and refused to join them.

On December 23, Fisher's Texans invaded Mexico and occupied Meir just across the Rio Grande. They captured supplies and quickly returned across the border to Texas.

On Christmas Day, the Texans under Fisher received information that a 700-man Mexican Army had come to the aid of Meir and was now occupying it. Although vastly out-numbered, Fisher's Texans re-crossed the border and attacked, but this proved to be a miscalculation. The Texans were forced to surrender.

The White Bean

Sam Walker was actually captured before the attack while part of a scouting expedition. He marched along with his 175 companions into captivity. On March 1, 1843, Santa Anna ordered the execution of all 176 Texans. Governor Mexia refused to obey the outrageous order, believing to obey such an order would commit his soul to Hell.

Instead of execution, the Texans were marched to Rancho Salado, where another order from Santa Anna was awaiting their arrival. There was no Governor Mexia to protect the Texans here; however, Santa Anna modified his order, demanding every tenth man be executed.

Each of the Texan prisoners was required to reach into a jar containing 176 beans. Most of the beans were white, but every tenth bean was black. Anyone picking a black bean was summarily executed.

As Sam Walker's turn came, he picked a white bean. He was made to stand by helplessly and watch as his friends were gunned down.

Commander Fisher managed to pick a white bean, but his fate was already sealed. The elected leader of this failed raid was executed.

Escape and Return to the Rangers

While in custody, the Texans were repeatedly beaten and enslaved. They were required to work, sometimes unto their death. Walker waited for an opportunity, and on July 30, 1843, he escaped from his captors. He managed to make his way to the Gulf of Mexico and sneak aboard a ship bound for New Orleans. As soon as Walker arrived in the Crescent City, he worked his way back to Texas.

Sam rejoined the Texas Rangers and was welcomed back to his unit commanded by Hays. Walker took part in many fights with Hays, including the historically significant Battle of Walker Creek. Neither the creek nor the battle was named after Sam.

The Comanche charged, expecting to ride through one volley and subsequently overwhelm the vastly outnumbered Rangers. In prior fights the Comanche warriors could fire five or possibly six arrows before the Rangers could reload their single-shot weapons.

This was the first fight where the Rangers were armed with their new five-shot Colt Paterson revolvers. Each Ranger was armed with two of these devastating weapons plus pre-loaded cylinders that could be loaded into an empty revolver with relative ease.

Though the Rangers routed the Comanche in this battle, Walker was wounded.

After the "Battle of Walker Creek," Walker was wounded repeatedly thereafter. Some men cautioned others in jest to stay clear of Walker. He was wounded so often he was dubbed "Unlucky Walker."

In one moment of combat with a Comanche, Walker took a warrior's lance in the side. The Comanche who delivered the wound fared worse. Each time Walker was wounded, he would recover and climb back into the saddle to rejoin his brother Rangers, undeterred.

Walker made no secret of the fact that he hoped to exact justice from the Mexican Army for the murder of his fellow Rangers at Rancho Salado and for his mistreatment as a prisoner of war. The opportunity came after the United States annexed Texas as its twenty-eighth state on December 29, 1845.

Santa Anna viewed the decision to annex Texas as an invitation to war.

The Texas Rangers Return to Mexico

In 1846 Sam Walker and the Texas Rangers once again joined the war effort.

United States Army General Zachary Taylor utilized the Texas Rangers as a cavalry unit. In the war with Mexico, the United States Army supply line was long, and it took great effort to keep arms, ammunition, gun powder, and rations supplied. Mexican Guerrillas constantly pecked away at this line trying to cut it, but the Texas Rangers continually located and engaged these Guerrillas. In this way they were able to maintain the flow of supplies to the army. The commands of both Walker and Hays excelled at this type of warfare.

While Walker and his men were in the rear of Taylor's army, their scouts discovered a Mexican army under General Ampudia on the march. This army was moving into a position to strike a heavy blow on Taylor's unguarded flank. The attack had potential to be a devastating surprise unless desperate actions were taken by Walker.

With the fate of the U.S. Army hanging in the balance, Walker led his men on a dramatic ride. They rode through the night and cut headlong through the Mexican lines. Walker and his Rangers arrived in time to warn General Taylor of the impending ambush.

After receiving the intelligence, Taylor prepared a surprise of his own for the Mexican Army. General Taylor was waiting for General Ampudia on terrain of Taylor's choosing. Thanks to Sam Walker and his Texas Rangers, the Battle of Palo Alto was a decisive victory instead of a possible campaign-ending defeat.

Zachary Taylor recognized the invaluable skills and tactics employed by the Texas Rangers. He directed Walker to return to the United States to raise and train a contingent of "Mounted Rifles." Though Walker was still officially a Texas Ranger, during this period he was given a commission as a Lieutenant Colonel in the United States Army. Sam immediately headed northeast to accomplish his assigned task.

The stories of Walker's exploits had spread throughout the nation. During the fundraising effort, Walker discovered he personally had become lionized by the press in the East. This popularity enhanced his ability to raise funds. One benefactor not only donated money for the cause but also presented Walker with a magnificent war horse which Walker named Tornado.

The Colt Walker

While in the East, Walker met Samuel Colt, the developer of the Colt Paterson revolver, which Walker and his Rangers used with such lethality. Walker immediately shared with Colt his ideas on how to make the Colt Paterson revolver an even more formidable battle weapon.

Samuel Walker was just what Samuel Colt needed at this moment in his life. Colt's weapons had made him at once famous and bankrupt. Colt and Walker became friends, and their collaboration in developing the weapon Walker envisioned would change Colt's fortunes.

Sam Walker had carried his Colt Paterson revolvers in battle for years, and although these five-shot revolvers were a remarkable advancement in fighting technology, he was aware of their shortcomings.

The Colt Paterson had no trigger guard. The trigger remained folded inside the weapon until the bearer cocked it, which caused the unguarded trigger to rotate down to allow for firing. Rangers would sometimes carry the weapon half-cocked, exposing the trigger. This allowed for quick acquisition of the trigger in a fight. It also resulted in too many weapons going off "half-cocked."

Another shortcoming of the weapon was that it fired a .36 caliber without as much knock down power as Walker wanted. A properly placed shot would do the job on a human, but Walker's men needed a caliber that could knock down the horse as well as its rider.

Sam Walker was also troubled that even though the Colt Paterson fired five rounds, most Rangers carried only four to allow the hammer to ride on an empty cylinder to prevent unwanted discharges. Walker envisioned a revolver that could safely carry six rounds. Walker gave Colt input on how to modify the weapon into the perfect Holster Model Pistol.

Sadly, Colt's financial circumstances were such that he no longer had a lab, a factory, or even a spare Colt Paterson to modify. However, Colt did possess the energy and the know-how to turn the Paterson into a hand cannon, and Colt realized Sam Walker had connections to make it happen.

Walker also represented a source for sales once the modifications were made. Walker's Mounted Rifles would need to be armed. If they were going to ride with Sam Walker, they would have to be equipped with at least two pistols each.

Walker arranged a meeting between President James Polk and Colt that led to an order of one thousand Holster Model Pistols that Walker envisioned. Colt was back in business.

Since Colt had no factory, Walker convinced Eli Whitney, of cotton gin fame, to allow his factories to produce the weapon. Walker's hand-held battle weapon became a reality.

The Walker-Colt partnership gave birth to a four pound, nine ounce, six-shot revolver, the precursor of the weapon that would be carried by law enforcement for the next 135 years.

Walker specified that the weapon possess "a bore suited to carrying round balls, fifty to a pound." This gave birth to the .44 caliber round. This handgun proved to be as accurate as a rifle at up to 200 yards in the hands of a trained Ranger.

The six shot revolver would literally change the course of history for the United States.

Walker Returns to the Fight

While Walker was helping to develop this weapon, he also raised and trained his new unit of Mounted Rifles. There was a war that still needed to be won.

On May 10, 1847, Walker's Company C, First United States Mounted Rifles, landed at Vera Cruz. He was in time to join the advance of General Winfield Scott's army. Even though Walker's unit was in the United States Army, he and his men considered themselves to be "Texas Rangers." This irked some of his commanders.

Upon landing in Mexico, Walker's Rangers led the way in the initial fighting. Company C fought their way to Perote, Scott's army's first foothold beyond the reach of the navy's guns.

Walker's Rangers became feared and respected as one of the best fighting units in the American Army. These Rangers defeated both regular Mexican army units as well as guerillas. Walker and his men were so successful Walker was allowed to call his Company C, "Texas Rangers."

On October 4, 1847, a special messenger reached Walker carrying two Colt-Walker pistols, which Sam Walker had designed. These pistols were an advanced shipment of the 1000 pistols that would follow. Walker would be the first to fire this pistol in combat.

The Death of Sam Walker

On October 8, 1847, Sam Walker was attached to U.S. Army General Lane's advance. Lane decided to attack the 4000-strong Mexican army at Huamantla. This army was directly commanded by Santa Anna himself. Lane ordered Walker to remain in close support of Lane's army.

A short time after receiving this order, however, Walker's scouts discovered a force lying in wait to ambush General Lane's army as it advanced. Walker realized if he did not attack immediately, the forces under Lane's command would be in great danger.

Walker led a charge and the Rangers cut deeply into the Mexican lines. The fighting was vicious with no quarter given on either side. After a stiff fight, Walkers men broke the Mexican lines. This occurred at the exact moment the rest of General Lane's force hit, resulting in a disorganized rout.

In the battle the Mexicans suffered 461 casualties. The Rangers lost 27 with an additional 47 wounded. Among the 27 killed was Colonel Sam Walker. Sam had been in the forefront of the fighting when he was shot from his saddle by a Mexican soldier who fired a shotgun from a balcony.

At the time of the Battle of Huamantla, Sam was either 30 or 32 depending on the teller. Colonel Sam Walker's fame was so widespread that his death made headlines in every newspaper in the nation.

No one, even in the military, argued the fact that he died in combat leading his famous Texas Rangers. Sam Walker's body was transported and buried in San Antonio, Texas.

After Huamantla, Santa Anna fled to Jamaica and General Lane moved his army into Puebla. Walker's Rangers would continue to fight, imbued with the courageous spirit breathed into them by Sam Walker.

Legacy

Although this chapter seems more of a tribute to a military commander than a law enforcement officer, the Texas Rangers were a unique law enforcement organization. They started out not as the guardians of a community, a county, or even a state. They were the frontline of defense of an independent nation, the Republic of Texas.

In order to protect their countrymen, Texas Rangers had to confront threats not only as law enforcement officers but as warriors as well. In both venues they set a standard while proudly wearing the Lone Star of Texas.

Colonel Sam Walker earned his place in the Texas Ranger Hall of Fame. Sam Walker lived hard, lived fast, and lived a life worth remembering. His legacy is not just the pistol that bears his name. The United States Cavalry also traces its birth back to Sam Walker and John "Jack" Coffee Hays.

Walker's legacy of excellence is felt by the Texas Rangers to this day. The Texas Rangers have had many shining stars in its history. None have burned so quickly nor shined so brightly as Sam Walker, the Texas Ranger's shooting star.

CHAPTER 3

JAMES BUTLER "WILD BILL" HICKOK

What narrative of great law enforcement officers would be complete without paying homage to James Butler "Wild Bill" Hickok? The problem with documenting Wild Bill's life is that he was a legend in his own time, and he was the closest thing to a rock star in his day.

When journalists told his story, since he was bigger than life in person, the writers felt compelled to make the stories they wrote bigger than life as well. This was a time when lines were blurred between journalism and entertainment. It was acceptable to enhance, embellish, and downright invent what was purported to be "the truth."

Sadly, in Wild Bill's case, the truth was fascinating enough and has been substantially obscured by myth. This story shall endeavor to come as close as possible to the true James Butler Hickok, the man who became the iconic "Wild Bill."

Early Years

James Butler Hickok was born May 27, 1837, to William Alonzo Hickok and Polly Butler-Hickok in Homer, later named Troy Grove, Illinois. Although it was a quiet farming community, William Alonzo introduced a touch of intrigue and danger into the

Hickok family's existence early in young James' life. William Alonzo became involved in a Quaker organization that helped transport escaped slaves from the South, through the North, and into Canada. The Hickok farm became a stop on the Underground Railroad. William Alonzo fashioned a hidden room in the cellar to serve as a secret room for slaves on the run. James' parents thus instilled in him a penchant for protecting innocents.

As James Butler matured, he helped on the farm and brought home meat for the table by hunting. He was clearly an excellent shot, even at a young age. Hickok was stronger and bigger than most boys his age. He could have chosen to be a bully, but instead, he used his size, strength, and absence of fear to defend those who could not protect themselves.

A local story relates James tossing a bully into a lake to protect a youngster who was being picked on. In 1854 he took a job as a wagon driver on the Michigan and Illinois Canal. He lost this job when he tossed his employer into the canal for mistreating a team of horses. It would become a Hickok habit to put himself in the middle of a fray where the odds were stacked against someone. Hickok would not stand idly by and watch one person tormenting another.

Rock Creek Station

As tensions rose between the North and South, twenty-one-year-old James Butler Hickok gravitated toward the eye of the storm. He chose sides early when he traveled to Kansas in 1858 and joined Jim Lane's Kansas Free Staters, who engaged in skirmishes against the pro-slavery group the Missouri Border Ruffians. In that same year he took his first known law enforcement position as constable of Monticello, Kansas.

The position apparently did not pay the bills, for between 1859 and 1860 Hickok also worked hauling freight on the Santa Fe Trail. During one of these excursions, he was quite famously attacked by a bear. He battled with the bear, but the enraged beast would not be stopped by gunshots alone, so the battle became a close-quarter encounter. Hickok finished the bear with his knife but not before he was the recipient of a significant mauling. Hickok was so badly injured he was laid up for months.

In the meantime Hickok's employers, the Overland Stage Company, allowed him to continue working light duty at Rock Creek Station. The duty would turn out to be anything but light.

In 1861, while serving in this capacity, friction developed between Hickok and a man named David McCanles (also spelled McKandles). McCanles was the former owner of the station property, and he complained that he had not received the full payment promised to him. If that was not cause enough for confrontation, McCanles had taken to calling Hickok "Duckbill" because of the shape of Hickok's nose. The label was not welcomed by Hickok; however, he did not pursue a fight over this open display of disrespect. Additionally, McCanles and Hickok may have been courting the same young lady, according to local lore. Suffice it to say, the two had personal and business conflicts.

In 1861 McCanles was considered to be the more dangerous man of the two. He was widely known and feared by many. Hickok, on the other hand, was virtually unknown.

One fateful day, McCanles went to the Rock Creek Station with two friends hungry for a confrontation. No gambling man in that region would have put down money on James Butler "Duckbill" Hickok to win the impending fight. McCanles went there to settle the financial disagreement between himself and Hickok's employers. The employers were not even present at the time.

There have been several versions of the final meeting between Hickok and McCanles told over the years making it impossible to say exactly what transpired. What is known is there was a deadly gunfight. When the only sound remaining was the ringing in the ears of the surviving combatants, Hickok was still standing while McCanles and his two friends lay dead. Although it was not the reason for the gunfight, no one would ever call James Butler Hickok "Duckbill" again.

What has often been lost in the re-telling was the fact that Hickok had two fellow employees with him who also engaged in the short-lived but intense gun-battle, J. W. Brink and Horace Wellman. Hickok, Brink, and Wellman later testified that their station came under attack, and it became a fight for their lives. McCanles and his friends went to Rock Creek Station looking for a fight, but they got more than they bargained for.

Hickok submitted himself to the law, but no charges were filed against any of the Rock Creek employees. The magistrate came to the conclusion that Hickok, Brink, and Wellman were in the right and were defending themselves as well as their employer's interests.

No matter which version of the events of that deadly encounter are true, few would remember Brink, Wellman, McCanles, or his friends. Based on the way he would live his life thereafter, the name Hickok would be permanently etched into Wild West History.

The Civil War

When the Civil War began, Hickok joined the army that was out to set men free. He despised slavery and knew the fight was coming. He was perfectly suited to be of great assistance to the cause.

There are many tall tales of Bill's service during the Civil War. One story told of his performance at the Battle of Pea Ridge. Hickok reportedly took a position lying behind a log as he calmly returned fire until he had killed "35 confederate soldiers." Every time Bill squeezed the trigger, another rebel fell.

One casualty Bill was said to have inflicted was none other than former Texas Ranger, Brigadier General Ben McCullough. While Bill undoubtedly wreaked damage on the Confederates that day, the general was most probably shot by Peter Pelican of the 36th Illinois.

What is factual is that Bill was a valuable member of the Union army in the West. He certainly had the skill to inflict terrible damage on his enemies, whose lines were as compressed as they were in the early battles of the Civil War. For Hickok, it would have been like shooting fish in a barrel.

J. B. Hickok was a reliable scout and spy, riding behind enemy lines for Union General Samuel Curtis. It was during this time that he took to wearing his hair long in a similar fashion to the southern guerillas who called themselves the Partisan Rangers, under the command of William Quantrill. During the war, James Butler Hickok took on the name Bill Haycock, possibly because he was operating behind enemy lines.

One much-told tale occurred when Bill was a spy. Taking the name of the brother of a dead Confederate, he enlisted in the Confederate Army to spy on their movements. When he had gathered enough information on the position, strength, and intentions of the enemy, he looked for an opening to reach the Union soldiers bivouacked directly across the river from the rebels.

An opportunity presented itself when a particular Confederate sergeant began harassing Hickok about his hair and questioning Bill's manhood. Bill challenged the abrasive sergeant to see who could get closer to the river's edge on horseback. Arriving at the river's edge would have put them within range of the Union guns on the other side.

The sergeant took the challenge, and the two galloped toward the river in a dangerous game of chicken. As the story goes, when Bill approached the river's edge, a Union soldier recognized Hickok and called out his name.

Realizing Bill was a Union spy, the sergeant growled, "Yer a Yank!" The sergeant drew his weapon, but he underestimated the speed of Bill's draw. Bill drew and shot the Sergeant through the heart.

Bill immediately came under fire from the rebels, who saw what had transpired. The river was very high at the time, and although it was dangerous, Bill had but one option. Bill and his horse entered the water with one great leap.

When Bill and his horse resurfaced, Bill's horse was swimming and Bill had hold of its tail. The rounds were buzzing by his head like hornets as Bill called out to the Union troops, "Don't shoot! I'm one of you." The Union boys were confused, but they held their fire.

This story was confirmed after the war by those who saw it, and versions of it were passed along by many others who wished they had. One very credible witness to the event was Union General Samuel Crawford who said that he personally witnessed the act of undaunted courage.

Bill also served as a provost marshal (similar to a military policeman). In 1862 Hickok was serving in this capacity in Independence, Missouri, when he came upon a large crowd. The crowd had gathered because a bartender had bested some of their number in a fight. The few who had caused the initial disturbance had been ignominiously tossed out of the bar. Now they were gathered, along with some supporters, and determined to do harm to the bartender.

Hickok arrived on the scene and placed himself, alone, between the crowd and the bartender. When the crowd did not respond to his order to disperse, he drew his twin Colt 1851 Navy Revolvers and fired them into the air. During the quiet that followed, Hickok stood alone and defiant as if to say, "Your move, gentlemen." The crowd turned and drifted away. A female onlooker, so impressed with the display of individual courage, called out, "Way to go, Wild Bill." Some people believe this is how he earned his famous handle "Wild Bill." There are other less dramatic stories, but this one fits the "Wild Bill" persona the best.

Even Bill's horse "Black Nell" was legendary by the end of the war. She was well trained and, according to legend, was taken as a war prize after Bill killed its Confederate rider and two other rebels in a sudden encounter while scouting for the Union.

Wild Bill had a restless spirit and changed his occupations often before the war, so it is not unreasonable to believe he would do so while serving in a war that lasted for four years. Wild Bill Hickok was a skilled wagon master, excellent shot, gifted lawman, and reliable scout. Bill most certainly served the Union in each of these capacities. His application of these skills would draw attention throughout the war.

When asked at the age of twenty-eight how many men he had killed, Wild Bill said in a matter of fact manner that it had been at least one hundred. Considering his legendary accuracy as well as his consistent placement in tight places, sometimes alone in enemy territory, this number is plausible; however, it is neither possible to confirm nor refute its accuracy.

James Butler "Wild Bill" Hickok's reputation by the end of the war was firmly established. A soldier named William Darnell was accompanying a wagon train near Fort Zarrah on April 9, 1865. He especially noted the rider who announced the surrender of Lee's army and identified him as "Wild Bill." This is Darnell's account describing Bill's appearance during this period in an admiring manner:

> When about a half mile from the fort "Wild Bill"
> Hickok, on a dandy horse, came riding by on the run,
> shouting out as he rode by, "Lee's surrendered! Lee's
> surrendered!" He was a striking figure as I noticed

him, a large broad-brimmed hat on his head, long drooping mustache, long flowing hair that fell about his shoulders, a brace of ivory-handled revolvers strapped to his waist, and an extra pair in holsters that fitted about the horn of his saddle where he could reach them instantly. These latter were long-barreled ones, capable of carrying quite a distance. It was common talk that he had got many an enemy with them just on account of their long-range qualities.

The unadulterated fact was what Hickok served his country honorably in the War Between the States. Hickok was highly regarded as an exceptional warrior by those who observed his service, both those who fought along-side him as well as those who fought against him.

By April 1865 James Butler Hickok was already a legend in his own time. To both stranger and friend he was then and forever "Wild Bill."

The David Tutt Affair

After the war ended, Hickok found himself mustered out of the service and out of work. He took his pay and tried to multiply it by gambling. Hickok was a man of his times, and he loved gambling and saloons. When the cards were falling right, Bill found he could make a fair living playing cards.

One night in Springfield, Missouri, Hickok was playing cards at a table with a recently paroled Confederate named David Tutt. The two did not like each other. Some believe their paths crossed during the war, as adversaries.

To make matters worse, at times Hickok and Tutt fancied the same woman. Hickok was also said to have taken an interest in Tutt's sister. Considering that Hickok was not known for having sustained relationships with women, this alone would have been enough to enrage Tutt.

These brewing animosities gave the two all the more reason to want to play cards at the same table. It was an opportunity for the each antagonist to take the other's money. What could be more satisfying?

On one particular night, Tutt was winning and committed a gambling faux pas; he abruptly quit early. As Dave Tutt gathered his winnings, he snatched Hickok's personal watch. Tutt claimed it was collateral for the money Wild Bill owed him.

In those times a personal watch often had great sentimental value to a man. To take a man's watch as collateral without first having it agreed upon could trigger a deadly fight between men in that era. Tutt was doing what would be called in law enforcement, "poking the bear."

Hickok held fire, however. He assured Tutt that he would pay what he owed and reclaim his watch. With great earnestness Bill cautioned Tutt, "Don't wear my watch in public." Doing so would be a deliberate affront to Hickok; however, Tutt declared that he would wear the watch if he wanted to wear the watch. Hickok closed the conversation by promising Tutt if he wore the watch in public, "There will be trouble."

Even though friends cautioned Tutt against wearing the watch, David Tutt was unimpressed with the man people called "Wild Bill" and foolishly disregarded the warning. David Tutt had also killed men in the war and was confident in his skills as a pistoleer. Tutt felt he was the man to be feared, not Hickok.

On the very next day, Tutt went to the public square in Springfield flaunting Hickok's watch. Tutt bragged about the manner in which he had come into possession of it as well as how Hickok had warned him not to wear it. Tutt had to know that his decision to wear that watch on the square could lead to gun play. To not wear the watch, however, would be an admission that David Tutt, "the good old rebel," was afraid of "that damned Yankee Hickok." To Tutt, that would have been intolerable.

As promised, Hickok arrived on the opposite end of the square wearing his pistols butt forward in a bright red sash, as he preferred. He was said to have developed a lightning-speed underhand draw.

Realizing there was a possible confrontation between a Kansas Yank and a Missouri rebel, a crowd had gathered on the square to watch. Most of the gawkers knew that both antagonists had deadly reputations. If this contest had been promoted as a paid event, it would have drawn a standing-room-only crowd in any venue in the nation in 1865. It was about to become the most famous duel since Vice President Aaron Burr shot Alexander Hamilton dead.

If David Tutt was frightened when he spotted Hickok across the square, he did not show it. Witnesses agreed, Tutt looked confident and unbowed. There was a pause after Tutt's eyes met the piercing blue eyes canopied by Hickok's distinctive heavy brows. Suddenly, Tutt strode toward Bill picking up his gait.

Hickok stood his ground but took a stance with his body turned sideways toward Tutt. He maintained his gaze, however, facing his approaching adversary. Hickok's subtle turn of his body was deliberate for it made him a smaller target.

In a quick and sudden jerk, Tutt drew his pistol, aimed, and fired. Hickok did not draw until after Tutt, but when he did, his movement was smooth and deliberate. Bill, steadied his pistol a fraction of a moment on his left forearm and fired. According to some witnesses, Tutt's bullet kicked up dirt in front of Hickok; others were certain it whistled by Wild Bill's head. How Tutt missed mattered little, for he would not get another chance.

Although Hickok drew after Tutt, witnesses claimed that the shots were fired almost simultaneously. This was a testament to Hickok's efficiency in the draw and coolness under pressure. Hickok's round spiraled 75 yards into Tutt's heart. David Tutt spun and fell face down, never to rise again.

Certain of his skills, Hickok did not wait to see whether his shot hit its mark. He turned to face Dave Tutt's friends. By now, Wild Bill was armed with two pistols since the men behind him appeared inclined to take up Tutt's cause. Some were even in the process of drawing their weapons.

His voice deep, Hickok calmly cautioned, "Return your pistols to your holsters, gentlemen, or there will be more dead men in this square before the end of this day."

All present reholstered their weapons, for they were certain Hickok was not making an idle threat. They would not underestimate Bill's capabilities.

The large crowd had watched Hickok allow the deadly David Tutt to draw first. In the next moment they saw Hickok draw with the speed of a teamster's whip-crack, take aim, and shoot Tutt straight through his heart. This story would not be embellished upon as there was no need for embellishment. The truth was impressive enough to stand on its own.

After neutralizing the crowd, Hickok crossed the square and retrieved his watch. With that accomplished, James Butler "Wild Bill" Hickok turned himself over to the law for adjudication.

Two days later Hickok was cleared of a charge of illegal dueling. The ruling was that there was technically no duel since duels had rules and protocols. The jury also cleared Hickok of all potential charges regarding the homicide. All were in agreement that the fight had been started by David Tutt and finished by Hickok purely as a matter of necessity. The jury believed this to be a clear-cut case of self-defense.

Modern western historian/poet Lowell "Zeke" Ziemann described the Hickok versus Tutt gunfight like this:

When the duel commenced, each man fired one shot.

Tutt's bullet missed. Hickok's did not.

Hickok's shot through the heart was easily seventy-five and quite possibly one hundred yards. Any person who has fired a pistol knows how difficult this shot is to make, especially while being shot at. Though Hollywood would replicate the Hickok-Tutt gunfight over and over again on television and in the movies one hundred years later, this gunfight was one of the few that actually occurred in the West in this manner.

Hickok Post War Scout and Military Lawman

After his vindication, Hickok immediately left Springfield for Fort Riley, Kansas, where he served as Deputy U.S. Marshal. Shortly thereafter he transferred to Fort McPherson. Here, Bill pursued horse thieves and mule thieves. Hickok also served as a cavalry scout, first for William Tecumseh Sherman and then for the famous 7th Cavalry with none other than George Armstrong Custer.

During his time with Custer, he managed to make a lasting impression on Custer's wife Libby. Custer's wife clearly sounded a bit smitten by this charming frontiersman who was quite famously a woman's man. Libby Custer's book, Following the Guidon, was published in 1890. This was fourteen years after her husband's miscalculation at Little Big Horn. In the book she described how the 6'3" Wild Bill Hickok appeared to her when he served as a scout for her husband:

> Physically, he was a delight to look upon. Tall, lithe, and free in every motion, he rode and walked as if every muscle was perfection, and the careless swing of his body as he moved seemed perfectly in keeping with the man, the country, the time in which he lived. I do not recall anything finer in the way of physical perfection than Wild Bill when he swung himself lightly from the saddle, and with graceful, swaying step, squarely set shoulders and well poised head, approached our tent for orders. He was rather fantastically clad, of course, but all that seemed perfectly in keeping with time and place. He did not make an armory of his waist, but carried two pistols. He wore top-boots, riding breeches, and dark-blue flannel shirt, with scarlet set in the front. A loose neck-handkerchief left his fine firm throat free. I do not at all remember his features, but the frank, manly expression of his fearless eyes and his courteous manner gave one a feeling of confidence in his word and in his undaunted courage.

It is unique that both a husband and wife would write memoirs of the times. It just so happens that George Armstrong Custer wrote a book, *My Life on the Plains*, and was also moved to describe Hickok.

His description gives great insight into what made Bill effective as a lawman:

> His influence among the frontiersman was unbounded, his word was law; and many are the personal quarrels and disturbances which he has checked among his comrades by his simple announcement that "this has gone far enough," if need be followed by the ominous warning that when persisted in or renewed the quarreler "must settle it with me."
>
> "Wild Bill" is anything but a quarrelsome man; yet no one but himself can enumerate the many conflicts in which he has been engaged, and which have almost invariably resulted in the death of his adversary. I have personal knowledge of at least half a dozen men whom he has at various times killed, one of these being at the time a member of my command. Others have been severely wounded, yet he always escapes unhurt. On the Plains every man openly carries his belt with its invariable appendages, knife and revolver, often two of the latter. Wild Bill always carried two handsome ivory-handled revolvers of the large size; he was never seen without them.

Bill Hickok Inspires another Bill

A chance meeting in the summer of 1868 became a life-long memory for a certain twelve-year-old boy destined to follow in Hickok's boots. When Hickok rode into Atchison, Kansas, on the trail of some bad men, he stopped to ask some youths if they had seen anything of the men he was pursuing. One boy was transformed by this encounter.

Bill Tilghman later wrote of the already-famous lawman, "He was mounted on no prancing charger, only a sturdy government mule, but he rode with the easy grace of a plainsman. Tall, he was over six feet tall, splendidly built, and his face as handsome as in form, with strong clear-cut features and keen dark blue eyes, long drooping mustache and hair curling upon his shoulders. He spoke in a slow assured manner, 'Good morning boys and young ladies,' he said."

That chance meeting with the twelve year old had an incredibly profound impact, altering forever the course of that boy's life. Young Billy Tilghman not only decided to be a lawman, but he wanted to emulate his hero Wild Bill Hickok. Tilghman would grow up to be one of the most famous lawmen of his times, with a career spanning four decades (see chapter on Tilghman).

Hays City

In 1867 Hickok, ever the wanderer, left the cavalry and took a job as Deputy U.S. Marshal in Hays City. The good citizens of Hays hoped the famous lawman would bring peace back to their rowdy and dangerous existence.

In September of that year, a local ruffian named Samuel Strawhun (also spelled Stringham and Stranhan) took it upon himself to create a loud disturbance in John Bitter's Beer Saloon while Marshal Hickok was on duty. Apparently, the group with Strawhun had loudly been chanting "Beer! Beer! Beer!" They were also emptying the saloon of its supply of beer glasses. The rowdies with Strawhun would fill them up, carry them outside to drink, and then leave them lying about.

Hickok heard the commotion and moved in, intent on returning peace to the saloon. Upon arrival, Bill initially tried to avoid a confrontation and even took it upon himself to gather and return many of the glasses to the saloon.

Meanwhile, when Strawhun was told the law was coming, he threatened there would be trouble if anyone tried to interfere with his fun.

Entering the saloon with an arm full of glasses, Hickok spoke specifically to Strawhun, "You hadn't ought to treat a poor old man in this way." Bill was referring to John Bitter, the bar owner.

Strawhun showed total disrespect when, speaking of the glasses Hickok had just painstakingly gathered, he assured Hickok, "I'm just going to throw them out again."

Hickok would not abide a bully, nor could he stand by while another was being bullied. Hickok was there to stop the ruffians from bullying John Bitter. Now, Samuel Strawhun was trying to bully Hickok. That would never do.

Hickok's eyebrows dipped low and heavy over his dark blue eyes. He answered Strawhun slowly, giving great significance to each of his words, "Do, and they will be carrying you out."

A man possessing a nickel's worth of caution and a penny's worth of common sense would have backed down. If Strawhun possessed a measurable portion of either of these qualities, alcohol had since washed them away. After sizing up the marshal, Strawhun made the same fateful miscalculation David Tutt had made.

Strawhun went for his pistol, but Hickok was much faster. In the blink of an eye, Wild Bill executed his underhand draw, twisted the pistol into position to fire, and shot Strawhun in the head, dropping him on the spot.

The shooting occurred at 1:00 AM, and by 9:00 AM a coroner's jury presided over by Hays City Justice Joyce concluded that Samuel Strawhun died from wounds suffered at the hands of J. B. Hickok and the shooting was justifiable. The deceased bully was in the ground by 1:00 PM.

A Second Gunfight in Hays

A short time after his deadly encounter with Strawhun, Marshal Hickok had a similar occurrence with a man by the name of Bill Mulvey. Mulvey also created a disturbance bringing Marshal Hickok to the scene. Wild Bill tried to reason with the man, but Mulvey suddenly attempted to draw on Hickok.

Mulvey's last experience in life was witnessing the speed of Wild Bill Hickok's draw and suffering the effect of Bill's incredible accuracy. Mulvey fell irrevocably dead.

Word spread quickly throughout the territory that it was suicidal to challenge Wild Bill Hickok face to face.

In spite of his successes, Hickok was greatly impacted by the assaults on his life. The marshal took to walking down the middle of the street when on foot patrol in Hays. It gave him a better vantage point to see the big picture. His dark eyes were said to dart about, always on the look-out for danger.

When Wild Bill heard disturbances in a saloon, he would end them "Hickok style." Bill approached the swinging doors and pushed them open hard as he entered, slamming them loudly against the walls. In this way he would burst in, startling all present inside to silence. By allowing the doors to hit the walls, it also assured there were no back-shooters occupying the blind spot on either side of the entrance.

After this dramatic entrance, Wild Bill would stop in the doorway and order them all to quiet down. In most cases, that is exactly what they would do, and the problem was solved. Everyone was aware of what was in store for someone who fought Bill. At 6'3" Bill was a large man in his time. He was also as good with his fists as he was with his guns.

The town became a much more peaceful place to live within months of Marshal Hickok's arrival. His mere presence served to deter rowdy and violent behavior. Bill could often be seen leaning back against a wall in his chair with his eyes darting about checking every man and movement on the street. At times he would perch on the boardwalk of an intersecting corner allowing him to watch two streets at once. Some described him as having "the look of an angry bull."

In spite of this, Bill was remembered to be very good with children. Urchins seemed to bring out a soft side of the man. He could make children smile, and whenever possible he did so.

The people of Hays were happy with Wild Bill's taming of the town. In the local newspaper they referred to Wild Bill Hickok as their guardian. There was just one problem. Hickok was absolutely necessary for lawless towns, but after he tamed them he became obsolete. Shortly after Hays was declared peaceful, its citizens thanked Bill by voting him out as city marshal.

Bill's Fight With the 7th Cavalry

A few months after Bill left Hays, he returned for a visit. During this visit he was in a local saloon talking to the bartender. Unbeknownst to Bill, at least two (some say five) troopers from the 7th Cavalry entered the bar. These men had a run-in with Marshal Hickok in the past. The troopers were Private John Kile (also spelled Kelley and Kelly) and Jeremiah Lonergan. Both were dissatisfied with the outcome of their previous meeting with Bill, so they decided to take advantage of the marshal while his back was turned.

The troopers attacked, and Private John Kile began strangling Hickok from behind. After placing both arms around Bill's neck,

Kile violently "bulldogged" Hickok to the floor. The beating which commenced was as brutal and life threatening as it was unprovoked. While the soldiers were pummeling him, Bill was able to draw a pistol, but Lonergan grabbed and held his wrist.

Even though his wrist was being held, Bill twisted the gun into firing position with the muzzle directed at Kile. Hickok fired the gun in a final effort to save his own life. Kile slumped forward. Lonergan tightened the hold he had on Bill's wrist, but Bill was able to re-direct the muzzle toward Lonergan's leg. He fired again. The shot blew Lonergan's knee cap off and put an end to the beating.

Bill was dazed and realized that if two boys from the 7th were in town there were likely more. Hickok fled Hays rather than submit to the marshal on this occasion. He was not trying to escape justice. He fled expecting an entire company of cavalry would shortly be on his trail and out for vengeance, not justice.

There are tales of Bill taking all his weapons and as much ammunition as he could muster to the cemetery in Hays. He spent the night using the headstones as cover awaiting the arrival of the 7th Cavalry, but they never arrived. Bill did not know that Lonergan and Kile were the only soldiers from the 7th in town; both were absent without leave. Kile died, but Lonergan survived.

Although Bill was not on the Hays city payroll at the time, this assault came as a direct result of his employment as an officer of the law. Bill must have been justified in his actions for neither the 7th Cavalry nor the townsfolk pursued any legal action against Bill. There were no attempts at retaliation against Bill by the men of the 7th either.

Abilene

The town of Abilene had just lost their marshal, Tom Smith. Tom was a good man who had a peculiar idea about enforcing the law. Tom strongly felt that he could inspire the cooperation of even the worst of men with his amiable nature. He had an aversion to gun play and believed you couldn't get into a gunfight if you didn't have a gun.

Marshal Smith, who refused to "go heeled," was partially right; he did not die in a gunfight. Marshal Smith was nearly beheaded after he was attacked by someone wielding an ax and was unable to defend himself during the fatal assault.

Wild Bill filled the open marshal's position in Abilene after the tragic death of Marshal Smith.

Hickok was definitely a different type of marshal than Smith. Abilene would develop a love-hate relationship with Wild Bill Hickok depending on the community member's point of view. Abilene was a wild "cow town," and during the summer months, cattle were driven from Texas to Abilene. When the cowboys arrived, they expected unfettered access to their brand of raucous fun.

MARSHAL TOM SMITH

As was the case with every cow town in the West, the citizens were conflicted. They loved the money the cowboys spent in town on supplies, alcohol, women, and gambling, but they hated their out-of-control and destructive behavior. Wild Bill was called upon to dial down the rowdiness as he had in Hays.

Upon arrival, Wild Bill began enforcing ordinances that would set him at odds with some in Abilene. He suppressed the use of guns within the city limits. He ended unfair gambling practices, the most notorious being the practice of getting cowboys so drunk while they gambled that in one sitting they would lose every cent that had taken the cow hands months to earn.

In a unique move, Wild Bill even supervised the editing of a Longhorn steer painting in one saloon which had outraged the people of Abilene. The steer had originally been painted anatomically correct, and the well-endowed Longhorn's male-member was painted over.

Often, Hickok would not arrest nor fine the disorderly cowboys. He determined this would just create a revolving door in the jail. His preference was to run the troublemakers out of town, which was an even worse punishment for the cowboys. They had money to spend on fines, but there were no other towns close by where they could party with their fellow cowboys. Word of this policy spread, and the cowboys instantly became more subdued in Abilene. It was

Hickok's active presence that had an immediate positive effect on the cowboys' behavior.

Just as Bill Hickok could scout to find wild game on the frontier and the enemy during times of conflict, Bill could find trouble as a lawman. When he found it, he would stop it before it got out of hand.

Hickok's aggressive form of peacekeeping was clearly effective, and people could see an immediate impact. The Mayor of Abilene described Hickok as, "The squarest [most honest] man I have ever known."

Hickok had his detractors, however. The cowboys were not happy with Bill's overbearing presence. Understandably, the cow hands much preferred free rein to having Hickok holding the reins.

There was a former Confederate saloon owner who especially disliked Hickok. Phillip Coe was a gambler-gunfighter who profited from the cowboys and did not appreciate Bill's interference. It was Coe's painting which had been edited.

Hickok had many run-ins with Coe. During one, Phillip Coe made a veiled threat which included the boast, "I have hit a crow on the fly with a pistol." If this was supposed to leave Hickok shivering in his boots, it didn't have the desired effect.

Bill replied, "Crows don't shoot back."

The antagonism came to a head October 5, 1871. The town was filled with cowboys, and Bill heard a single shot come from the area of the Alamo Saloon. Bill had been talking with his deputy Mike Williams and told Williams to stay put at the hot spot they had been watching. This was not unusual since a single fired shot did not necessarily mean a disaster in the making. Bill told Mike that he would check it out.

As Bill neared the area of the Alamo Saloon, he found a very large crowd of intoxicated cowboys spilling into the streets around the Alamo. There were a variety of reactions to Bill's arrival ranging from drunken jocularity to hard looks. Bill was concerned that he was about to become tonight's entertainment.

Phil Coe stepped purposefully forward out of the crowd. Coe took credit for the shot explaining sarcastically, "I was just shooting at a dog,"

There was a long moment of silence as the lawman and the gunfighter stared at each other from across the street. The tension hanging over that moment was palpable. Without another word, Phil Coe drew his pistol and fired at Wild Bill.

Bill Hickok was not a harmless crow on the fly; Phil Coe missed.

Bill drew his revolvers and returned fire. Coe was hit twice in the stomach. Coe dropped his gun, clutched his stomach, and stumbled forward, finally falling into the street.

Hickok was keenly aware of the fact that this gunfight had taken place where Coe's friends were rather than where Hickok's friends were. He was in a state of heightened alertness for possible retaliation. Shortly after Hickok's rounds cleared his muzzle, an armed man ran toward Hickok from his flank. Bill sensed imminent danger, so he instinctively turned and fired, dropping the man in his tracks. The man Hickok shot and killed was his own deputy, Mike Williams.

Hickok flew into a rage. He shouted for everyone to disperse and shut down the saloons. His manner coupled with his reputation had the same effect that one hundred Hickoks would have had. The crowd slunk away.

It took Coe days to die from his stomach wounds. To be "gut shot" was a bad man's Purgatory on earth.

Ultimately Hickok's type of policing brought peace to Abilene, and once again Bill found himself mustered out. It was just as well. After the Coe gunfight, Abilene had enough of Marshal Hickok, and Hickok was done with Abilene.

Hickok's Last Days

Bill was as famous in the East as he was in the West, and for a time he performed in Wild West shows. People paid money in the East to see Wild Bill Hickok; however, this was not a satisfying life. Bill had a passion for his work in the West. In the East his performances on stages were lackluster even when he was at his best.

His time in the East was not without passion. He fell in love with Agnes Thatcher-Lake. Wild Bill first met the talented performer and business woman when her circus passed through western towns on tour. The two exchanged letters afterward. Bill's letters to Agnes during the times they were separated reveal a man deeply in love. His prose was notably eloquent. When Bill moved East after the Phil Coe gunfight, Hickok and Agnes reconnected.

On March 5, 1876, Bill and Agnes married. Bill could easily have lived out his life as a showman like his friend Buffalo Bill. People all over the world would have paid money to see the real Wild Bill Hickok ride his well-trained horses and perform trick-shooting. People were enthralled by everything Western and Wild Bill was the real deal.

Agnes could have been his manager, and he could have traveled with her show. He could have had the greatest love of his life at his side for his remaining days. He could have written a biography that would still be selling to this day. Wild Bill Hickok did not need another adventure to secure his place in history.

AGNES THATCHER-LAKE

It was not to be.

You don't get a name like "Wild Bill" by choosing life's easiest path. Bill was hungry for more adventure. Some would argue that Bill headed to Deadwood for the cards because there was a lot of money to be lost in this mining boom-town. Others would say that he headed to Deadwood in pursuit of striking it rich in his own mine.

If you follow the pattern of Wild Bill Hickok's life, you may draw another conclusion. Bill was quite possibly looking for one more helpless population of hard working citizens living under the tyranny of disorder. If he went there, they might ask him to pin on a badge one more time and make things right the way only Wild Bill could.

Whatever his motivations, Bill kissed Agnes goodbye and told her he was off to Deadwood where lesser men than he were becoming rich. After exchanging passionate farewells, Bill road west one last time.

Deadwood, South Dakota, in the summer of 1876 was as wild as any western town had ever been. Word of Wild Bill Hickok's arrival spread through town like water through a sluice. The criminal elements, which were becoming vicariously rich off the miners, were probably somewhat alarmed. Their shady business deals, gambling establishments, opium dens, and whore houses were taking hard-earned money from the miners the easy way. No matter why Wild Bill Hickok came to Deadwood, these crooked operators must have suspected that Hickok intended to bring law and order. Law and Order was bad for business.

Bill spent most of his waking hours pursuing riches at a card table. During his time away from the card table, he wrote Agnes letters professing his enduring love for her. There was an ominous tone in one of these letters indicating Bill may have had a premonition of trouble on the horizon. He wrote:

> Agnes, darling, if such should be we never meet again, while firing my last shot I will gently breathe the name of my wife—Agnes—and with wishes even for my enemies, I will make the plunge and try and swim to the other shore.

On August 2, 1876, Wild Bill Hickok entered the Number Ten Saloon and asked to join a game in progress. Someone had the seat he usually would have taken so that his back could be against the wall. The man in that seat was winning and did not want to change, even for Wild Bill Hickok. There was a time when Bill would not have sat at a table under such circumstances. On this day Hickok did not press the issue and sat down to play cards with his back exposed.

After a bit, a man named Jack McCall quietly entered Number Ten Saloon. Slipping unnoticed behind Hickok, McCall pulled out a pistol and put it but inches away from the back of Hickok's head. Pulling the trigger, McCall sent Hickok swimming to the other shore. Hickok never saw it coming.

Quite famously, Hickok's final hand, black Aces and Eights with a Jack of Diamonds, would be forever known as "The Dead Man's Hand."

Jack McCall's motives are speculated upon to this day.

Did his desire to be remembered as "the man who killed Wild Bill Hickok," motivate him to end the life of this great man? Was he paid by the criminal elements to prevent Wild Bill Hickok from cleaning up Deadwood? Was Jack the relative of someone Hickok had killed in the past?

Jack McCall's true motives are now and will remain a mystery, for McCall would hang before making them clear to anyone.

James Butler "Wild Bill" Hickok

There is a continual pattern of James Butler "Wild Bill" Hickok standing up for the oppressed and the persecuted. He would not tolerate bullies. He and his family protected runaway slaves. As a youth he stood up for bullied children and animals. He fought in a storied manner during the war to free men, women, and children from bondage. After that war he expertly scouted for Custer and Sherman during the Indian Wars. He protected embattled citizens in some of the most lawless towns in the Old West.

In taming these towns he put forth a template for others to follow. Where others had failed, he achieved success in just weeks. Part of his strategy was to have laws, enforce them, be present when lawlessness occurred, and bring back order to the street. The most important part was to be fearless and indomitable when confronted with people who would kill in an instant. When they attempt murder, shoot faster and straighter every time.

Wild Bill Hickok was not famous for the unbelievable feats journalists of his time said he did. Wild Bill Hickok was famous for the things he actually did. He was a gunfighter, a soldier, a scout, a spy, a wagon master, and even a gambler. He excelled in every category.

He was all of those things, but he will always be remembered as the man with a star on his chest, two pearl-handled guns tucked into a red sash, butts forward, staring down a crowd of bad men with piercing dark-blue eyes squinting ominously beneath his heavy eyebrows saying, "Your move, gentlemen."

CHAPTER 4

DEPUTY U.S. MARSHAL BASS REEVES, A REAL LONE RANGER

Historian and professor Art Burton has pondered whether or not Deputy U.S. Marshal Bass Reeves may have been the real-life inspiration for the Lone Ranger. If so, he lived a life more dangerous, more challenging, and definitely more interesting than the legend he inspired.

In 1838, Bass Reeves began life as a slave in Crawford County, Arkansas. His duties varied, but he was known to have been gifted with great talents. Bass developed incredible strength and was a brilliant horse trainer. Reeves also possessed an innate skill with firearms. Bass was so naturally talented, his master entered him in marksmanship contests which Bass would win handily.

The historical record is murky and conflicted about Bass's life during the Civil War. There is consistency in the all accounts, however, that Bass was known to have accompanied Colonel George Reeves, the son of his master, as he raised a company for the Eleventh Texas Cavalry at the onset of the Civil War.

In an interview in 1907, Bass Reeves told a reporter he fought along-side Colonel Reeves in the Battle of Pea Ridge as well as other battles. It was not unusual for a slave to assist his master in this manner, but Confederate records fail to document such loyalty.

Accounts vary on how Bass escaped from slavery. Some say he escaped after an argument between the Colonel and Bass over cards. Other accounts attribute his dash to freedom as inspired by the Emancipation Proclamation.

His actions after he escaped slavery are also a puzzle. Some stories place him fighting with Creek Indians, loyal to the Union, toward the end of the war.

What is known is that Reeves' flight to freedom eventually landed him in Oklahoma Territory, where he was immediately embraced by the Cherokee. It was here that he learned to track and speak five Native American languages fluently — skills that would serve him well.

Bass Reeves, Deputy U.S. Marshal

At the war's end, Reeves married and began raising his children and working his own farm. Occasionally, Reeves earned additional money hiring on as a scout for lawmen who were hunting wanted criminals in Indian Territory. An extraordinary man-hunter, Reeves' skills were in high demand, and he made a fair living tracking criminals. He was also good in a fight when the object of the pursuit chose to resist.

In 1875, Judge Isaac Parker hired Bass Reeves as one of 200 deputy marshals in the Oklahoma Territory who were sent out to tame "Indian Country." This was a tough assignment. During the years Judge Parker occupied the bench, an estimated 65-100 Parker Deputies were killed in the line of duty working in this hostile environment.

The "Indomitable Marshal"

At a time when the average man was about 5'6," Reeves was a towering 6'2." He was broad at the shoulders, narrow at the hips, and was said to possess superhuman strength. He was quite possibly the first black lawman west of the Mississippi. Reeves cut a striking figure on his large gray horse (some said it looked white in the sun light) while wearing his trademark black hat. He carried two Colt Peacemakers cross-draw style. One was a Colt 45, the other a .38 caliber. One caliber could easily bring down a man, and the other could bring down his horse.

Reeves' pistols did not have pearl handles; they were black, not silver like the Lone Ranger's pistols. When choosing weapons,

Marshal Bass Reeves preferred functionality to appearance. Reeves did not give out silver bullets, but he did pay for everything, including information, with silver dollars. In his time a silver dollar could buy a thick steak and solid information, and he was always in search of both when on a bad man's trail.

Reeves became well known among criminals for his skills and relentless pursuit. Although shot at many times, he was never touched by a single bullet earning him the moniker the "Indomitable Marshal." One woman said he was so tough he could "spit on a brick and bust it."

A contemporary newspaper lauded his dogged pursuit of criminals by reporting, "Place a warrant for arrest in his hands and no circumstance can cause him to deviate." Considering the times during which he lived and the criminality of the suspects he pursued, those were tall words to live up to, but Bass never failed.

Even though he pursued some of the most dangerous men in the territory, no records report him to be anything but absolutely fearless. The *Oklahoma City Weekly Times-Journal* reported, "Reeves was never known to show the slightest excitement, under any circumstance. He does not know what fear is."

Chances are Reeves was as human as all Law Dogs who do not show fear. They feel it, experience it, overcome it, and channel it into action. Fear is like an invisible companion that urges some men forward with a cautious determination while it screams *run* to others. If fear accompanied Reeves, no one was the wiser.

This was never truer than the case Reeves described during a newspaper interview in 1906. A reporter asked, "What was the tightest spot you were ever in?"

Reeves answered by telling the story of a time in 1884 when he was in pursuit of wanted criminals he referred to as the "Brunter Brothers." At one point on the Seminole Whiskey Trail, he was ambushed by these three men who ordered him off his horse at gunpoint. Initially, Reeves felt compliance was his only option, so he climbed down from his horse. As he did, he formed a plan that would have seemed foolhardy except for the fact that he was otherwise most certainly about to die.

Upon dismounting, Marshal Reeves seemed to ignore the guns pointed at him and nonchalantly reached into his coat pocket. To the dismay of the brothers, Bass removed the warrants he had for them, along with a pencil. With pencil in hand the marshal asked them, "What is today's date?"

"What?" the leader asked.

Bass explained that he wanted to make a note of the arrest date on the warrants he had to turn in after he took them to jail.

The leader chuckled and cleverly retorted, "You are just ready to turn in now," causing all three of the Brunters to laugh in premature triumph.

Taking advantage of this momentary distraction, Bass made his move. One of the brothers was covering him on foot, and Bass grabbed the gun barrel, managing to keep the muzzle directed away from his own torso as this brother fired off three shots. The bullets went harmlessly wide. Simultaneously, Bass drew his own pistol and shot one of the brothers off his horse.

The other brother still on horseback brought his weapon to bear on Reeves, but the marshal fired again. This second bandit rolled off his horse, dead by the time he hit the ground.

With two down and one to go, Reeves turned his complete attention to the third Brunter, who was even more frantic than ever to break his pistol free from Reeves' vice-like grip. Reeves did what seemed easiest at the time. He brought his smoking pistol crashing down on his adversary's skull.

All three warrants were served by Deputy U.S. Marshal Bass Reeves, but he delivered them to face justice in a higher court than Judge Parker's.

Capturing the Murderer of Reverend William Steward

The determination of Bass Reeves was especially evidenced in the case of James Webb.

There was a circuit preacher/land-owner named Reverend William Steward who had decided to do a controlled burn-off on a patch of his land for future planting. The fire got away from him and spread to land on the Washington-McLish range.

Jim Webb, a cowboy with a mean streak and a notoriously bad temper, became enraged by the preacher's unintentional transgression. Often sparked into violent action, Jim exploded in an uncontrollable rage, then shot and killed the preacher.

Days later, Reeves, with warrant in hand, rode up to the ranch where Webb was working. As Reeves and his posse-man Floyd Wilson approached, Webb was standing on the porch with another cowboy, Frank Smith. Webb and Smith held their unholstered pistols as nonchalantly as if they were branding irons instead of shooting irons. The two cautiously watched Reeves and Wilson with great interest, as if a steady glare held long enough could reveal a person's intentions.

Reeves had worked out a plan in advance with Wilson. They would pose as two hungry drifters looking for work. If there was none to be had, they would ask if they could at least share a meal in the bunk-house.

Upon reaching the house, Reeves dismounted, then pulled his rifle out of its scabbard and leaned it against a nearby wall. This non-aggressive action caused Webb and Smith to relax a bit and holster their weapons. Reeves was not yet ready to make his move because he was uncertain what Webb looked like. He did not want to trigger a confrontation with innocent ranch hands.

Webb invited the two hungry drifters in for breakfast, which the cook was about to serve. The two lawmen, still concealing their identities, entered the kitchen end of the bunkhouse and sat down at the table. Marshal Reeves assumed a character far from his own and began chattering away non-stop. During his friendly banter, he discovered that the man he was dining with was indeed Jim Webb, the object of his pursuit.

With Webb right next to him, Bass just needed to wait for the right moment to make his move. For a time Bass continued his chatter. At some point during the meal, Reeves noticed Webb pass some quiet murmurings to Smith, and the marshal concluded that sly Webb was on to him. Reeves decided to take action and hope that Wilson would follow suit.

In the flap of a hummingbird's wing, Reeves secured Webb's throat with one hand, drew his weapon, and pressed the muzzle against the wanted killer's forehead as he said, "I'm Deputy U.S. Marshal Bass Reeves and you, sir, are under arrest."

The plan had been for Wilson to cover Smith when Bass made his move; however, Bass had acted so suddenly Wilson sat startled with his mouth agape.

Reeves had inspired the opposite reaction in Smith, who drew his weapon and fired twice at Reeves. Both rounds, fired in the fury of the moment, missed the marshal.

Deputy U.S. Marshal Bass Reeves maintained his grip on Webb's throat as he turned his pistol toward Smith and fired once. Smith died in his failed attempt to defend a murderer.

With Smith killed right before his eyes, Webb gurgled out his assurance that he would come along peacefully.

Webb Flees

After the shootout in the bunkhouse, Reeves transported Webb to Fort Smith to be held for trial. However, a benefactor posted $17,000 for Webb's release, and the alleged preacher-killer was set free to await trial. When Webb did not appear on the date of the first hearing into the matter of the death of Reverend Steward, the bond was forfeited and another warrant was issued for Webb.

Most lawmen would probably be perturbed at having to go into the territory a second time after the same man. The practical application of the concept "innocent until proven guilty" caused occasional inefficiency, but Bass Reeves was, as always, undeterred. All Bass ever really needed for proper motivation was the warrant in hand.

This time, however, would be different than the last since there would be no opportunity for subterfuge. Both Reeves and Webb were well acquainted with each other. Whether that would make the apprehension harder or easier was yet to be determined as Bass rode out to the territory attempting to locate James Webb.

Reeves entered the Chickasaw Nation on the hunt for Webb. One of his many informants was certain they would find the fugitive hanging about Jim Bywater's General Store, located in modern day Woodford, Oklahoma. Reeves and his posse man Jim Cantrell spurred their mounts toward Bywater's General Store. The store was one of many watering holes in the nation which had not yet earned a place on a map, but Bass knew it well.

As they arrived in the vicinity of the general store, Reeves hung back. He sent Cantrell in to scout since Webb did not know Cantrell. Riding slowly, Cantrell approached the store. He saw Webb seated inside through the front window then signaled to Reeves to move in. Reeves tapped his heels lightly against the sides of his horse and rode toward the store.

Webb easily spotted the big man approaching on his grey horse. Even silhouetted by the sun, the man was unmistakably Bass Reeves. Webb sprang to his feet and filled his hands with his Winchester. Jumping out an open window, he broke into a dead run toward his horse in hopes of a fast ride to freedom.

It was not to be. Reeves anticipated his move and rode to a point between Webb and his horse, cutting off his escape. Instead of turning and running, Webb chose to advance and give fight. He swung his weapon up to his shoulder as he ran toward the marshal and opened fire. Luckily, he was pointing, not aiming. This, coupled with the bouncing movement of his run, caused Webb to miss as he fired. He continued closing the distance between himself and Reeves and fired three more times. One bullet cut a button off Reeves' coat, another chipped the pommel on his saddle, while the third cut his reins.

In the meantime, Reeves had spun his Winchester up to his shoulder and returned two quick shots, both of which lodged into the torso of the charging killer. Skidding to a stop in the dust, Webb fell and drew his revolver. Approaching, Reeves ordered Webb to let loose of his revolver.

The fight quickly drained out of Webb like water spilling from an upended canteen, and he tossed his gun out of reach into some tall grass. Webb had used up all the meanness in his life and knew he was a dying man. He called to Bass, who was the closest thing to family or friend he had at this juncture of his life, and said, "Take my hand."

Reeves took the dying man's hand, and Webb declared, "You are a brave man. I want you to take my revolver and scabbard as a present and you must accept them. Take it, for with it I have killed eleven men, four of them in Indian Territory and I expected you to be the twelfth." Webb's final wish was that the guns he wielded as a bad man would find their way into the hands of a good man.

Bywater, the store keeper, wrote down Webb's dying declaration for Reeves. Bass would later make a declaration of his own in his twilight years. He declared, "Jim Webb was the bravest man I ever met."

A Lawman of Many Faces

Deputy U.S. Marshal Bass Reeves was famous for his use of cunning disguises.

Bass was in pursuit of two criminals who were holed up in a cabin with such a view it would be impossible to approach unseen. Bass devised a plan. He took a hat and shot three holes in it, then changed into tattered clothing and hid his handcuffs in a bag. He left his posse men behind along with his horse and wagon and set to walking.

The distance he walked varies depending on the storyteller. Bass walked as few as three and as many as twenty-eight miles to get to the cabin. He did this to sell his subterfuge. To fool these men he not only had to say he walked a long way, he had to look like he had walked a long way. The only way to do that was to actually walk the distance.

Finally, Reeves staggered up to the cabin appearing exhausted. The wanted men listened to Reeves' fantastic tale. He told them he had been captured for crimes he had committed and managed to escape. He said he had ridden a long way, but his horse gave out. The two men were mesmerized as Reeves showed them his bullet-riddled hat, confirming the story.

So impressed were these men in Bass Reeves' story, they offered him food and drink and a place to sleep in their cabin. After dinner they shared a drink or two, and during the robust conversation they asked Bass to join them in their next robbery.

That night, as the fugitives slept in a drunken stupor, Reeves quietly handcuffed both of them and then let them sleep through the night. In the morning he woke them and explained that he'd let them sleep so they would be rested for their long ride back to the jail in Fort Smith.

In another case Bass dressed like a farmer and drove a wagon into a ditch in front of the cabin where the men he was looking for were holed up. As the men came out to see what the commotion was, he asked them for help pushing his wagon out of the ditch. The men helped push the wagon out, and while their hands were still empty and on the wagon, Bass produced his weapon and told them to keep their hands where they were; they were under arrest. The men were taken into custody without a shot having to be fired.

The Accident

In April 1884 Bass Reeves was involved in what was ultimately ruled to be a tragic accident while on the trail with a number of prisoners. His cook, William Leach, was shot dead. Two years later Reeves was arrested and charged with the murder.

This incident would impact heavily on Bass Reeves both financially and emotionally. Until the case was heard Bass Reeves was made to sit in jail among men he had arrested. Reeves had no money for bond because he had to use every cent he had saved for his defense. He also had to sell the fine home he had made for his family.

Bass was on trial for his life.

During this sensational trial, Reeves testified in his own defense. Reeves explained that he was seated near the cook fire and Leach was going about his business. It was Reeves' habit to inspect his weapons at the end of each day to make sure they were functional, just in case. On the trail it was not unusual for trouble to come calling at night.

On the night in question, he discovered his Winchester had an oversized bullet jammed into the chamber. He could not eject the round by working the action. Reeves took a knife and tried to pry the round out, but it would not budge.

During the process of attempting to free the round from the chamber, somehow Bass accidentally engaged the trigger. To his horror, the gun went off and the bullet hit Leach in the side of his neck. Reeves said he rushed to Leach's assistance, but there was nothing he could do to save the man.

The criminals he was transporting gave a different account, claiming Reeves deliberately killed Leach. These men had a score to settle with Bass Reeves and saw an opportunity to bring him down. They testified that Marshal Reeves was no better than themselves, for he had done murder.

After hearing all the testimony, the jury deliberated and reached a verdict. They based their ruling on two factors:

First, the witnesses against Reeves lacked credibility since all of them were criminals who had been arrested by Bass Reeves. They had reason to want to see Reeves suffer.

The second factor in their decision was based on Reeves' known accuracy with all firearms. They concluded that Bass Reeves, wielding a Winchester from such a short distance, would not have made such a shot with the rifle if killing Leach was his intent. The trajectory of the killing round supported Bass Reeves' version of the event. They concluded that if Bass had intended to kill Leach, the round would have been better placed and Leach would have died instantly.

Bass Reeves was found innocent of the murder of William Leach.

Since the criminals Reeves arrested lined up to testify that he had done murder in the William Leach case, historians are in a quandary about whether to believe the version Bass Reeves told, which the jury believed, or to believe one of the versions told by the criminals, who sorely wanted to see Reeves hang.

All should conclude that the death of William Leach was an accident. It is easy to come to the conclusion that Bass Reeves was a man of high integrity when one hears of an arrest he made in 1902.

Reeves' Most Difficult Case

In 1902 Bass Reeves served the most difficult warrant of his life. The warrant was for murder, and the suspect was his own son Benjamin, Bennie, who he loved dearly.

Bennie was a hard working young man. He married an extremely beautiful woman, and in an attempt to give her everything she needed, Bennie worked multiple jobs and long hours. Due to the long hours away from home, the two grew apart. There were rumors of infidelity on the part of Bennie's wife. Finally, Bennie confronted his wife, and this is Bennie's version of what transpired taken from his contemporary statement:

> On the morning of June 7, 1902, at 11:00 AM, I called upon my wife at her cousin's house in Muskogee asked her if it was true she was having or did have improper relations with John Wadly. She answered me that she thought more of his little finger than she did my whole body. By constant worry over her actions and breaking up of my home and receiving such an answer, I lost all control and shot her.

After shooting his wife, Bennie attempted suicide, but the round was a glancing blow. There are several versions of what happened next. All of the versions end the same. Benjamin fled the scene and a warrant was issued for his arrest. There was concern about the fact that he was Bass Reeves' son and that in Bennie's current state of mind he would not come along peacefully.

Bass knew what had to be done. He picked up the warrant and went into pursuit. In short order he located Bennie and brought back him back to face justice.

Bennie was convicted, sentenced, and sent to Fort Leavenworth Federal Prison. He served his sentence and returned home. Bennie became a barber and a pillar of his community. He never committed another crime. Bass remained close with Benjamin, as he did with all of his family throughout his life.

Law Enforcement Officer

In telling the story of a lawman like Bass Reeves, great attention and detail is most often given to the intense moments when lives hung in the balance and guns were blazing. The truth of the matter is that much of Reeves' time was spent entangled in the routine. For every arrest there was the long transport back to Fort Smith. Reeves accomplished efficiency by taking out "posse men" to assist him as well as a transport wagon and cook wagon. He, at times, was known to bring back as many as twenty-four wanted criminals on one trip, which could easily take a month or more.

The criminals' crimes included murder, illegal whiskey sales, horse stealing, larceny, incest, hog mutilation, and aggravated assault, to name a few. The long trail would finally come to an end after which came the dictating of reports and courtroom testimony. Reeves' life consisted of quiet routine punctuated by moments of indescribable intensity. It was a young man's job, but Reeves did it nearly his entire life as a free man.

In 1907 Oklahoma became a state, and the job of day to day law enforcement was no longer the responsibility of federal law enforcement officers. That responsibility transferred over to the state and municipalities. After thirty-two years of federal service as a deputy U.S. Marshal, Bass Reeves became the last and longest serving of Judge Parker's deputy marshals to retire. After retiring from the U.S. Marshals service, Bass took a position with the City of Muskogee Police Department.

As a city police officer, Bass abandoned the long trail rides for working a beat and shifts. He calmed domestic disturbances, broke up saloon fights, and instead of riding the endless trails on his grey sorrel, he rode about town on his "wheel." The wheel was the early twentieth century name for what would eventually be called a bicycle.

In Muskogee, Bass's reputation preceded him. It was said that criminals took the day off when Bass was working, but Bass still managed to collar his share of rough characters.

While in the twilight of his career, Bass was interviewed a number of times. He was a law enforcement legend in his own time, and his storied career was made even more amazing when considering that he performed these deeds as a black man during an age of unfathomable inequities. In a time when a black man was expected to bow his head when passing a white man on the street, Bass Reeves bowed to no man.

Reeves possessed the authority as well as the will and the skill to take dangerous men of all colors into custody. Reeves accomplished this more than just about any other man in his time with the possible exception of Deputy U.S. Marshal Bill Tilghman.

In one story about Reeves, a newspaper reported that Bass had brought in three thousand dangerous felons during his days as a deputy U.S. Marshal. This, without a doubt, was both a phenomenal number as well as an accurate estimate. In the same story, it was reported that Bass had killed twenty men in the line of duty.

Bass read the account and could not abide the unnecessary exaggeration that needed to be corrected. He confirmed the number of three thousand arrests but said that he had not killed twenty men. To Bass Reeves, taking a life was no insignificant consequence of the pursuit of justice. Reeves did not want the truth to be a casualty of his story. Reeves contacted the reporter and demanded that he make a correction of the record. He had indeed found it necessary to kill bad men in defense of himself and others. The number was not twenty but fourteen. This incident stands as one more testament to Bass Reeves' veracity.

In 1910 Bass Reeves died in his home surrounded by his family.

Deputy U.S. Marshal Bass Reeves' funeral was widely attended. The color of those attending did not matter for they were all members of a community and state that benefited from the firm but fair protection Bass Reeves had provided over the years. The funeral was also attended by the many officers who had served with him.

Whether or not Reeves was the basis for the Lone Ranger character doesn't really matter. Reeves was clearly a lawman of the highest order. He had ingenuity, courage, skills, honor, and a sense of duty that the actor Clayton Moore, who played the Lone Ranger on television and radio, could only aspire to portray. Bass Reeves lived and breathed these ideals, turning them into reality.

Bass Reeves, a former slave, was arguably one of the most able of all the great peacekeepers to ever strap on a Colt Peacemaker. From that day to this, some might argue that there were others as good, but none could be better than the great Bass Reeves.

Reeves would have been humbled by the glowing tributes written upon his passing. One of the lines, however, would probably have made him smile and nod his head in quiet satisfaction. In one lengthy and glowing obituary Deputy U.S. Marshal Bass Reeves was described as "absolutely fearless and knowing no master but duty."

A very special thanks to Professor Art T. Burton, author of Black Gun Silver Star. Professor Burton has authored articles about Bass Reeves that significantly assisted in retelling the story of this great officer. It was an honor to meet the man who has revived Bass Reeves' memory, Art T. Burton.

CHAPTER 5

DEPUTY U.S. MARSHAL GRANT T. JOHNSON, THE BEST LAW DOG YOU NEVER HEARD OF

On Christmas Day, 1900, John Tiger rode into to Eufaula, Oklahoma, drunk. Tiger was brandishing firearms intent on committing a Christmas day massacre. This was nine decades before Harris and Klebold entered Columbine High School shooting, inspiring the term "Active Shooter." John Tiger had the idea first.

For no apparent reason, other than to say he did it, Tiger opened fire with his Winchester and pistol shooting randomly at anyone in the street. His opening barrage shot the waist buttons off a small boy's pants, killed three men, and sent people running for their lives.

Marshal Grant T. Johnson heard the commotion and ran toward the sound of the gunfire. Upon spotting John Tiger, Marshal Johnson diverted him from his smorgasbord of death by engaging him in a sustained gunfight. His first shots succeeded in pinning Tiger down and covering the escape of innocents. Tiger momentarily stopped shooting to find cover.

As Tiger moved behind a large tree, Johnson took up a position behind another tree within range. It was here the two engaged in a fight that could only accommodate one winner. The sound of Christmas carols was replaced by the sound of bullets slapping into the trees.

Finally, the killer made a mistake. Between shots, John Tiger would duck behind his tree, but at one point he left his arm exposed. Marshal Johnson seized the opportunity and took careful aim at the target provided. He lined up his sights, took in a breath, let half of it out, and squeezed the trigger. His Winchester barked as the bullet spun straight and true.

Screaming in pain, Tiger dropped his rifle and gathered up his badly shattered arm. When Marshal Johnson called for Tiger to give it up, John Tiger surrendered.

The enraged citizens of Eufaula gathered and demanded Johnson give over his prisoner for immediate execution. They found a rope and chose a tree. Fire raged in their hearts that they believed could only be extinguished with the death of John Tiger. "An eye for an eye," was the only Bible verse any of them could remember this Christmas Day.

The townspeople were not prone to join a lynch mob, but each man in this crowd was willing to personally place the noose around John Tiger's neck and hoist him ignominiously aloft. It appeared that John Tiger was about to die. Only one man stood between Tiger and the mob, Deputy U.S. Marshal Grant Johnson.

Johnson would not save John Tiger for the sake of John Tiger. If it were legal, Johnson would have hung the man himself. John Tiger would be saved in the name of justice.

Johnson could not stand for one lawless act to be followed by another lawless act in his presence. He had not risked his life to have justice cheated by a lynch mob. Johnson faced down that mob ever-faithful to his oath and told them to go home. He reminded them of the fact that it was Christmas.

As the marshal delivered his Christmas sermon on justice, he stood before them with weapons reloaded. His determination to defend justice was equal to his defense of Eufaula's people. He assured them John Tiger would have his day in court and justice would be done.

Every man and woman present was aware of the content of Grant Johnson's character; the man was as good as his word. They were personally witnessing his legendary calm and courage under pressure as well as his skill as a communicator.

Deputy U.S. Marshal Grant Johnson was one of the only men in Oklahoma Territory that could have prevented the screaming assemblage from decorating a tree with John Tiger's lifeless body on that Christmas day. One man standing firm before them. One man telling them to go home.

One good man was all that was needed. They melted away like the Christmas snow in the afternoon sun rather than defy Deputy U.S. Marshal Grant T. Johnson's quiet, but effective, insistence.

By Christmas Day of 1900, Grant T. Johnson had already served and survived fourteen years wearing a deputy U.S. Marshal's badge in Oklahoma's unforgiving and hostile Indian Country. There may have been some deputy marshals as good as Johnson, but few were better in law enforcement at the dawn of the twentieth century.

Grant Johnson Early Years

Grant T. Johnson, whose parents were slaves to the Chickasaw and Creek Indians, was born in 1858. He was a black man, yet he also possessed striking Native American features. He wore a broad white hat, a black bandana, and a pistol deliberately positioned on each hip. He drew the pistols both smoothly and quickly.

Johnson would often travel with two saddled horses, a black horse and a bay. He was known to tie one up at one side of town while he rode to the other. This gave the appearance that he was in two places at once. While mounting his horses, he would confidently slide his Winchester into its scabbard without the slightest hesitation, as if he had practiced this particular movement a thousand times.

Johnson felt that this observable proficiency with his weapons helped achieve his ultimate goal, to bring his prisoners and himself in alive and without a fight. Johnson believed that appearing unbeatable went a long way toward discouraging resistance.

Marshal Johnson also felt the way you treated people could either calm or awaken the beast in a man. Marshal Johnson, at 5' 8" and 160 pounds, felt that he could accomplish this with his quiet, always respectful demeanor. He treated all people of the territory with a dignity he believed all men deserved. The way he treated men was at once his signature trademark as well as his secret weapon. Grant Johnson was described by Judge Isaac Parker, "The Hanging Judge," as one of his best marshals.

During Johnson's tenure as a deputy U.S. Marshal, he became one of the legends of law enforcement to come out of this wild, as yet unsettled land called Oklahoma Territory. Johnson often shared the trail with his counterpart Deputy U.S. Marshal Bass Reeves, who noted historian Art T. Burton believes may have been the real-life inspiration for the beloved character the Lone Ranger. If that was true, Professor Burton suggests Grant T. Johnson could possibly have been the inspiration for Tonto.

The real Grant T. Johnson, however, played second fiddle to no man wearing a badge. Johnson was a powerful example of law enforcement at its best in his own rite.

Muskogee Train Gunfight

Deputy U.S. Marshal Johnson lived in a violent time when gangs of dangerous armed men rode through the West contemptuous of laws and the lawmen who enforced them. These men took what they wanted and killed anyone who stood in their way.

Johnson not only dared to stand in their way, he also pursued them to the far corners of the Oklahoma Territory. When outlaws were on the run, it was figures like Johnson who put the fear into their hearts.

Even though Marshal Johnson wanted to bring his prisoners in alive to face justice, Oklahoma Territory was filled with men who made bringing them in alive an almost impossible task. On one occasion in 1891, Marshal Johnson was a passenger on a train when a rough-looking character boarded it near Checotah, Indian Territory. Marshal Johnson was almost certain he recognized the man through the trail dust and whiskers as a wanted man. After the man passed the seated marshal, Johnson decided he needed a closer look.

Attempting to be nonchalant, Johnson stood, walked past the man, and exited the door out of the train car and onto the exterior platform. There, Johnson paused, satisfied in the knowledge that the roughly hewn passenger was indeed the wanted man he thought him to be.

Convinced of the suspect's identity, Marshal Johnson drew his pistol and prepared to re-enter the car to take the man into custody. This moment of personal preparation was suddenly interrupted when the door to the car burst open and the wanted rogue exited, shooting wildly. Johnson instantly returned fire while simultaneously twirling to avoid the spray of bullets. During this short but violent engagement, at least eight shots were exchanged. The wanted man either deliberately jumped or fell wounded from the speeding train. Johnson was uncertain of which.

Due to Johnson's quick reaction to the sudden assault, all of the suspect's rounds went wide. However, Johnson could not be certain if the man was killed or wounded by his return fire. Quite possibly, the fall from the train may have killed him. Johnson sent a message to the engineer to stop the train, but the engineer refused to do so.

This was a time of frequent train robberies, and the wary engineer felt the arrival of an armed, wanted man on the train was a precursor to a train robbery. To stop the train would only facilitate the robbery. Instead of stopping, the engineer continued down the track faster than before.

Johnson could not argue with the engineer's reasoning.

One of two things ultimately happened to the man who fought with Marshal Johnson. Either the man died and his remains were taken into custody by many ranging scavengers in the territory, or the close call served to rehabilitate the dangerous man. He was never heard from again.

The One He Couldn't Save

In 1892 Marshal Johnson received a request to investigate a domestic violence case. The request came through Deputy U.S. Marshal Bass Reeves from Mattie Bittle, a woman seeking relief from the incessant beatings she was receiving from her husband. The most recent of these nearly killed her.

After gathering the facts from the battered and frightened wife, Johnson asked the court for a warrant to arrest Mattie's perennially violent husband, George Bittle, for brutally beating Mattie. The reason the court denied the request for a warrant is lost to history, but nonetheless, it was denied.

In speculation, the ruling was possibly due to the prevalent attitude toward domestic violence in the nineteenth century. It was the age of the "rule of thumb." In 1891 a husband was expected to "discipline" his wife occasionally. Sadly, in both the cases of a man beating his wife or a mule, neither was considered cruel nor socially unacceptable in those days. As long as the switch the husband chose was no thicker than his thumb, the beating was defensible. This is how the term "rule of thumb" came to be coined.

Whatever happened to Mattie Bittle was severe enough, even considering these barbaric guidelines, that Johnson felt prosecution was in order.

Mattie's husband George was a cruel man, undeserving of this good woman's love. As in so many modern cases, the next beating George administered killed Mattie. After beating his wife to death, George fled into the territory.

Mattie's death now constituted probable cause to arrest George. Marshal Johnson made another request for a warrant for George

Bittle, but this time the warrant was for murder. With warrant in hand, Marshal Johnson personally tracked down Bittle into the territory and brought him to back to face justice. Johnson would always be haunted by the murder of this young woman, which could have been prevented.

The Whiskey Gunfight

Whiskey, then as now, was federally regulated. Due to the public perception of the death and destruction the demon drink caused, deputy U.S. Marshals were expected to vigorously enforce these laws. The Prohibition Movement had its roots firmly planted in the frontier towns of the West. Many Oklahomans wanted new laws written and old laws enforced to end the sway "John Barleycorn" had on so many in the territory.

The enforcement of liquor laws would seem to be a routine task of law enforcement; however, nothing in law enforcement is routine.

In 1895 Marshal Johnson located and challenged three illegal whiskey peddlers to surrender. Instead, the three smugglers offered a galling fire which threatened to shorten Johnson's career and life. Marshal Johnson, who was a crack shot, returned their fire and killed their leader outright.

After looking into the face of their dead partner, the two surviving whiskey smugglers abruptly opted to abandon the fight and surrender. Landing in a jail at the end of the trail was preferable to landing in a grave beside the trail.

After going through the surrender ritual, Johnson granted the two men a request. He allowed them to bury their leader and say a few appropriate words over their fallen friend. The ceremony was followed by the long trip back to Fort Smith to face justice. Their leader was arraigned in a higher venue.

In 1896 the federal court in Fort Smith lost jurisdiction of Johnson's bailiwick, which covered Muskogee and Eufaula. This could have meant the end of Marshal Johnson's career, but the citizens of Eufaula were so appreciative of Marshal Johnson's performance, they requested that he be transferred permanently to the jurisdiction of the Muskogee-Eufaula Court. Their request was granted.

Gunfight on Horseback

On September 6, 1901, the local newspaper in Eufaula reported Marshal Johnson's attempt to break up a fight between two men. As he arrived, the disturbance was just then turning from fisticuffs into a gunfight. Frank Wilson and Wade Smith sincerely wanted to kill each other.

Wilson, thwarted in his attempt to kill Wade Smith by the timely arrival of Marshal Johnson, jumped upon his horse and spurred it on. This may have solved the problem if not for the fact that as he rode away Wilson fired two shots at Wade Smith in one last attempt to kill his rival.

Johnson could not tolerate an attempt to commit murder made in his presence, so he went into pursuit of Wilson. Johnson fired a warning shot and called out, "Stop, or I'll shoot."

Wilson answered, "I would rather die than surrender." After shouting his preference, Wilson turned in the saddle and took deliberate aim at Johnson, who was already prepared for such an eventuality. Johnson fired first in defense of his life while at a full gallop; Wilson tumbled off his horse.

Marshal Johnson rushed Wilson to a doctor, but Wilson died the next day after lingering for twenty-four hours.

A Career to Remember

The yellowing newspapers of his day relate numerous detailed accounts of Marshal Grant T. Johnson. He quelled riots with his decisive presence and diffused tribal uprisings with his considerable communication and intervention skills. He put a run on rustlers and outlaw gangs while helping to tame a wild territory. Johnson brought all manner of criminals to justice, from meat thieves to murderers, risking his life while never faltering from his duty.

In an obituary in 1927, the *Indian Journal* reported, "Johnson, although a Negro, was a fearless, courageous officer and had many friends both among the colored and white citizens of the state."

Additionally, the *Journal* reported Johnson "…will go down as one of the best peace officers this section of the state ever had." In a state which touts names like Bass Reeves, Bill Tilghman, Chris Madsen, and Heck Thomas, that is high praise indeed.

THE EARPS OF TOMBSTONE

ven though the Earps spent only a portion of their lives as lawmen, they have captured and held the interest and imagination of Americans ever since that fateful day in Tombstone when three souls were "hurled into eternity" in a matter of thirty seconds. No compilation of influential lawmen could be complete without paying homage to the legacy of the Earps sealed in a dusty alley in Tombstone, Arizona, in 1881.

Where does one start with the Earps? How about in 1862? It was in this year that three of the Earp brothers, James, Warren, and Virgil, enlisted in the Union Army. Virgil was married at the time, so he kissed his wife Magdalena and their infant baby daughter Nellie goodbye.

Wyatt, who was incredibly close to his brothers, was too young to enlist. The boy was beside himself as he watched his brothers leave without him. After they left, Wyatt would run away to join his brothers time and time again. Each time, his father Nicholas tracked him down and brought him back to the farm.

Virgil's Tragedy

The older Earp brothers were mustered into the 83rd Illinois. While Virgil was away at war, Magdalena's father, who was against them marrying when they were only sixteen years old, told her a lie. She was told Virgil had fallen in battle in Tennessee and was killed in action. In reality, Virgil's unit was involved in garrison duty holding the city of Nashville at the time, and Virgil was alive and well.

Perceiving herself a widow, Magdalena re-married. Magdalena and Virgil's daughter moved west with her new husband after shedding many a tear for Virgil. She believed her Virgil lay buried in a grave on a far-away battlefield. Magdalena eventually settled in Oregon.

When Virgil returned from the war, he discovered his wife and daughter were gone. Since she thought Virgil was dead, she had left no forwarding address other than saying she was going west. The heartbroken Virgil Earp turned west also, determined to make a new life.

Wyatt's Tragedy

After the war, Wyatt Earp was drawn to a career in law enforcement. He took a position as a constable in Lamar, Missouri. It was in Lamar where Wyatt met, fell deeply in love with, and married Urilla Sutherland. They bought a home and began their life together. He was thrilled when he discovered his beautiful wife was expecting their first child. By all accounts, Wyatt and Urilla were blissfully happy together.

Prior to the birth of their child, life for Wyatt and Urilla took a tragic turn. Urilla was struck down with typhoid fever. After just one year of marriage, Wyatt lost his wife and the unborn child they were expecting to raise together.

Wyatt Earp was devastated. He left the memories of Lamar and also headed west. He floundered inside the bottle for a period. He even had some scrapes with the law. Eventually, he hit bottom and lifted himself up. He came out the emotional haze serious, focused, and sober. For the rest of his life, he swore off alcohol and preferred ice cream instead.

The Earps Established as Lawmen

Like many in the West, Wyatt and his brothers initially worked a variety of jobs outside of law enforcement, but they were gradually drawn to it and were good at it.

It was actually Virgil, not Wyatt, who had the longest career in law enforcement. Virgil was sucked into the career in the heat of the moment. He saw Arizona's Yavapai County Sheriff Ed Bowers in the midst of a running gun battle with armed robbers. Virgil offered his assistance to the sheriff with his Winchester at the ready. It seemed like a good idea at the time, so Bowers deputized Virgil on the spot.

Virgil's first action as a deputy sheriff was to take careful aim at one suspect and fire twice. Both shots struck the desperado in the head, marking the end of one career and the beginning of another. Virgil probably holds some sort of record for engaging in his first gunfight seconds after he was sworn in as a law enforcement officer.

Wyatt, on the other hand, established a solid reputation as a law enforcement officer first in Wichita and then in Dodge City. "Cow Towns" desperately needed men like Wyatt. He was known for his apparent lack of fear as well as for having a steely gaze that could stop a man in his tracks. Even though Wyatt was an expert shot, he was also a talented pugilist. He had been a boxer in his teens and a referee on occasion throughout his adult life. When needed, he knew how to apply the art of self-defense to facilitate the arrest of a non-cooperative belligerent. He preferred this to gun play.

In all cases but one, prior to Tombstone, when suspects resisted Wyatt's efforts to place them under arrest, Wyatt battled with his fists rather than bullets. He also was known to occasionally "bash" or "buffalo" a man with his pistol. Although it sounds harsh nowadays, it was an acceptable, less-than-lethal alternative for law enforcement back then.

Wyatt's first and only use of deadly force prior to Tombstone occurred when he was in Dodge City. A cowboy named George Hoyt was riding wildly about the town, shooting in every direction and endangering every soul. The rounds were not directed into the air but toward businesses and people. Hoyt appeared determined to kill somebody, anybody.

Hoyt disregarded all calls to cease and desist from his deadly escapade, so Wyatt could see that he had but one option. He took careful aim at the out-of-control gunman and fired. George's horse was in full gallop through the streets of Dodge City as Wyatt shot. The round knocked the drunken shooter out of the saddle. Hoyt was rushed to a doctor, but he later died from his wounds.

The Earps Arrive in Tombstone, Arizona

Virgil, in the meantime, had become constable for Prescott, Arizona. He proved so effective there he was appointed Deputy U.S. Marshal by U.S. Marshal Crawley Dake.

Marshal Dake directed Virgil to Tombstone, Arizona, where a loosely organized but truly lawless group of cross-border raiders hung their hats and corralled their horses. These rustler/raiders called themselves the "Cowboys." They were armed and dangerous men who were running roughshod over the law in two nations, rustling cattle on both sides of the border.

The Cowboys viewed lawmen as individuals who, in the course of their business, needed to be owned or intimidated into allowing the Cowboys to have free rein. This world view would go a long way toward creating friction between themselves and the Earps. It was not in the Earps' nature to be bought nor intimidated.

The local sheriff of Cochise County, John Behan, made no effort to rein in the Cowboys. Some believed he was in collusion with them. If this was not the case, at the very least he allowed them room to operate unfettered by the law.

Wyatt headed to Tombstone to join Virgil and was, once again, drawn into the law enforcement business. Upon arrival, there was immediate friction between the Earps and the Cowboys.

In later testimony, Wyatt traced the genesis of the conflict to July 1880 when Virgil, Morgan, and Wyatt joined Captain Joseph A. Hurst, Commanding Officer at Fort Bennett, in an effort to locate stolen mules. The trail led to the McLaury Ranch.

The posse utilized a branding iron that changed the "U.S." brand to "D.8." After locating the evidence, tension built toward confrontation. The Earps were ready to proceed with the investigation, but Captain Hurst was not so inclined.

Captain Hurst agreed to back down since he was not prepared to possibly kill, or die, over a mule. A verbal agreement was reached whereby the Cowboys would return the stolen mules to the military. The captain as well as the Earps would leave the ranch rather than pursue the investigation further. Hurst withdrew his complaint after the McLaury's promised to return the mules, but the mules were never returned.

This incident would lead to the Cowboys feeling empowered enough to continually threaten the lives of the Earps in an attempt to intimidate them into inaction.

The Death of Fred White

Another tension-building event was no small deal. On January 6, 1880, one of the Cowboy's most notorious members, Curly Bill Brocius, and five other Cowboys began shooting up Tombstone for the pure fun of it. Tombstone's City Marshal Fred G. White intervened and ordered Brocius to relinquish his pistol. Curly Bill appeared to comply, but as he turned his pistol over to White, it discharged, striking White in the groin.

Wyatt, who was unarmed at the time, borrowed a pistol and knocked Brocius unconscious with it. With this done he backed the rest of the Cowboys down and, in an undeniable act of courage, hauled Brocius to jail for murdering Marshal White.

Ironically, just days later, it was Deputy U.S. Marshal Wyatt Earp who saved Curly Bill from an enraged lynch mob by sneaking him off to Tucson for his trial. Tombstone loved Fred White, and although Brocius claimed the shooting was an accident, many did not see it that way and wanted Brocius to pay. Many of the townspeople were tired of the lawless Cowboys having their way.

A court of law was convened, and ruling the death of Fred White as accidental, a jury acquitted Brocius of all charges. The jury arrived at this verdict because of a death bed statement made by White in which he reportedly said the shooting was indeed an accident.

In the wake of Fred White's death, Virgil Earp was appointed to replace him as city marshal. In effect, it was Virgil who was the Chief of Police in Tombstone, not Wyatt. Virgil also retained his position as Deputy U.S. Marshal.

Wyatt, as always, was determined to help his brother in any way that he could. He also held positions as a deputy U.S. Marshal, deputy sheriff for Pima County, and deputy city marshal for the City of Tombstone. This was not at all unusual for the times, especially for individuals with a reputation like Wyatt Earp.

Having expanded jurisdiction helped a great deal when lawmen were in pursuit of criminals who had a tendency to avoid prosecution for their crimes by merely changing names and jurisdictions.

Tension Builds in Tombstone

Prior to the arrival of the Earps, the Cowboys had a sweet deal, which allowed them to come and go as they pleased in Tombstone. That changed when the Earps arrived. The rift was not just between the Earps and the Cowboys. The town was divided in their support between the Cowboys and the Earps.

This allegiance came about because, for the most part, the Cowboys committed their crimes elsewhere, and when they returned home to Tombstone, they spent their ill-gotten gains. Businessmen liked the Cowboy's money. Also, not all of the Cowboy's enterprises were illegal. These men had supporters, as did the Earps.

The conflict between the Cowboys and the Earps started with the stolen government mules, but other events, such as the death of Fred White, a crooked election, and an unsolved double-homicide stagecoach robbery, added fuel to the fire. There was also the appearance that the courts would not convict a Cowboy of anything requiring more than a small fine as punishment.

Over and above all of these issues, the Earps were growing weary of having their lives threatened on a daily basis. A fight was brewing in Tombstone.

All of these broken fences could have been mended if only the Earps would have put aside the law and bowed to the gang, paying them homage as did Behan. The Earps, however, would rather die first, and the Cowboys would give them the opportunity to do so.

Gunfight at the O.K. Corral

The night before the famous gunfight, Ike Clanton was in the middle of the street drunkenly brandishing a weapon and shouting threats. Virgil came up behind him and hit him with his revolver over the head. Ike was taken to jail, and the next day he pled guilty to carrying a concealed weapon and paid a fine of $25.

That morning, October 26, 1881, Wyatt confronted Tom McLaury about carrying a pistol in town. Even though Wyatt could see the pistol in McLaury's belt, Tom McLaury denied that he was armed. With lightning speed, Wyatt slapped McLaury with one hand then pulled out a revolver and hit him over the head. Instead of arresting McLaury, however, Wyatt left him lying in the street.

Eventually, the Cowboys gathered near C. S. Fly's boarding house and photographic studio, which was a short distance from the O.K. Corral. Tom McLaury and Ike Clanton were sporting head wounds received from the Earps, and they were angry. Word reached Virgil Earp that the group was armed and threatening the Earps once again.

This could have been just another day in Tombstone except Virgil, Wyatt, and Morgan were bone-tired of the constant threats. The building tension was coming to a head.

There was an ordinance in Tombstone against people carrying guns in town. Virgil decided to take action against the group of Cowboys, who were armed and hanging out by C. S. Fly's.

Virgil Earp deputized Wyatt, Morgan, and their friend Doc Holliday. On Virgil's command, the four began the long walk toward the O.K. Corral, intent upon disarming the Cowboys gathered there. They probably suspected this would trigger a fight, but there must have been some consolation in knowing it would come on their terms. They knew the Cowboys were not above back-shooting the Earps, and their chances for survival were much better if the fight took place face to face.

As the four lawmen walked steadily toward their destiny, the watching townspeople realized a moment of reckoning was imminent. Word spread through Tombstone that there would be a fight today. By walking four abreast, it confirmed everyone's suspicions.

When the group approached Fly's Lodging House, the Earps saw Sheriff Behan talking with the Cowboys. Behan approached the Earps and did something unforgivable for one law officer to do to another. Behan told the Earps, "I have disarmed them." This was a lie, and he knew it. The Cowboys were still armed.

Sheriff John Behan accomplished little with his statement, however, because no one in the Earp entourage believed or trusted him. Behan may not have been the enemy, but he was no friend.

Behan was told, "If you have disarmed them, Johnny, then there will be no trouble."

With that said, the law officers, bypassed Sheriff Behan and stopped about ten feet from the Cowboys. Standing before them were Ike Clanton, Billy Clanton, Frank McLaury, Tom McLaury, and Billy Claiborne.

Virgil called out to them, "Throw up your hands!"

To this day, there has been much debate about this incident. What is overlooked in all the controversy is this simple fact: if the Cowboys would have complied with Virgil's lawful command, this moment would have passed unnoticed by history. The Cowboys did not comply.

Instead, witnesses agreed that Virgil's command was followed by the Cowboys reaching for their weapons and cocking them. In spite of the fact that this action could have caused a deadly response, Virgil tried one more time to avoid the fight by calling out, "Hold. I don't want that!"

There was another tense pause. Suddenly, two shots rang out fired simultaneously by Frank McLaury and Wyatt Earp. These shots were immediately followed by general firing from both sides. Wyatt's first shot mortally wounded the person he believed to be the most dangerous man present, Frank McLaury. Frank was shot in the stomach, but even so, he was still in the fight.

With the first sound of gunshots, Claiborne and Behan fled. Ike ran toward Wyatt. Grabbing him, Ike begged him not to shoot because he was not armed. Wyatt shrugged him off and said, "The fight has commenced, Ike. Get a gun or get out." Ike ran like the wind. Little is said about this moment, but it speaks volume about Wyatt and the intent of the Earps. Of all the Cowboys, the Earps disliked Ike the most. Yet because Ike was not armed and presented no threat, Wyatt spared him.

As the fighting continued, Holliday was on the move inflicting a great deal of damage. He killed Tom McLaury with a double barreled shotgun blast to the chest as McLaury was reaching for a rifle in its scabbard on his horse. That done, Doc tossed the shotgun aside and opened fire with his pistol. Billy Clanton fired at Wyatt, missed, and was immediately hit in the right wrist by Morgan Earp.

Still not acknowledging defeat, Billy transferred his pistol to his left hand and continued the fight. Doc was grazed in the hip, Virgil was shot in the calf, and Morgan had a round travel across both shoulders before the guns of Billy Clanton and Frank McLaury were silenced forever by the combined fire of Virgil, Wyatt, Morgan, and Doc.

Finally, it was over. Just thirty seconds had passed, thirty seconds that would inspire books, movies, television shows, magazine articles, historical re-enactments, and passionate discussions from that half minute to this one.

Sheriff Behan Arrests the Earps

Immediately after the shots stopped echoing through the streets of Tombstone, Behan emerged from hiding and attempted to arrest the Earps. Wyatt coldly answered the sheriff with a smoking gun still in hand, "I don't think I'll let you arrest me today, John." Behan took one look into those fabled eyes of Wyatt Earp and backed down.

Eventually, after assuring that their families were safe, Wyatt, Morgan, Virgil, and Doc submitted to arrest, and there was a hearing in front of Judge Wells Spicer. After a month of testimony, Judge Spicer ruled:

> "I am of the opinion that the defendant, Virgil Earp, as chief of police, subsequently calling upon Wyatt Earp, and J. H. Holliday to assist him in arresting and disarming the Clantons and McLaurys— committed an injudicious and censurable act, and although in this he acted incautiously and without due circumspection, yet when we consider the condition of affairs incidental to a frontier country, the lawlessness and disregard for human life; the existence of a law-defying element in [our] midst; the fear and feeling of insecurity that has existed; the supposed prevalence of bad, desperate and reckless men who have been a terror to the country, and kept away capital and enterprise, and considering the many threats that have been made against the Earps, I can attach no criminality to his unwise act. In fact, as the result plainly proves, he needed the assistance and support of staunch and true friends, upon whose courage, coolness and fidelity he could depend, in case of an emergency."

No charges were filed.

It was hardly over.

Ambushed

On December 28, 1881, Tombstone Chief of Police Virgil Earp was on foot patrol in the streets of Tombstone. He was shot in the back and arm with buckshot from an ambush. He would survive but lose permanent use of one arm.

Ike's hat was found lying at the scene, but Pete Spence, Johnny Ringo, Johnny Barnes, Ike, and Phin Clanton had the charges dismissed against them.

On March 18, 1881, while Wyatt was watching his brother play pool, the Cowboys struck again. One round hit the wall just above Wyatt's head; another round was buried deep in Morgan. Morgan died in Wyatt's arms.

Deputy U.S. Marshal Wyatt Earp, while engaged in an effort to get Virgil, his family, and Morgan's body out of the territory, spotted an impending ambush in the Tucson railroad yard. He was able to break up the ambush and prevent further death and injury to his family members on the train.

It is not hard to analyze what happened to Wyatt in that railroad yard. Someone had ambushed one of his brothers, disabling his arm for life. If that was not enough, they shot Morgan dead while he was playing pool. Everyone knew who was responsible, but in both cases charges were dismissed in spite of the fact that the Cowboys said they were going to do it, did it, and even left a hat at the scene of the crime.

Now, in the railroad yard in Tucson, Wyatt spotted one of the men involved in the ambushes lying in wait. He could only draw one reasonable conclusion. The men, Frank Stillwell and Ike Clanton, were there to ambush and kill the Earps.

Witnesses saw armed men chasing other armed men in the railroad yard. Shots were heard shortly thereafter, and the next day Frank Stillwell was found dead of very unnatural causes. His body had many bullets in him. Stillwell was not only a suspect in the previous ambushes, but he had also been tried and acquitted of two homicides and a stage robbery in separate incidents after other Cowboys had given him a false alibi.

Stillwell's death was anything but a "whodunit." Stillwell had escaped justice too many times and then attempted to ambush the remnants of the Earp family. Frank Stillwell was shot to death by his judge, jury, and executioner, Wyatt Earp. Holliday had no love lost for Stillwell and may have fired a round or two into the Cowboy as well.

This, by today's standards, may be considered excessive. Stillwell should have been brought to justice, but the courts had had the opportunity to deliver justice and had failed.

After Frank's shot-up body was found the next morning, a warrant was issued for Earp and his posse. The lawman was now a wanted man. Earp was still undeterred. The rounds fired into Stillwell constituted merely the opening volley in what some people refer to as the Vendetta Ride.

After Stillwell, Wyatt and his posse found another Cowboy involved in Morgan's murder. Wyatt located Florentino Cruz in a logging camp. One version of the events is that Cruz went for his gun and was shot down.

Accurate details of what transpired are lacking since police reports were not written on any of these events. What is known is that Cruz was found shot dead near a campfire in the logging camp.

Two More Dead

After the death of Cruz, the Earp posse arrived at a watering hole called Iron Springs. They were operating under the supervision of U.S. Marshal Crawley Dake and were expecting to be re-supplied. Instead of allies with supplies, they were met by a yet another Cowboy ambush.

The Cowboys were led by none other than the killer of Marshal Fred White, Curly Bill Brocius. This man, who Wyatt had saved from a lynch mob, was now lying in wait to kill Deputy U.S. Marshal Earp. Brocius and his men laid down a barrage on the Earp posse.

One member of the posse, Texas Jack Vermillion, went down with his horse; the others took cover. Wyatt, however, was focused. He ignored the gunfire even though by all accounts bullets were hitting all around him. He had his sights on Curly Bill Brocius, determined he would pay for his crimes here and now.

Wyatt and Brocius saw each other across the battlefield. Just as if Earp had thrown down a gauntlet, Brocius left cover to advance on Wyatt as he fired from his Winchester. (Another account maintains he was firing from his shotgun.) Curly Bill Brocius fired repeatedly at Wyatt but missed each time. Wyatt calmly turned in his saddle, aimed, and fired once, both barrels of his shotgun hitting Brocius squarely in the chest. Brocius was killed instantly.

With their leader dead and Wyatt Earp in the open, the Cowboys focused their fire on Wyatt hitting Wyatt's boot heel, saddle pommel, and the coattails of his duster, but once again, Wyatt escaped unscathed. Not a bullet touched him. Wyatt returned their fire with as much vigor and more accuracy. He killed one more of the Cowboys, Johnny Barnes. With two cowboys down, Wyatt turned to rescue Texas Jack with the assistance of Doc Holliday, and all three retreated to cover while firing at the Cowboys. With two of their number either dead or dying, the remaining Cowboys lost their enthusiasm for this poorly executed ambush and scattered.

The close call would mark the end of the Vendetta Ride of Wyatt Earp. Wyatt had the financial and moral support of the territorial U.S. Marshal Crawley Dake, but Sheriff Behan was leading the local anti-Earp faction.

During the Earps' time, there were many who felt they were courageous and honorable law enforcement officers placed in an incorrigible, corrupt environment. Others felt the Earps were as bad as the men they were arresting. Which version of the story is the truth is up to the reader. Some insight can be gained from the resignation letter submitted by Virgil and Wyatt when they resigned as Deputy U.S. Marshals:

> Major C. P. Dake,
> United States Marshal,
> Grand Hotel, Tombstone—
>
> Dear Sir:
> In exercising our official functions as deputy United States marshals in this territory, we have endeavored always unflinchingly to perform the duties entrusted to us. These duties have been exacting and perilous in their character, having to be performed in a community where turbulence and violence could almost any moment be organized to thwart and resist

the enforcement of the process of the court issued to bring criminals to justice. And while we have a deep sense of obligation to many of the citizens for their hearty cooperation in aiding us to suppress lawlessness, and their faith in our honesty of purpose, we realize that, notwithstanding our best efforts and judgment in everything which we have been required to perform, there has arisen so much harsh criticism in relation to our operations, and such a persistent effort having been made to misrepresent and misinterpret our acts, we are led to the conclusion that, in order to convince the public that it is our sincere purpose to promote the public welfare, independent of any personal emolument or advantages to ourselves, it is our duty to place our resignations as deputy United States marshals in your hands, which we now do, thanking you for your continued courtesy and confidence in our integrity, and shall remain subject to your orders in the performance of any duties which may be assigned to us, only until our successors are appointed.

Very respectfully yours,

Virgil W. Earp.

Wyatt S. Earp.

Ultimately Wyatt decided that if he continued there would be no good end to it all. He disbanded his posse after his resignation as marshal and left the state. The warrants for his arrest were never served.

One More Body

One major actor in the ambush of Virgil Earp was found alone with a bullet in his head on July 14, 1882. Johnny Ringo had been present at the ambush and was disappointed that he missed the "Gunfight at the OK Corral." The death was ruled a suicide, but to this day there is a great deal of conjecture about Ringo's death. Some believe he was the last victim of the Vendetta Ride.

It makes a most interesting conclusion to the story to believe Wyatt secretly returned to Arizona and met the deadly gunfighter Johnny Ringo in a face to face contest of arms. The truth is most likely that Johnny Ringo, a chronic brooder, took his own life.

Some may feel that there never was justice for the deaths of Brocius, Barnes, Stillwell, Cruz, and possibly Ringo. Others assert that their deaths were justice served up Earp-style. The argument continues to this day.

Post O.K. Corral Virgil

Virgil traveled to California with his family. His arm, which was wounded in the ambush, would be supported by a sling the rest of his life, but this did not prevent him from serving as a railroad detective, Colton, California, city marshal, and a deputy for Esmeralda County, Nevada.

In 1898 Virgil received a letter from someone in his past. As it turned out, his first wife happened to read accounts about the Earps and realized it was her "deceased" husband they were talking about. She sent him the letter after discovering he had not died in the Civil War.

As soon as Virgil received the letter from Magdalena, he packed a bag, boarded a train, and rode it to Portland, Oregon, to reunite with his wife. She introduced him to his daughter, now all grown up. Virgil's daughter was married and, ironically, acquired the name Mrs. Nellie Law.

In a glorious moment in Virgil's life, Nellie introduced Virgil to his grandchildren. The family separated by war was once again together. It must have been a cheerful and tearful reunion to say the least.

Although Virgil and Magdalena had found separate lives after their tragic parting, the family maintained a relationship throughout the remainder of his life.

In 1905, Virgil died at the age of sixty-two. His body was claimed by his daughter, who brought her father back to Portland, Oregon, where he was buried according to his wishes. He wanted to be close to his grandchildren.

Post O.K. Corral Wyatt

Wyatt lived out the remainder of his life with his common law wife, the beautiful actress Josie Marcus. He met her in Tombstone, where he had won her away from Sheriff John Behan. Every trail he rode after Tombstone, he rode with Josie. His pursuits included being a saloon keeper, sporting man, and occasional gold miner.

Wyatt came to the forefront of the American Press one more time in 1896. Wyatt was hired to referee a Heavyweight Championship Fight between Bob Fitzsimmons and Sailor Tom Sharkey.

The fight sparked an intense controversy when Bob Fitzsimmons struck a blow somewhere into Sharkey's mid-section. Sharkey dropped to the canvas and held his groin, calling foul. Fitzsimmons claimed he hit Sharkey in the solar-plexus. Half the crowd thought it was indeed a groin shot while the other half did not see at that way. Wyatt ruled that it was a punch to the groin and gave the championship to Sharkey because he was hit by an illegal blow and could not continue.

The most telling moment in that fight night, however, did not take place in the ring. It was the moment when, even though Wyatt Earp was a thousand miles and fifteen years removed from the dusty alley in Tombstone, he was still scarred by the events that took place in that period of his life. Even though he was surrounded by a cheering crowd of people who admired him, he found it necessary to have a pistol at the ready.

Before the fight had even started, as Wyatt was entering the ring he was contacted by a police captain and disarmed of the pistol he had concealed upon his person. Apparently Wyatt was still prepared to defend himself.

Last Words

After Tombstone, Wyatt Earp never again wore a badge, but he and his brothers' determined, albeit controversial, effort to bring justice to a lawless land secured their place in law enforcement history.

Wyatt Earp died in 1929, the last remaining survivor of the Gunfight at the O.K. Corral. His last words, like his life, are up for interpretation. He turned to his wife Josie as she sat next to him and said, "Suppose… suppose….," and then he died.

Deputy U.S. Marshal Wyatt Earp, like Virgil, was a man of action not of words. He left some timeless wisdom, however, for any law enforcement officer to take with them into any gunfight. Wyatt Earp, the legend, learned the hard way that in a gunfight, "Fast is fine… accuracy is final."

A television show, which ran from 1955 to 1961 starring Hugh O'Brian as Wyatt Earp, had a theme song that went like this:

I'll tell you a story, a real life true story,
a tale of the Western Frontier.
The West it was lawless, but one man was
flawless, and his is the story you'll hear.
Wyatt Earp, Wyatt Earp, brave, courageous, and bold,
Long live his fame, and long live his glory,
and long may his story be told.

Wyatt's story can never be just a story of Wyatt. It will always be a story of the Earps. This story will always be told because it is one part American history and one part American legend. It features love, hate, and the timeless battle between good and evil.

Whether the story of the Earps is told as history or legend, it is a story that people never tire of hearing. Americans love stories about underdogs taking a stand and facing overwhelming odds even though they would be better off, and much safer, to back down. Virgil, Wyatt, Morgan, and their good friend Doc took a stand, fought a good fight, and "long will their story be told."

CHAPTER 7

BILL TILGHMAN.
THE BEST OF US ALL

In the lawless West there was a breed of men who could not stand by and do nothing in the midst of lawlessness. Coming forward to pin on a badge, these men made a difference. Bill Tilghman's name must be given a prominent place on every list of names identifying the men whose courage and six-guns transformed the Wild West from a graveyard of lost souls into a place you could raise a family and prosper.

Bat Masterson, a man who bore witness to the deeds and character of Bill Tilghman, once said of him, "He was everything you would want in a hero. His sense of justice and fairness separated him from all the other lawmen like night and day."

Early Years

Bill Tilghman was born on a farm in Iowa on July 4, 1854, and two years later his family moved to a farm in Kansas. At seventeen, Bill headed west eager to leave the monotonous rows of corn in pursuit of adventure. In the decades that followed, Bill would bite off more adventure than any ten men could chew. Bill would thrive on the life he pursued and live it to the fullest, all the way to the very end of his trail.

Bill Tilghman was skilled with both his long guns and the pistols he carried and was not afraid to use them in a just cause.

He initially applied those skills as a buffalo hunter. In those early years it must have seemed to Bill that there was an endless supply of the large beasts, which populated the plains in numbers impossible to count. Each day, Bill would venture out into the wilderness and shoot and skin until he ran out of daylight. Each night he would return to his camp to eat and sleep so he could do it all again the next day. When he filled his wagon, he would return to civilization and trade his buffalo hides for cash and supplies.

The Cheyenne had a different point of view. They perceived that the white men were not engaged in the hunting of buffalo but the extermination of them. The end of the buffalo meant the end of their way of life.

While hunting in Kansas in 1872, Bill's camp was targeted by the Cheyenne. Upon returning to his camp from the day's hunt, Bill discovered that raiding Cheyenne had carried off or burned everything he owned. Many hunters receiving such a warning would have counted their blessings and skedaddled, glad to be alive and still attached to their scalp.

Bill refused to run and failed to see it from the Cheyenne's point of view. In his defense, few white men in 1872 did. From Bill Tilghman's point of view, his property had been destroyed, his livelihood threatened, and if there was to be justice in a wilderness such as this, he would have to pursue it himself.

Bill and his fellow hunters stretched out their new skins to dry and re-supplied themselves. Then, instead of hunting, Bill hid close by and waited until the Cheyenne raiders returned. Bill assumed they were the same Cheyenne raiders, back to repeat their performance. As the group began looting Tilghman's camp, Bill decided this was the raiding party he had been waiting for. In his mind, Tilghman tried them and found them guilty. His Sharp's rifle barked out their sentence. The Cheyenne raiders fought back, and although they outnumbered Tilghman seven to one, they were shocked by the sudden, unexpected ferocity and accuracy of Bill's fire. When the smoke cleared, Bill Tilghman was four ponies richer. Only three of the raiders escaped with their lives and a hard lesson.

Bill's personal battles with the Cheyenne did not always land in the win column. At one point during this period, Bill was joined by his brother Richard in the lucrative Buffalo hunting business. Bill and his brother were attacked one day by raiding Cheyenne, and although the warriors were driven away, Richard lay dead on the field after the skirmish.

Possibly inspired to change his career by the loss of his brother, Bill left buffalo hunting as the raiding turned into an all-out war with the Cheyenne. Having covered the territory far and wide as a hunter, Bill expertly served as a cavalry scout during the hostilities.

Dodge City

As the buffalo herds were depleted by over-hunting, Bill left the isolated life on the frontier. He had always been frugal with his money, and he determined that since he did not drink, entering the saloon business would be a wise way to prosper. He set up his business in Dodge City.

In his buffalo hunting days, Bill met and befriended a pair of brothers, Ed and Bat Masterson, who also hunted buffalo. In 1877 Bat Masterson was sheriff of Ford County, in which Dodge City was located, while his brother Ed was marshal of Dodge City. Bat convinced Bill to join him and appointed him as a deputy sheriff of Ford County. Bat had faith in Bill's great potential as a lawman, knowing well his courage, determination, and skill with his fists and firearms.

Bill took on the position of deputy when Dodge City was in its heyday. Bill immediately took to the life of a peacekeeper. He loved the action but discovered that he was as good a communicator as he was a fighter. He was able to diffuse potentially violent situations with words more often than with fists and bullets.

While taming this wild town, Tilghman worked alongside other notables like Wyatt Earp, Bat Masterson, Ed Masterson, Larry Deger, and Ned Brown. Eventually, Bill was appointed marshal, the chief law enforcement officer in Dodge City, Kansas.

Hard Lesson

Even though Bill found himself to be as deft with dialog as he was deadly with his pistols, he learned the hard way in 1877 that a lawman could not rely on one without the other. Dodge City Marshal Ed Masterson was as affable a man as ever pinned on a badge in the country. He wore pistols but primarily relied on a handshake, a smile, and his ability to sooth a beast with gentle verbal offerings. In modern law enforcement, he would have been considered an expert in the tactic "Verbal Judo."

Ed Masterson was repeatedly warned by his brother that his friendly nature put him in a terrible position with bad men too often. Since Ed was not inclined to practice with his firearms as often as Bat and the others did, Bat worried Ed would end up being "managed" by bad men. Bat and Bill believed that practice made good better and fast faster.

In 1878, Ed Masterson approached two cowboys, Walker and Wagner, who had not turned in their firearms while they were drinking in town, which was a violation of the ordinance. To make the situation worse, they had been warned earlier. Ed made contact with the two, and after a brief conversation, the two cowboys drew on the marshal and shot him. Ed drew and returned fire while staggering away. Witnesses later said that it looked as if for some reason Ed was holding a bad cigar to his body, but it was actually his clothes burning from a contact shot delivered by one of the two trail hands.

After the assault, Ed staggered away, traveling nearly 200 yards before falling. Bat, who was also on duty, came running after the shots were fired and shot both men. Since Ed, Bat, and another deputy named Heywood all fired at the men, it is not known for certain which lawman killed Wagner and mortally wounded Walker. The newspapers of the day gave credit to Ed Masterson, but some historians believe Bat was the marksman who ended the confrontation. If today's forensic pathology existed then, it would probably be discovered that all three men were responsible for the wounds in the killers.

Bill Tilghman would not abandon his gentlemanly ways just because they failed Ed Masterson. He would neither put himself in a bad position nor abandon his practice with firearms as Ed Masterson had.

While serving in a town that used a "Dead Line" to delineate the part of town good citizens should not cross into, Tilghman effectively used his soft spoken, gentlemanly style backed up by sheer toughness to help make Dodge City safe for all citizens and visitors. Tilghman quickly gained a reputation for avoiding gun play if at all possible. He was widely recognized, however, to be deadly efficient with a firearm when called upon to use it as a last resort.

The Three Guardsmen

In 1889, Tilghman felt inclined to move again as he established a homestead near Guthrie, Oklahoma. Tilghman was a successful rancher and raised Jersey Cattle, Poland Hogs, and horses. Bill could have attended to his successful ranch exclusively, but Bill felt he could not ignore the outlaw gangs that seemed to run untethered throughout Oklahoma Territory. Besides, Bill's reputation as a lawman was known far and wide. Bill was recruited and appointed as one of Judge Isaac Parker's Deputy U.S. Marshals.

Bill teamed with Chris Madsen and Heck Thomas (see chapter eight). The three formed a powerful alliance and relentlessly pursued and captured individual members of the gangs terrorizing the territory. Tilghman, Madsen, and Thomas would affectionately become known as the Three Guardsmen for their successful dismantling of the Wild Bunch as well as the Doolin Gang.

While Hollywood and historians still speculate about the end of Butch and Sundance, the other members of the gang were killed or captured by the Guardsmen.

The Guardsmen split the Oklahoma Indian Territory into three areas. They specifically targeted gangs and their members. As a team, they apprehended an estimated 300 desperate criminals and killers. The most wanted criminal of this era was the gang leader Bill Doolin.

The Doolin Gang

Some say in his fifty-one years of law enforcement Bill Tilghman may have arrested and brought more bad men to justice than any other lawman in his era, which spanned from the Wild West Era into the era of Prohibition.

Tilghman was not just a gunfighter. He was a solid lawman as well as a leader, possessing a great tactical mind. He had a stellar reputation for finding criminals and skillfully maneuvering into the best possible position to ensure a reasonable man would elect to surrender and live. Tilghman was lauded for targeting and dismantling the Doolin Gang.

Bill Doolin had been a member of the Dalton Gang until it raided Coffeeville and attempted to rob two banks at once. The citizens of Coffeeville shot the gang into eternity, but Doolin had sat out that day.

Doolin chose to assemble a gang of his own and for years robbed banks, stage coaches, and trains. The Doolin Gang escaped an attempt to capture them at Ingalls, Oklahoma, when they engaged a posse in a gunfight and killed or wounded six members of the posse. Only one member of the gang was captured.

Tilghman was not involved in the failed Ingalls raid but felt even more inclined to end the gang's reign of terror. Tilghman, along with Heck Thomas and Chris Madsen, systematically pursued, captured, or killed many members of the gang. Tilghman preferred capture to killing.

He brilliantly exhibited his ability to do this when he tracked Bill Doolin to Eureka Springs. Tilghman located Doolin sitting in a hot springs bath healing from wounds he received at the shootout in Ingalls.

In a move of tactical brilliance, Tilghman waited to make the apprehension until Doolin was soaking in a hot tub. Tilghman entered the establishment dressed as a minister and had his pistol on Doolin before the criminal could suspect something was afoot.

When Doolin saw the pistol directed at his head, he considered going for his own pistol, but one look in Tilghman's determined eyes inspired him to surrender. Besides, who wants to die in a gunfight while naked as a new born?

There was a crowd of five thousand gathered to watch Deputy U.S. Marshal Tilghman bring the notorious outlaw gang leader to justice.

Typical Tilghman

When Tilghman apprehended Doolin, the desperado was in possession of a small silver mug, which Doolin said was a present for his newborn son. In a gesture typical of Marshal Bill Tilghman, he personally delivered the mug to mother and child.

Jail, however, would not hold Bill Doolin. Six months after his capture, Doolin orchestrated an escape. This time, Heck Thomas tracked Doolin down and justifiably shot-gunned the fugitive to death after Doolin responded to a call to surrender by firing his rifle at Heck Thomas.

Even though it was Bill's preference to bring criminals to face justice upright in the saddle, it was not always possible. Bill found it necessary to shoot and kill Arizona Wilson after giving him an opportunity to surrender.

Two of Arizona Wilson's cohorts saved the marshal from having to track them down. They were so angry at the demise of their accomplice, they actually chose to pursue Tilghman to exact revenge. Tilghman detected their approach and was ready for them. Bill called for their surrender, but Wilson's friends, Crescent Sam and Calhoun, chose to open fire rather than open a dialog. During the short gunfight that ensued, Bill Tilghman shot them both dead.

Two women who had attached themselves to the Doolin Gang, Cattle Annie and Little Britches, became quite famous for their involvement in the gang's crimes. Bill was relieved to capture them without killing them.

Little Dick West, a criminal whose name belied his expertise as a killer, did not come along peacefully. Little Dick chose to fight Tilghman and died as result—his last bad choice in life.

Little Dick West's partner Raidler also shot it out with Marshal Tilghman. The gunfight ended with Raidler lying helpless and badly wounded; his death appeared imminent.

After the fight, Tilghman showed great humanity by setting up a long-term camp similar to those he made during his Buffalo hunting days. Tilghman nursed the wounded man back to a condition healthy enough to take the long ride to face justice. Raidler was convicted of his crimes and served his sentence. He was released from prison in 1903. He owed the remainder of his life to Bill Tilghman, a man Raidler had tried to kill. Raidler never returned to crime.

Gunfight Advice From Tilghman

For sidearms, Tilghman carried a Colt SA .38 Special with a 5½-inch barrel as well as an engraved nickel plated Colt 45 with a pearl handle. Modern day firearms trainers have many opinions about where a gunfighter should aim on a human being. Many people have strong opinions on the topic but have never been in an actual gunfight. Bill Tilghman, on the other hand, survived many gunfights. He shared his view of target acquisition on one occasion saying, "I would always shoot for the belt buckle because it was the broadest target from head to heel."

President Theodore Roosevelt once asked Bill Tilghman how, "… a gunman on the side of law all of his life was still alive after so many experts had tried to kill him."

Marshal Tilghman replied making a strong point that could be taught in a modern day police academy ethics class, defensive tactics class, as well as a firearms class. He said, "A man who knows he's right has an edge on a man who knows he's wrong."

Offices

Tilghman's tenure as a lawman spanned fifty-four years, but his place of employment changed often. He was a city marshal in Dodge City and served as a deputy U.S. Marshal in Oklahoma Territory. He was elected as sheriff of Lincoln County, Oklahoma, as well as a state senator in Oklahoma. He left the senate, however, to become the chief of police for the Oklahoma City Police Department. These are but a few of the positions which he held.

Bill Tilghman Lawman to the End

In 1924, at the age of seventy, Tilghman could have retired on his laurels. He was widely respected as an honorable lawman.

It is difficult to comprehend what drew him to attempt to tame one more town at the age of seventy, but he did. The citizens were tired of the lawlessness in Cromwell, Oklahoma. They pleaded for his help. They felt that the name of Bill Tilghman was enough to get the job done.

No man, however, is the same at seventy as he was at thirty. Chris Madsen, one of the Three Guardsmen cautioned his friend against taking the position, "You are not so young and your draw is a little slow." Chris, with great care and candor, added, "Someone might kill you."

Bill would not be deterred. He responded, "It's better to die in a gunfight than in bed like a woman."

A few weeks after reporting for duty in Cromwell, Tilghman heard gun shots in the street and ran to investigate. When he arrived on the scene of the disturbance, he discovered Federal Prohibition

Agent Wiley Lynn was the cause of the disturbance. Lynn was a thoroughly corrupt agent, and at the time, he was also thoroughly drunk.

Bill saw Lynn staggering down the street with a pistol in one hand and a prostitute in the other. Lynn had the prostitute in tow as a patron, not as a policeman. Bill Tilghman approached the fellow "lawman," disarmed Lynn, and placed him under arrest. Since Lynn was a fellow lawman, it is probable Bill lowered his guard, for his search was not as thorough as it normally would have been.

While leading Lynn toward jail, the agent pulled a second weapon from his belt. There was a time when Tilghman would have easily handled Lynn in an encounter such as this, but that was decades past. After several moments of struggling over the weapon, Lynn shot Tilghman and ran off. Within twenty minutes, Chief Bill Tilghman, legendary lawman, husband, and father of three, died from his wounds.

Lynn was tried for killing Bill Tilghman in a legal setting as corrupt as Lynn himself. Amazingly, the federal agent was acquitted of all charges.

Due to his iconic status, Tilghman's body lay in repose in the Oklahoma State Capitol building. Thousands of citizens of Oklahoma gathered to mourn the loss of this great man. In life he was a buffalo hunter, cavalry scout, deputy U. S. Marshal, senator, city marshal, sheriff, and chief of police. He performed all of these tasks with great skill, touched many lives, and truly made a difference.

William Tilghman was laid to rest in Chandler, Oklahoma.

Once, at the age of twelve, Bill Tilghman had a chance encounter with the famous lawman Wild Bill Hickok. It was Bill's dream to someday be as great a lawman as Hickok. Even though Hickok may be better remembered than Tilghman, Bill's law enforcement career eclipsed Hickok's. In fact, the quantity and quality of work that Tilghman accomplished has been achieved by very few, if any.

Bat Masterson hunted buffalo with Bill, tamed Dodge City beside him, and knew Bill as a lifelong friend. When Bat became a writer, one of his favorite lawmen to write about was Bill Tilghman. While trying to compare Bill Tilghman to the rest of the lawmen who tamed the Wild West, Bat Masterson may have hit it on the head when he said, "He was the best of us all."

CHAPTER 8

DEPUTY U.S. MARSHAL "HECK" THOMAS, "TRUE GRIT"

Henry Andrew "Heck" Thomas was born in Georgia in 1850, but this Law Dog grew up early. At the tender age of twelve, he went off to war with his father and his uncles to fight for the Confederacy. Even as young as he was, Heck was not a bystander in this war. Heck found himself engaged in mortal combat at an age when most modern boys would still be playing little league baseball. Despite this, he would survive the entire war.

After the war, Heck's father became the City of Atlanta's marshal. Heck was still only seventeen, but he was mature well beyond his years, seasoned considerably by the conflict. He joined the force and was praised for showing great courage after he was wounded in the line of duty during a violent post-war riot.

Gunfight with Sam Bass Gang

After the war, many Confederates found their homes in the South so devastated they answered the call of the West. Heck heard that call as well. Something drew him irresistibly away from hearth, home, family, and a career he loved. After serving several years with the Atlanta Police Department, Heck resigned and set off to make his own life in Texas.

Heck was the proverbial sheepdog, drawn to the life of a protector. In Texas, he took a job serving as a railroad guard for the Texas Express Company. In 1878, the famous Sam Bass Gang attacked a train Heck Thomas was guarding. It was inconceivable for Heck to surrender money in his protection to train robbers. His job was to protect the money on that train with his life, odds of survival be damned. Heck proved throughout his life that he was prepared to die in defense of a cause, property, or person.

Immediately, Heck engaged the gang in a fierce gunfight. So fierce was the return fire, the gang was eventually driven off by Heck. Before that, however, Heck deliberately positioned himself to allow a gang member to reach the safe. The gang member was able to snatch the loot from the safe, but then Heck drove him off with another barrage. The robber tucked his winnings in his saddle bag and quickly rode off, assuring his companions he had the money. Due to Heck's galling fire, the gang took great haste in making their escape.

During this robbery, Heck demonstrated that there was more than one way to protect the money. While engaging the gang in a gunfight he had allowed that one member to think that he had penetrated Heck's defenses in reaching the safe. In the urgency created by Heck's relentless fire, the gang member was satisfied with just grabbing the money bag and running without checking the contents. Heck had bested Bass and his gang by hiding the real payroll in a stove while placing a dummy stash in the safe.

The train reached its destination, considerably shot up, but its large payroll was still intact.

Great Risk – Great Reward

Shortly after the robbery, Heck became a man-hunter. There was great money to be made pursuing wanted criminals who had large bounties on their heads. By 1885, Heck Thomas had become an experienced bounty-hunter while working for the Fort Worth Detective Agency.

Heck pursued the Lee brothers who had a $7000 bounty on their heads—a great deal of money for the times. Jim and Pink Lee had committed many crimes, but the high reward was due to their killing of Marshal Jim Guy and four members of his posse in their attempt to apprehend the brothers.

Heck had developed a penchant pursuing the most dangerous criminals while working for the Fort Worth Detective Agency. Heck discovered that a greater risk quite literally returned a greater reward.

Detective Heck Thomas and fellow Detective Jim Taylor trailed the brothers and cornered them in a hay field near Dexter, Texas. Even though the Lees were wanted "Dead or Alive," Heck chose to call for the Lees' surrender. Heck's offer was met with gunfire.

Heck had taken a superior position before delivering his call to surrender, so the matter was settled by the belch of Heck's Winchester. Heck Thomas had faced gunfire since he was twelve years old, and although he realized the danger he was in, it no longer shook him up as it would most men. He could remain calm in a gunfight. He realized that shooting was just useless noise unless the bullets hit you. The Lees went down in the first volley; Heck and his partners were $7000 richer.

Judge Parker's Deputies—The Best of Their Times

In 1886, Heck was drawn out of Texas to Fort Smith, Arkansas, by a job that was perfectly suited for his talents. Thomas was hired by Judge Isaac Parker as a deputy U.S. Marshal and moved to Fort Smith with his wife and family.

Readers who have faithfully followed this prose will realize that Heck Thomas represents the fourth of Parker's Deputy U.S. Marshals to make the list of great law enforcement officers, along with Bass Reeves, Bill Tilghman, and Grant T. Johnson. There is a practical reason for this. Judge Parker's marshals went into the most unforgiving places, facing incalculable dangers over and over again. They inspired an entire genre of movies and literature. What they actually did was much more interesting and dangerous than could ever be accurately depicted on film or in writing.

Many of Parker's Deputy U.S. Marshals gave their lives in this noble endeavor. Sadly, many of their names and the circumstances of their deaths have been long forgotten. Historians can't even arrive at an exact number of them.

Of this contingent of relentless man-hunters, the four chronicled here struck fear into the worst criminals of their day. The issue is not why four but why only four?

A Heavy Cost

It is hard to explain the Oklahoma Territory in the late nineteenth century. It was wide open, unsettled land occupied by good people trying to make a life; Native Americans trying to hold onto a life; and some of the cruelest criminals ever to take a dollar at gunpoint who wouldn't hesitate to take a life.

Heck Thomas came to this land to make it a safe place for good men and women to make their dreams come true.

Heck's first foray into Indian Territory while wearing a deputy U.S. Marshal's badge was fruitful. When Heck returned to Fort Smith, he had eight murderers, several hardened criminals, a horse thief, and a bootlegger in tow.

Heck thrived in this environment. He had barely turned the key on these prisoners before he was resupplied and on the trail again. More criminals captured and more miles traveled meant higher pay. Heck was driven and ambitious. The best always are.

Then, as now, law enforcement took its toll on a lawman's personal life. Upon returning home from one of his treks, Heck stood on the porch and shook the trail dust off himself. Entering, he discovered his wife Isabelle had packed up their five children and moved back to Georgia. She hated the life Heck loved and divorced him for leaving her alone for so long and so often. Heck was deeply saddened but did not pursue her. Although he loved Isabelle, he also loved his life as a deputy U.S. Marshal.

On June 27, 1888, Heck Thomas—along with Burrell Cox, Jacob Yoes, Hank Childers, and Jim Wallace—located the Purdy Gang. The Purdy Gang was a group of train robbers led by Aaron Purdy. Once again, Heck gave the gunmen an opportunity to surrender, but they opened up on the deputy marshals instead.

This time, Heck had shouted his commands from a rather precarious position and was shot twice. He managed to return fire along with other members of his posse, and together they killed the gang's leader Aaron Purdy. The death of their leader as well as the unforgiving return fire of the deputy marshals inspired the rest of the gang to surrender.

Heck was patched up on the trail and survived the hard ride back to Fort Smith where he was laid up for months recuperating from his wounds.

Heck was nursed back to health by a school teacher named Mattie Mowbray. Mattie was the perfect medicine for she not only healed his gunshot wounds but his broken heart as well. It seemed only appropriate that in Heck's case Cupid used two .45 caliber rounds instead of an arrow.

The two married, and from that day forward every dusty and dangerous trail would lead back to his Mattie. Mattie was the proverbial good woman behind the great man Heck Thomas.

The Three Guardsmen

In 1891, Thomas formed the famous alliance with Marshals Bill Tilghman and Chris Madsen. They felt they would be more effective in combatting criminal gangs if they worked as a team to bring them to justice. The impact of this powerful law enforcement triumvirate was felt immediately by the criminal gangs that were robbing and killing their way throughout the Oklahoma Territory. The trio came to be known as the Three Guardsman.

The Ingalls Fiasco

On September 1, 1893, Marshal E.D. Nix formed a posse to capture the Doolin Gang and descended upon Ingalls, Oklahoma. Members of the gang were hiding out in plain view. Enamored by their free spending ways, Ingalls' businessmen welcomed known outlaws into their town. It was a safe haven.

A young boy spotted the marshal's posse and rode hard to the town to warn the gang. The Doolin Gang members immediately saddled their horses but decided they had time to finish their card game.

With the hand completed, "Bitter Creek" Newcomb exited the saloon. He was instantly shot by Deputy U.S. Marshal Dick Speed. This opened a devastating twenty minute gun battle. During the subsequent gun fire, gang members Dick Clifton and Charlie Pierce were also shot.

Deputy U.S. Marshal Lafayette "Lafe" Shadley had a bead on Bill Dalton but mercifully shot his horse instead. In an incredible feat of skill, Dalton came off the horse in a standing position as the horse fell and shot Shadley dead.

In the meantime, Bill Doolin facilitated an escape immediately after Dick Speed had wounded Newcomb. Doolin took careful aim while simultaneously climbing upon another horse, then shot and killed Dick Speed.

As Speed slumped to the ground, Doolin spurred his horse to a fence and cut it open. The fence had been blocking the only avenue available for the gang's escape. Calling his gang members to follow him, Doolin fled the fight with bullets zipping everywhere. Following at a gallop were Bill Dalton, George "Red" Buck, "Tulsa Jack" Blake, Dan "Dynamite Dick" Clifton, Charlie Pierce, and wounded, but still riding like the wind, "Bitter Creek" Newcomb.

Left behind was Arkansas Tom Jones who had been in an upstairs hotel room. From this vantage point he was able to keep the posse pinned down with deadly rifle fire while the rest of the gang made good their escape. One of Jones' rounds killed Deputy U.S. Marshal Tom Hueston. Ultimately, Arkansas Tom realized that although his position enabled him to help the rest of the gang escape, it doomed his chances of escape. He surrendered to the posse that had him surrounded. Arkansas Tom was the only capture of the day, which all agreed was achieved at too great a sacrifice.

The good news for Arkansas Tom was that by being captured, he would outlive the entire gang. The bad news was he did so behind bars. He was given a fifty year prison term for his crimes.

Doolin's Demise

Bill Tilghman eventually captured Doolin on January 15, 1896, in Eureka Springs. On July 5, Doolin escaped Guthrie Federal Prison. Almost immediately, Heck Thomas was in pursuit of the most wanted man in the country.

Finding a "cold trail," Thomas became convinced Doolin would try to meet his wife at his father-in-law's homestead in Lawson, Oklahoma. Heck positioned his posse-men in wait around the farm. His hunch was proven right. After dark on August 24, Doolin appeared in the moonlight, nonchalantly walking along, whistling, and leading his horse.

Heck's call for surrender came out of the darkness and was met with Doolin's wild and frantic gunfire. Heck's rifle barked along with Deputy Bill Dunn's shotgun. Both blasts hit Doolin hard and square in the chest. He was probably dead before he hit the ground.

Heck Thomas Lives On

As the century turned, Heck could see the writing on the wall. Oklahoma was about to become a state. His job as Deputy U.S. Marshal would disappear because state and local authorities would take over policing in what had been a federal territory. Besides, the power of the outlaw gang had been regulated to the history

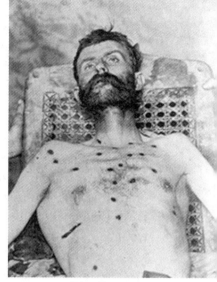

BILL DOOLIN

books by Thomas and his fellow lawmen. Those that were not dead or in prison were scattered to the wind.

Since the Wild West was tamed, Heck saw another opportunity. Forty years after Heck had taken a position on the firing line beside his father in the Confederate Army, Heck took the position of Chief of Police in Lawton, Oklahoma, in 1902. He continued in this capacity until his death of natural causes in 1912. He was a lawman to the very end.

Heck's legend lives on not only in history but also in fiction. Heck Thomas was the inspiration for John Wayne's portrayal of Rooster Cogburn in the movie *True Grit*. Cogburn does a short but truthful Heck Thomas-like call for the surrender of a criminal.

In the movie, the character Deputy U.S. Marshal "Rooster" Cogburn is in pursuit of a murderer and his gang. The way Rooster used his knowledge of the territory to deduce the criminal's next move was a classic Heck Thomas-style pursuit. Toward the climax of the movie, Cogburn cuts off the retreat of the escaping criminals, and instead of gunning them down, he endangers himself to give them the opportunity to surrender, as Heck Thomas always did. Cogburn shouts matter-of-factly to the leader of the criminals Ned Pepper, "I mean to kill you in one minute, Ned, or see you hang in Fort Smith at Judge Parker's convenience. Which will it be?"

In assessing the performance of Heck Thomas, one must consider the caliber of criminal Heck pursued. In both Texas and Oklahoma, a criminal had to leave a trail littered with carnage and destruction to warrant pursuit by this gifted man-hunter. When Thomas inevitably found them, as he always did, he would often put himself in greater danger in an effort to take them in alive. Heck would always offer them the simple choice, "Which will it be, justice or death?"

Those who chose to fight Heck Thomas often found both delivered by the guns of this courageous marshal.

PART TWO

THE GANGSTER ERA

CHAPTER 9

THE LEGENDARY
CAPTAIN FRANK HAMER

For some inexplicable reason, Hollywood has chosen to tell the stories of fictional lawmen while ignoring some of the best law enforcement officers in history. One, whose story is absolutely worth retelling, is Texas Ranger Frank Hamer. The problem is Frank's story may be too big for even the Big Screen.

Frank Hamer, a Hard Man to Kill

Frank Hamer and his career were larger than life. Frank started his crime-fighting on horseback pursuing rustlers with blazing six guns and ended it in careening cars facing gangsters armed with automatic weapons. In both venues he prevailed.

Who was Frank Hamer? That's a hard question to answer. He was extraordinary.

Frank Hamer would survive, by some accounts, fifty gunfights in his lifetime. According to some storytellers, he killed as many

as seventy-five bad men and one very bad woman. When asked to verify the numbers later in life, Frank refused to discuss the matter. Killing another human being, even when it was absolutely necessary, was too personal to talk about.

Frank faced many men who tried to kill him. These would-be cop-killers had the privilege to fight with the best, and when they did, they died like the rest.

The Beginning

Frank Hamer was born March 17, 1884, in Wilson, Texas. He was a farm boy who excelled with firearms at a young age.

His skill caught one bad man's attention. This unsolicited admiration led to Frank's first gunfight, which took place when Frank was but a teenager and before he ever pinned on a badge.

It happened when Frank and his brother Harrison were sharecropping some land for a man by the name of Dan McSwain. Although Frank was young, he had exhibited incredible skill with a firearm. In those days, in Texas, a firearm kept food on the table and trouble off your door step.

Knowing of Frank's skill, McSwain approached Frank one day and offered him a great deal of money to do a special job. Frank, possessing wisdom beyond his years, was suspicious. In response the sixteen year old jokingly asked, "Who do I have to kill for that?"

Frank stopped smiling when McSwain told him who he would have to kill to earn the money. McSwain had an enemy who he wanted dead and sought to hire Frank to do the dirty deed. McSwain felt a youngster such as Frank could easily be recruited by the lure of cash but would not be suspected of the crime because of his young age.

Frank answered without hesitation, "No!"

Frank was not and would never be a hired killer of innocent men. McSwain was surprised by Frank's unwavering resolve to do the right thing and became concerned that Frank might go to the authorities. He warned Frank not to tell anyone about his offer or Frank and his brother would be dead men.

Frank would always be able to read men. He concluded McSwain's threat was not an idle one, so Frank took to carrying a pistol, even while farming. This precaution would pay off.

Only a few days later, McSwain, armed with a shotgun, crept up behind Frank while he was plowing. He aimed carefully and shot Hamer in the back of the head. Frank went down hard. As McSwain approached to confirm that Frank was indeed dead, the badly wounded Frank Hamer drew his pistol, spun, and shot McSwain.

This proved more than the back-shooting McSwain had bargained for. While McSwain retreated to acquire his Buffalo gun to finish the job, Frank's brother Harrison ran to his brother's aid. Harrison assisted his wounded brother to escape.

FRANK HAMER (LEFT)

Hamer required quite some time to convalesce. Since no one wearing a badge came looking for McSwain, he believed he had sufficiently frightened the young farmer. After McSwain recovered from his wound, he returned to his day-to-day activities. He considered Frank Hamer to be a closed book.

To Frank, the Hamer-McSwain affair was not a book to close at all. It was merely a chapter in Frank's life, bookmarked until he healed. Frank Hamer planned to rewrite the ending.

The Thirst for Personal Justice

McSwain did not properly assess the resolve of this sixteen-year-old Texan. The moment Frank felt healthy enough, he strapped on his pistol, saddled his horse, and rode directly toward the place he felt most likely to find McSwain. Hamer had very strong feelings about right and wrong, justice and injustice. He knew he had been done wrong and felt he was entitled to seek justice. The only way for him to do that was Frank's way.

While Frank was recovering, he thought it out. If he went to the law, it would only be a matter of time before McSwain hired someone to have him killed. Frank wouldn't know when the hammer would drop. The only way to settle this debt was to meet McSwain face to face.

Hamer rode right up to McSwain's home. As Hamer looked the back-shooter in the eye, McSwain instantly knew the reason for the visit. McSwain said, "I thought I killed you."

Frank replied, "I'm afraid not," then announced, "I'm here to settle our account." With that said, both men drew and fired.

The account was settled.

Frank Hamer, Texas Ranger

Shortly after the Hamer-McSwain gunfight, Frank took a job as a hired hand for a rancher on the Pecos. It was during this period Frank assisted a local sheriff to track and capture some rustlers. After the partnership the sheriff was much impressed with Frank's tracking and the way he handled himself in a fight. He recommended Frank for the Texas Rangers and in 1906 Frank Hamer joined the storied law enforcement agency.

It is said that on his first action as a private in John H. Rogers' Company C of the Texas Rangers Frank distinguished himself. The Rangers were tasked to arrest a man for murder, but the wanted man commandeered a home and barricaded himself. He opened fire on the Rangers and told them he would not be taken alive.

Frank ran to a position close to the window the suspect was using as a gun-port. He waited for an opportunity, and when the killer exposed himself to fire his weapon, Frank fired one shot, putting it through the man's jaw and killing him instantly.

In those early years, Frank rode trails near the Rio Grande and captured countless rustlers, smugglers, bootleggers, and bandits with Company C.

Marshal of Navasota, Texas

In 1908, the town of Navasota was out of control. It had become a haven for rustlers, thieves, and killers. The good citizens of Navasota contacted the governor of Texas and pleaded that he locate a lawman who could stand toe to toe with the criminal element that had run every marshal out of town.

Frank was offered the opportunity and accepted the challenge. Frank took a leave from the Texas Rangers and became Marshal Frank Hamer of Navasota, Texas, at the governor's request.

As the marshal sent to tame this town, Frank preferred to solve problems without gun play. When it appeared gun play was on the horizon, but Frank was still talking, he would offer the bad man a unique opportunity at freedom. Frank would sincerely say, "If you put down the gun and fight me bare handed man to man and you beat me, you can walk out of here a free man with no charges. If I beat you, you will have to accompany me to jail and answer to the charges I have on you. It's your choice."

Many a man said, "That sounds fair enough." They put down their guns and put up their fists.

By the time the fight started, many townspeople had gathered to see the show. Their brave young marshal never failed to entertain them with a pugilistic display of excellence that was way ahead of its time. Frank was not only an expert at pummeling opponents with his fists, he could also thump them succinctly with his feet, striking vulnerable areas with the uncanny precision of a choreographed fight.

This approach would hardly cut the mustard in the twenty-first century, but it was quite humanistic for the early twentieth century. Frank's approach prevented many gunfights in Navasota which otherwise would have ended in death. It was potentially less damaging than a pistol blow to the cranium. Hamer was unbeatable in his time in a stand up gunfight. He was just as invincible in a contest of empty-hand combat.

As might be expected, some criminals did not accept Hamer's offer to fight their way out of charges. In these cases the men held their ground, pulled their weapons, and died in the dust. After three years, the town of Navasota was a place where young lovers could walk hand in hand and children could play in the street. It was a fine place to make a home thanks to Frank Hamer. Even though no town will ever be crime-free, Navasota was no longer a haven for rustlers, robbers, rapists, and murderers. They were either long gone, locked up, or laid to rest.

With an impeccable reputation for honesty and courage established, Frank was hired in 1911 as a special agent for the mayor of Houston. He was assigned to fight crime both inside and outside law enforcement. While in this position, Frank captured the killer of a police officer, broke up a burglary ring, and even arrested a police officer whom he had witnessed beating up a man without justification.

Hamer ran himself into a political buzz saw after an incident with a reporter. While conducting an interview, the reporter insulted Frank. The lawman answered the insult with a punch to the jaw. The governor sent Frank back to the Rangers. Frank had his fill of politics.

It is important to note that there is nothing in the record to indicate that Frank ever hit another reporter. With that said, there is also nothing in the record where a reporter ever showed Frank Hamer such disdain again, at least not when they were within arm's length of this Texas Ranger.

Old Lucky

During his career, Frank Hamer mastered and carried many firearms, but his personal favorite was "Old Lucky." Old Lucky was a Colt Single Action 45, C-engraved, 4 ¾" blued revolver with pearl handles.

Anyone beholding this weapon would be inclined to say, "That sure is pretty."

Frank would likely respond, "Pretty damn accurate."

Frank shared his philosophy on gunfights with an interviewer once. Frank said when he had a choice, he preferred to fight with a rifle, but he also practiced long-distance hand-gunning. When in a gunfight, Frank said he used his sights because he could not see, "spraying the countryside with lead when one shot would do the trick."

A Unique Honeymoon

Frank Hamer had one such one-shot gunfight in Sweetwater, Texas. Shortly after Frank and his wife Gladys Johnson were married, on October 1, 1916, Frank, his brother Harrison, Gladys, and her brother Emmett were on a trip when they stopped at a garage in the town square in Sweetwater because they had a flat tire.

Harrison and Emmett left to find a restroom while Frank went into the garage's office to take care of the flat. Gladys stayed in the car. When Frank exited the garage, he was approached by two men from different directions.

It is not known whether the two men had decided on the spur of the moment to try to kill Frank or if they were a paid team of hit men who had been assigned to kill him. Their motive in either case was to keep Frank from testifying in an upcoming murder case. Despite which possibility was the case, the two killers named Gee McMeans and H. E. Phillips spotted Hamer relaxed and unaware. They decided now was the time to kill this formidable gun-fighting lawman since his guard appeared to be down.

Intent on murder, McMeans approached from the front while Phillips, armed with a shotgun, approached from behind. As McMeans reached Hamer, the hit man drew his pistol and shoved it toward Frank. Frank reacted instinctively by grabbing McMeans' weapon. As the two grappled over the weapon, Frank was shot in the shoulder and the thigh. The wounds only served to spur Frank on.

Frank wrenched the weapon out of McMeans' hand and began beating the would-be killer viciously with it as McMeans tried to regain the momentum and his weapon. During this phase of the fight, Phillips approached from behind with a shotgun. Frank was unaware of this impending threat because he was so focused on his struggle with McMeans.

Hamer's wife Gladys, however, saw Phillips approaching and shouted "Look out, Frank!" Gladys was a woman of action. As she gave warning to Frank, she filled her hand with a pocket Colt and opened up incessant fire upon Phillips. The swarm of bullets buzzed by Phillips' head. Gladys did not hit Phillips, but she disrupted his aim enough so that the round he fired did nothing but destroy the brim of Frank's favorite hat.

With the tide turned, McMeans and Phillips appeared to abandon the failed ambush; they ran. Suddenly, when McMeans reached his car, he produced a shotgun and swung its gaping muzzles menacingly toward Hamer. Frank took deliberate aim at McMeans and fired. The shotgun clattered harmlessly to the pavement. McMeans dropped dead next to it. Hamer had placed his single shot into the dead center of McMeans' cold, hard heart.

Phillips had seen quite enough. He abandoned his partner as well as their car and fled on foot. Harrison Hamer, who had heard the commotion, arrived on the scene with a pistol in hand. He took aim at the fleeing Phillips, but Frank knocked the barrel of his brother's gun down causing Harrison to miss.

Frank explained that the true culprit was already dead. He said that Phillips did not need to join McMeans in eternity because, as he put it, "The man did nothing but ruin a good hat." Frank believed a hard lesson learned was better than a life taken.

Hamer family lore gives credit for the killing shot to Gladys. They say Gladys in every way possible saved Frank's life that day. Frank was said to have taken credit for the shot to save his wife from the unwanted attention that would have followed such a revelation.

Death Ruled Self Defense

It just so happened that while the gunfight was in progress there was a Nolan County Grand Jury in session. The jury had paused from deliberation in the case they were hearing and its members had the perfect vantage point to watch the street battle from upstairs windows across the street. They witnessed the entire event from start to finish and were especially moved by the mercy displayed by Frank Hamer. The Nolan County Grand Jury decided to take no testimony in the matter since they had witnessed the incident directly.

In a supreme example of the swiftness of Texas justice, which has to be a record to this day, the jury convened in the matter of McMeans death. Within minutes of the gun battle, the grand jury returned a "No Bill" in the shooting death of McMeans. The grand jury ruled that the killing of McMeans by Frank Hamer was a justifiable homicide and purely done in self-defense of his life and his family. The decision was made while Frank was still being treated for his wounds.

Violent Men From Across the Border

In 1915, most of the world was at war. The United States was at peace everywhere except the southern border. Bandits were crossing from Mexico into the Southwest United States and were dealing death wherever they went. Sergeant Frank Hamer led the fight against these raiders. To do this, he engaged the bandits on both sides of the border with his Rangers and the Mexican Police at his side. The Mexican lawmen were proud to fight alongside Sergeant Frank Hamer, who was famous on both sides of the Rio Grande.

The fighting came to an end after a full-scale battle at Candelia, Mexico, where dozens of Mexican bandits lay dead on the ground after the fire-fight. Frank Hamer had personally inflicted many of the casualties in this decisive victory.

Rafael Lopez

One bandit who had avoided death in the battle of Candelia was Rafael "Red" Lopez. He was responsible for many criminal atrocities and evaded capture for years. He was also one of Pancho Villa's generals.

One crime Lopez perpetrated occurred in 1914. Lopez and his men derailed a train and then robbed it. During the robbery, he and his men killed nineteen passengers. With the dirty deed done, Lopez and his accomplices fled to Mexico. Lopez avoided justice for this crime and many others for years.

In 1921, Frank Hamer was contacted by an informant and told that Lopez would be at a meeting at a particular location. The informant assured Hamer that if he placed men in an irrigation ditch close to the meeting place Frank would be in a position to capture or kill Lopez.

Frank did not trust the word nor the tactical acumen of the informant. He decided to arrive hours earlier with his men. After performing a scout of the area, he determined that the informant was turning the predators into the prey; it was a trap.

Hamer improvised his own trap. Unknown to the informant, he positioned his men in a vastly superior position.

Frank's instincts, as usual, were dead on. From the Rangers' new vantage point, they watched at least twenty bandits, including Red Lopez wearing his signature red scarf, crawling up to the irrigation ditch where the Rangers were supposed to be hidden. Next to Lopez was the treacherous "informant."

Hamer called out to the bandits "Manos Arriba! Esta Preso!" ("Hands up! You are under arrest!") Lopez, however, was not the surrendering type. His reaction was to spin and fire toward Hamer, who had stood up to give his command.

Lopez's bullet grazed Hamer's cheek, but Hamer didn't even flinch at this close call with death. His first shot fired from his Model 8 hit Lopez dead center in the chest. The rest of the Rangers took this as their cue and opened fire. Eleven bandits were killed before the remnants of Lopez's men surrendered. One of the dead bandits was the informant.

Frank's bullet killed one of the deadliest killers in the history of the Southwest United States.

Hamer's career was replete with desperate gunfights, the capture of criminals, the suppression of riots, and even the arrest of corrupt politicians. Frank Hamer was never one to shy away from either danger or controversy. The State of Texas knew that if conditions were out of control, if a person was bad beyond comprehension and somehow evading capture, or if there was corruption in the system itself, there was one man who they could count on in every case: Frank Hamer.

After a long and colorful career, Frank Hamer retired from the Texas Rangers in 1933 as a captain. This was not the end for Frank though. It was just a new beginning.

In retirement, Frank was sought after as a peace officer where there was no peace, a body guard where someone was in danger, and most notably as a man hunter when the safety of the community dictated that someone needed to be captured.

Bonnie and Clyde

The most famous of his post-retirement call-outs occurred in 1934. Frank Hamer was commissioned to attempt to end the crime spree of the Barrow Gang as a special investigator for the prison system. Bonnie and Clyde were not the laughing, loving, couple of kids driving recklessly through the country-side to banjo music as portrayed in the movie *Bonnie and Clyde*. Then again, Frank Hamer was not the bungling incompetent lawman Hollywood depicted him to be either.

Bonnie and Clyde were bank robbers and cold-hearted killers. Bonnie and Clyde killed three innocent civilians and were also responsible for the death of ten law enforcement officers. One of these officers was lying wounded on the ground when, according to witnesses, Bonnie walked up and cruelly delivered a shot into the officer's face. Some historians argue gang member Henry Methvin fired the finishing shot on the officer, but Bonnie most probably did the deed.

Frank Hamer was hired to bring Bonnie and Clyde to justice for their wanton lawlessness. The minute Frank was put on their trail, Bonnie and Clyde's days were drawing to a close.

Frank meticulously studied the gang's activity and movements. Frank Hamer did not catch criminals by rushing to where they had been, like most lawmen. Frank hunted men in a manner akin to Heck Thomas. He would attempt to ascertain where they were going to be and then be there waiting when they arrived.

During his initial investigation of the tendencies of the Barrow Gang, Frank was able to conclude they all still contacted members of their family. Armed with this information, he had to decide which family was the most vulnerable to an offer. Eventually, Frank was able to solve that puzzle. He decided the weakness in the Barrow Gang was the family of Henry Methvin.

The family loved Henry and did not want him to die nor spend the rest of his life in prison. They agreed to a plea bargain on Henry's behalf to cooperate in the capture of Bonnie Parker and Clyde Barrow. Hamer assured the Methvins that if Bonnie and Clyde could be captured or killed as a result of information he received from Methvin's father, Henry would receive leniency.

The capture of Bonnie and Clyde alive could not be accomplished easily because the two were always heavily armed with automatic military-style weapons. They were also quick to shoot when cornered. At one point during his spree, Clyde had broken into a United States Military Armory and stolen a cache of BAR's, Browning Automatic Rifles, and ammunition. Clyde oiled, wrapped, and hid each of them at different locations so that as he found it necessary to dump one, he always had another BAR and ammo waiting for him. Bonnie and Clyde shot it out with law enforcement repeatedly.

Frank wanted to have the upper hand so that any resistance would not lead to the death of law enforcement officers. Naturally, this consideration was more important to Frank than Bonnie and Clyde's life. Even so, Hamer truly did not want to have to kill Bonnie.

Hamer finally received information he could rely upon. Captain Frank Hamer was able to ascertain that Bonnie and Clyde would be traveling down a country road in Gibsland, Louisiana, on May 23, 1934.

He assembled a team which included ex-Ranger Manny Gault as well as Dallas County Deputy Bob Alcorn and Deputy Ted Hinton. Also included was the local sheriff, Henderson Jordan, who had been the primary negotiator with Henry Methvin's father.

As a part of the plan, Methvin's father set his vehicle up on a hoist as if it was disabled to induce the wanted bank robbers to stop. At 9:15 AM on May 23, 1934, Bonnie and Clyde came upon the trap and pulled over to assist the elder Methvin. There are varying accounts of what happened next.

One account says Sheriff Jordan called for their surrender and another says Hamer called for their surrender. It is most likely true that in the excitement of the moment both called out for the surrender of the notorious duo.

All accounts report Barrow made what modern law enforcement officers call "a furtive movement," toward one of the many loaded weapons in the vehicle. This movement was the go sign for every officer on the scene who perceived a deadly threat. A hail storm of lead poured into Bonnie and Clyde as well as their vehicle. In a matter of seconds, 150 rounds of varying calibers of ammunition were fired.

Then it was over. Frank Hamer had succeeded where many others had failed. Bonnie and Clyde were instantly transported from headlines on front pages to the footnotes of history books.

Frank Hamer Rides into the Sunset

After the demise of Bonnie and Clyde, Frank continued to take jobs that interested him. Even as Frank aged and his skills diminished accordingly, just having him at a scene made an impact. For example, in 1948 the living legend was a special guard during a hotly contested Senate race between Lyndon Johnson and Coke Stevenson.

At one point there was trouble brewing at a polling place where two opposing groups of armed men were facing off when Frank pulled up. The sixty-four-year-old Frank Hamer exited his car, strolled resolutely toward one armed group, and merely said, "Git!" The armed men scattered. With that accomplished, Frank sauntered over to the second group, lest they feel slighted, and snarled, "Fall back!" They did. A deadly confrontation was averted by the mere arrival of this legendary figure.

One year later, Frank Hamer retired entirely. Unlike Wyatt Earp and Bass Reeves, who were never wounded in their lives, Hamer survived seventeen wounds. In 1955 the lawman who had endured so much violence died peacefully of natural causes.

Captain Frank Hamer was laid to rest in Memorial Park Cemetery in Austin, Texas, next to his personal hero, his son Billy. Billy Hamer was a Marine killed in combat in 1945 on that barren island in the Pacific named Iwo Jima.

This should be the end of the Frank Hamer story, but it is not.

Got His Back One More Time

In the 1967 movie *Bonnie and Clyde*, Hollywood finally portrayed Frank Hamer. As mentioned previously, the makers of the movie showed great disrespect and disdain to the memory of Frank Hamer. It was something they would not have dared do to Frank in life.

The movie makers chose to use their literary license to fictionalize the character of this iconic lawman. They could have told the story the way it happened, which certainly would have been interesting enough for any theater goer. Instead, they chose to portray Frank in a way he had never been... inept.

In the movie, Hamer is portrayed by actor Denver Pyle who, as Hamer, is shown stumbling alone upon the criminals. During the encounter, he is captured, disarmed, and restrained with his own handcuffs. He is so frustrated by his circumstance, he spits in the face of Bonnie Parker. In spite of this indignity, the good looking bandits show mercy and set him afloat in a boat on a river.

The character played by Denver Pyle repays Bonnie and Clyde by assassinating them without giving them a chance to surrender.

In reality, the only officer kidnapped by Bonnie and Clyde was Motorcycle Officer Thomas Persell, who was held for twelve hours and released after they stole his gun. It was Persell's weapon which was pictured in the famous roadside photographs of Bonnie and Clyde. Frank Hamer was never kidnapped by Bonnie and Clyde.

The Hamer family was outraged. Just like Gladys did so many years before in Sweetwater, the family came to the defense of the man they loved. Gladys and Frank Hamer Jr. (Frank's son) filed a lawsuit for defamation against Warner-Seven Arts.

The family received an out-of-court, undisclosed settlement.

Frank Hamer

Historians argue whether Captain Frank Hamer killed a dozen men and one woman or seventy-four men and one woman. With the deeds past and all witnesses now deceased, no one will ever know for sure. Frank adamantly refused to talk about the human lives he had to take.

Frank especially refused to talk about Bonnie and Clyde, for it always troubled him deeply that he had to take the life of a woman.

Here are some facts: Frank Hamer willfully and deliberately pursued men who would kill without hesitation or regret. Some came along peacefully, but many who chose to fight lost.

Texas Ranger Captain Bill McDonald was talking about men like Frank Hamer when he said, "No man in the wrong can stand up against a fellow that's in the right and keeps on a-coming."

Frank Hamer was a Law Dog who kept on a-coming. When criminals were at their worst, Frank Hamer was always at his best.

A special thanks to the Texas Ranger Hall of Fame in Waco, Texas, for their gracious assistance.

CHAPTER 10

THE "G MAN"

In 1924 J. Edgar Hoover was appointed Director of the Bureau of Investigations (not yet called the Federal Bureau of Investigation). It was his dream to take this obscure federal agency and transform it from a disorganized, poorly led bureaucracy into the premiere law enforcement agency in the nation. In the end, the ultimate establishment of the FBI as a viable law enforcement agency depended less on J. Edgar Hoover's dream than on the outcome of the clash between his agents and the vicious men they battled in 1934. These agents initially stumbled and even fell. Nevertheless, they rose up again, stood tall, and established the FBI.

J. Edgar Hoover

When Hoover began, he relied on picking the correct "type" of agent. He proclaimed he did not want his special agents to look like "truck drivers." He chose college educated men that looked more like lawyers and accountants than cops. J. Edgar would learn that something more than a look and a pedigree was needed to aggressively go after the deadly criminals born out of prohibition and poverty in the midst of the depression. Sadly, he would learn this the hard way.

Very Bad Men

Banks were being robbed at an alarming rate. Due to widespread poverty, which led to countless foreclosures, banks were not popular. Many of the poor, who felt victimized by banks, romanticized the bank robbers even as they were ruthlessly mowing down law enforcement officers and bystanders all over the nation.

Some of the most notorious of these criminals were John Dillinger, Lester Gillis—also known as "Baby Face Nelson," and Charles Arthur "Pretty Boy" Floyd. They robbed and killed with an almost casual viciousness. On one hand, the public demanded action. On the other, they sat in movie theaters watching newsreel images while in awe of these men, like a crowd mesmerized at an out-of-control warehouse fire.

These bandits knew how to play to the crowd. Floyd captured attention by burning mortgages on the floors of the banks he robbed. Dillinger gained a popular following by giving a press conference standing with his arm around his prosecutor while smiling confidently. Shortly after the conference, he broke out of jail by using a wooden gun that he blackened with shoe polish. He made his getaway by stealing the sheriff's personal car. These killers caught the nation's attention with a violent panache.

G-Men

Stopping these heavily armed robbers was the challenge facing the Bureau of Investigation. It was during this formative era the name G-Man became linked to the Bureau because of George Francis Barnes Jr. He was more commonly known to his movie-going fans as "Machine Gun Kelly." Until his arrest, gangsters and thugs referred to all federal agents as "G-Men" including Secret

Service, Prohibition Agents, as well as Bureau of Investigation Special Agents. Machine Gun Kelly would forever link it to the Bureau.

Machine Gun Kelly was a wanted bank robber who got his name from his weapon of choice. The banks he targeted ranged from Minnesota to Texas. The fast cars of the day allowed criminals to be highly mobile. Multi-state crime sprees were also facilitated by the lack of coordination among local, state, and federal law enforcement agencies. There were also well known criminal safe havens in different parts of the country, which allowed these thugs to live high on their ill-gotten gains without fearing arrest.

Kelly branched out from bank robbery. He orchestrated an elaborate kidnapping of oil magnate Charles Urschel. Kelly succeeded in acquiring $200,000 in ransom, which was an incredible amount for the times. After he received the ransom, he released Urschel.

When Urschel was safe, special agents from the Bureau kicked into gear. They collected fingerprint evidence linking Machine Gun Kelly to the crime. They interviewed the victim, who had paid particular attention to everything said around him and remembered clues to indicate his location. The investigation ultimately led special agents from the Bureau as well as Tennessee authorities to arrest a disoriented Machine Gun Kelly in Memphis, Tennessee, without firing a shot.

As the story goes, George Francis Barnes Jr. "Machine Gun Kelly" came out with his hands up pleading, "Don't shoot, G-Men." The Bureau instantly took ownership of the word. The process leading to the arrest of Machine Gun Kelly created the template for kidnapping investigations, which would result in the Bureau becoming the most successful agency in the world at managing kidnappings.

In a way, Kelly benefited from his arrest by outliving all of his contemporaries. Kelly was a model prisoner in the infamous prison at Alcatraz. At the time of his death in 1954, Kelly had so tamed his personal wild side the other inmates took to calling him "Pop Gun Kelly."

1934, the Year of the G-Man

1934 was a year of reckoning for bank robbers and the coming of age for the agency that would eventually be known as the FBI. It would be of a year of devastating losses as well as soaring successes for the Hoover's special agents. It was the year of the G-Man.

Due to the dangerous men and women the special agents of the Bureau were pursuing, Hoover also expanded his search for candidates to serve as special agents. He began looking for special agents who were more than just highly educated men in suits. He recruited local officers with a prior history of success while facing down deadly armed criminals.

This search lead to the acquisition of Charles Winstead, a Texas lawman. His pursuit and apprehension of Kelly associate Harvey Bailey in Rhome, Oklahoma, led to the arrest of Machine Gun Kelly. Winstead would play a leading role in the birth of the G-Men aura.

Others sworn in as agents during Hoover's talent hunt were Clarence Hurt and Delf "Jelly" Bryce (see his chapter). These men were excellent man-hunters as well as deadly gunfighters.

The first of many tests for the G-Men in 1934 would occur at a barely perceptible dot on the map. It was at a sleepy little community in northern Wisconsin called Manitowish Waters in quaint little lodge called Little Bohemia.

CHARLES WINSTEAD

Little Bohemia: April 20, 1934

When John Dillinger, Baby Face Nelson, Homer Van Meter, John "Red" Hamilton, Tommy Carroll and two women rented out Little Bohemia, the lodge owners thought them to be well dressed travelers. When the owners saw the hardware these men constantly carried, they realized who these people really were.

It was impossible for owners Emil and Nan Wanatka to get a message out when they initially discovered the identities of their guests because the gang always watched them. After a time the gang members came to trust the couple, so they actually allowed Nan Wanatka to attend a family gathering where she smuggled a note to be delivered to the Federal authorities. She had seen the armaments of the criminals and thought they were too heavily armed for the local sheriff.

The note reached the Bureau of Investigation, and the tip sounded credible. A "Flying Squad" was mobilized.

Assistant Director Hugh Clegg was in charge of the Bureau team that flew to Rhinelander in northern Wisconsin. Although it was fifty miles from Little Bohemia, it was the closest airport. When the team arrived, they rented cars to transport the agents and the local law enforcement to the Little Bohemia Lodge. As luck would have it, the weather was so unseasonably cold two of the rented cars would not even start. Some of the team members had to ride on the running boards of the cars for the drive to Manitowish Waters.

In the very early morning hours of April 20, 1934, the team rolled into the area with lights out and descended upon the lodge. Due to faulty intelligence, the approach plan was flawed from its inception. It was thought that the lodge's lakeside was blocked by the lake itself, so no agents were assigned to cover this avenue of escape. In reality, it was the perfect escape route. This miscalculation played into the gang's pre-arranged emergency escape plan perfectly. The raid was doomed to failure from the very beginning.

Even so, there was one other problem with the planning. The members of the raiding party did not realize that even if the gang members had gone along peacefully they were still under equipped and under manned. They could neither secure the lodge nor effectively arrest and transport the number of bad people housed therein. Things did not go well for the special agents and the local officers with them.

As the special agents stepped off the running boards of their cars, the area dogs started barking incessantly. While the agents were moving in to secure the perimeter, three men carrying rifles exited the front door of the lodge. They climbed into a 1933 Chevrolet Coupe and began to leave.

The agents wrongly perceived these were the wanted criminals making their escape. They shouted for the car to halt, but the driver of the car kept going. Due to their blaring radio and the low visibility in the poorly lighted North Woods location, they neither heard nor saw the agents. The men in the car failed to comply, and the agents opened fire on the hapless occupants.

Special Agent Melvin Purvis later said that the agents meant to shoot the tires out on the vehicle. Even if this was their intent, rounds penetrated into the passenger compartment of the vehicle. All three men in the car were hit.

The vehicle's driver, John Hoffman, and passenger John Morris stumbled out of the car, both bewildered and badly wounded. They tried to escape the death trap by scrambling into the darkness. A third innocent man, Eugene Boisneau, died in the front seat of the car without having any idea why his life was so abruptly ended.

In the minds of the agents at the scene that night, escape was a concern. Dillinger had escaped from jail twice, slipped out of surrounded banks on a number of occasions, and in March shot it out with special agents in St. Paul. Dillinger was hard to catch, hard to hold, and he had killed one police officer already. He and the men he traveled with were as skilled with weapons as an army platoon, but there was one major difference: they operated with no rules of engagement. When the agents opened up on that car, they truly thought they had Dillinger and he was getting away. They were dead wrong.

As it turned out, Dillinger and his gang had not been alerted by the dogs. In the days leading up to the raid, they had become numb to the barking dogs. The dogs barked incessantly on a regular basis for every guest, patron, mailman, squirrel, and rabbit.

LITTLE BOHEMIA

The gang was, however, alerted by the one sided gunfight directed at the innocent salesman and two unwitting Civilian Conservation Corps members. The fugitives had prepared an escape plan on the day of their arrival and followed it almost instinctively. As they leapt up, machine guns in hand, they sent an initial burst of automatic weapon fire from the upper windows and roof of the lodge.

With that done, they climbed out onto the side roof and lowered themselves to the ground. Their female companions hunkered down and stayed put. The wanted men, however, hit the ground still heavily armed and running toward the lake into the pitch black northern Wisconsin woods.

The agents' plan proved critically flawed. They thought no escape was possible on the lake side when, in reality, there was an embankment which provided cover and concealment almost instantly as the men cleared the lodge—an ideal escape route.

Securing the perimeter around the lodge was impossible at any rate due to the number of agents Assistant Director Clegg brought on the raid. The agents made this task more difficult by shooting before anyone was in position.

Even if there had been enough men to secure the perimeter it would have been difficult to get into position. A ditch as well as barbed wire that no one knew existed served as obstacles for the agents when moving about in the darkness. The agents returned fire at the criminals, but most rounds were fired at the lodge after the criminals had abandoned the hideout. Almost as fast as the agents had returned fire, Dillinger and his friends were disappearing into the darkness along the lake.

Clegg sent two agents and a local constable to get more help and to cordon off the area with a road block. By the time Clegg gave this order, it was like trying to catch a train that already left the station.

On the way to summon help, Special Agent Jay Newman, Special Agent W. Carter Baum, and their local law enforcement liaison Constable Carl Christensen came across an occupied parked vehicle a short distance from the lodge. Constable Christensen recognized it as belonging to a neighbor, and Newman, who was driving, pulled up side by side with the parked car. The man behind the wheel asked something to the effect of, "Who are you gentleman?" The strange man's pleasant countenance and young looking face raised no alarm in any of the three officers in the car.

The agents identified themselves without taking any special precautions. In a blink of an eye, the man displayed a pistol and ordered the three lawmen out of their vehicle. As Special Agent Jay Newman began getting out of the car, as ordered, the stranger shot him in the head.

The man with the gun was no gentleman. He was Lester Gillis A.K.A. "Baby Face Nelson." The head shot skipped off the agent's skull, but the grazing impact of the bullet rendered Newman unconscious and temporarily incapacitated. He was lucky though, for he would survive.

Without a pause to reflect, Nelson killed the second agent W. Carter Baum and severely wounded Constable Christensen. The entire gang escaped that night except for the two women who had accompanied them to the lodge.

The special agents were left to shake their heads, mourn their dead, and attempt to recover from this unmitigated and tragic failure.

W. Carter Baum

The Biograph: July 27, 1934

The Bureau of Investigation was undeterred by the events that took place at Little Bohemia. If anything, it made every member of the Bureau more resolute than ever to put a stop to Nelson, Dillinger, and their murderous ilk.

Melvin Purvis, head of the Chicago office, shared a leadership role with Samuel P. Cowley. They were desperate to capture Dillinger and Nelson following the loss of their agent. Their big break came in the person of Ana Cumpănaş, also known as Anna Sage.

It was late summer in Chicago, and Anna, an immigrant Romanian prostitute in danger of being deported, was desperate to stay in the United States. When she discovered her friend Polly

Hamilton was having an affair with Public Enemy Number One, John Dillinger, she saw an opportunity to make a bargain. She met with Agents Cowley and Purvis and later claimed to have made a deal with them. She would receive a $10,000 reward and be allowed to stay in the country if she served up Dillinger.

On July 27, 1934, Anna accompanied John Dillinger and Polly Hamilton to the Biograph Theater on Lincoln Street in Chicago. The night was hot and the theater, which advertised itself as "air cooled," seemed the perfect spot to be. They watched a gangster movie called *Manhattan Melodrama* starring Clark Gable.

After the movie ended, Public Enemy Number One left the crowded theater and walked casually into the hot Chicago night with a woman on each arm. It appeared to the surveillance team, headed by Samuel P. Cowley, that Dillinger was totally unaware that all avenues of escape were blocked by special agents of the Bureau of Investigation.

When Melvin Purvis recognized the Dillinger, he lit a cigar. This was the team's signal to converge. At that very moment, Dillinger's sixth sense detected something was terribly wrong. John Dillinger let loose of his companions, drew a pistol from his pants pocket, and ran down an alley to make his escape.

Shots cut through the Chicago heat and echoed between the buildings. Dillinger skid to an abrupt stop, falling face down in the alley. One of the shots fired by Samuel P. Cowley went through the back of Dillinger's neck. Two others fired by Special Agents Charles Winstead and Clarence Hurt also helped nudge Dillinger toward the hereafter.

Word spread instantly that it was John Dillinger who lay dead in the alley. Bystanders crowded around, pushing forward to dip their handkerchiefs in the blood of the famous John Dillinger.

John Dillinger's death in Chicago without any police casualties was reason for celebration; however, even though Public Enemy Number One was down there were more to go.

Pretty Boy Floyd

After the death of John Dillinger, the Bureau of Investigation named Pretty Boy Floyd as Public Enemy Number One. Baby Face Nelson may have earned that title, but Floyd had an edge. He was then and is now suspected of masterminding the Kansas City Massacre.

The massacre occurred on June 17, 1933, when Kansas City officers along with Bureau of Investigation special agents were escorting prisoner Frank "Jelly" Nash. After the officers arrived by train at Union Station in Kansas City, they cautiously transferred their prisoner to one of two waiting cars to finish their transport.

Men carrying machine guns suddenly moved in. A violent gunfight ensued, during which Kansas City Detectives William Grooms and Frank Hermanson were killed instantly. McAlester, Oklahoma, Chief of Police Otto Reed and Bureau of Investigation Special Agent Ray Caffrey were shot and killed as well.

Frank Nash also fell victim to the failed attempt to free him from custody.

Pretty Boy Floyd, Adam Richetti, and Vernon Miller were thought to be involved. Floyd was identified as one of the shooters by eyewitnesses.

Vernon Miller was able to escape justice for his part in this crime, but he did it the hard way. Miller was later found beaten and strangled to death. His death was not related to the Kansas City Massacre but was the harsh payment of an unrelated underworld debt.

The Bitter End for Floyd: October 22, 1934

One year later, Richetti and Floyd were still a team when, on October 18, 1934, the car they were driving slid off the road and hit a telephone pole. No one in the car was hurt, but afraid that they would be recognized, Richetti and Floyd sent the women with them on a hike to bring back a tow truck.

On October 19, a passing motorist, Joe Fryman, saw two men lying by the roadside in suits. This struck him as suspicious, so he contacted Westville, Ohio, Police Chief John Fultz. The chief went to the scene to investigate taking three officers with him.

As the chief and his officers approached the two men, Richetti fled into the woods. Two officers went after him. Fultz began to question the remaining man. As the conversation started, Floyd drew a weapon and opened fire on Chief Fultz, who returned fire. Fultz was hit in the foot. After wounding the chief, Floyd also fled into the woods.

The two officers in pursuit of Richetti enlisted the aid of former chief Chester Smith, who had been a sniper in World War I. After searching the woods, they located Richetti and took him into custody. He would ultimately die in the gas chamber of the Missouri State Penitentiary in Jefferson City in 1938 for his role in the Kansas City Massacre.

Floyd continued to avoid capture until October 22, but by then Melvin Purvis was leading a combined team of local law enforcement and federal agents. They combed the Westville area believing Floyd was still on foot in the vicinity.

Purvis, four agents with him, and four local officers spotted a car pulling out from behind a corn crib. When the driver saw the officers, he stopped and backed up in an apparent effort to hide the vehicle again.

The agents cautiously approached, and as they neared the vehicle, Floyd bolted from the car with a .45 in hand. He fired wildly at the officers while attempting to run into the woods.

Federal agents and local officers returned fire at Floyd, and he went down. While Floyd lay helpless on the ground, his last words came out breathlessly, "I'm done for. You've hit me twice."

There exists at least three varying accounts of this shootout. All three versions disagree on who shot Floyd, when he was shot, and even what his last words were. One thing all accounts agree on is that Charles Arthur A.K.A. "Pretty Boy Floyd" died in the shootout that took place on October 22, 1934.

To the Bureau of Investigation, this meant they had once again suffered no casualties. There were two down, but the Bureau's work continued. Baby Face Nelson had not yet given up the gun. With the passing of Pretty Boy Floyd, Baby Face was now promoted to Public Enemy Number One.

On May 24, 1934, Bonnie Parker and Clyde Barrow were killed by the team headed by Frank Hamer. With the passing of Dillinger, Floyd, as well as Bonnie and Clyde, many career bank robbers were gone. Due to the pressure that was being brought to bear on the remaining armed robbers, they were losing their support as well as their safe havens.

Dillinger's compatriot Carroll was killed in Waterloo, Iowa, and his partner in crime Van Meter was killed by the St. Paul police.

Dillinger's buddy Harry Pierpont, who had been captured with Dillinger just prior to Dillinger's escape from jail in Indiana, was executed in the electric chair in October 1934.

The G-Men were fast becoming the best show in town, nationwide. J. Edgar Hoover was promoting his agency proudly like a circus barker. The nation has probably never seen a law enforcement administrator who was such an adept, even formidable, political animal as Hoover. He reserved the wielding of his political clout on behalf of his one passion in life, the Bureau of Investigation.

Many historians try to speculate on Hoover's other passions. There is only definitive proof of two loves in J. Edgar Hoover's life. One was the love he had for his mother, and the other was the undying love he had for the Bureau. The FBI was his life.

Nelson's Last Gunfight: November 27, 1934

After the demise of Pretty Boy Floyd, Hoover directed his Flying Squad to concentrate on two remaining high priority targets: Baby Face Nelson and the Barker-Karpis Gang.

On November 27, 1934, Samuel P. Cowley in the Chicago office received information that Nelson had been seen driving a stolen car near Barrington, Illinois. He and Special Agent Ed Hollis headed to the area.

On the day Nelson would do final battle with the G-Men, he was traveling with John Paul Chase. Chase, who J. Edgar Hoover referred to as "a rat with a patriotic name," had been a wheelman during bank robberies for the Barker-Karpis gang, Homer Van Meter, and John Dillinger himself.

Ultimately, Special Agent Thomas McDade and Special Agent William Ryan spotted Nelson in a stolen car near Barrington. A series of bizarre U-turns were made by both vehicles, which resulted in Baby Face Nelson in pursuit of McDade and Ryan. A fierce, rolling gun battle ensued during which Special Agent Ryan fired a round that destroyed the water pump in Nelson and Chase's car.

Shortly after this occurred, Cowley and Hollis joined the pursuit. They followed Nelson and Chase until Nelson veered off Northwest Highway at the entrance to Northside Park in Barrington, Illinois. Nelson and Chase opened up on the agents with automatic weapons. The sustained gunfight lasted between four and five minutes. Nelson was hit and mortally wounded, but there was still fight left in the determined killer. He fired back hitting both agents.

Both Cowley and Hollis were mortally injured by the end of the fight. Chase, Nelson, and the woman with them transferred their weapons to the FBI vehicle then fled the scene leaving the bleeding agents dying on the roadside.

As assistance arrived, Cowley bravely told them to "take him first," referring to his partner and friend, Special Agent Hollis, who had been shot in the head. Cowley had a stomach wound, and because of his concern for Agent Hollis, he was transported later. Hollis was dead on arrival. Cowley lingered a bit but died the following day. Both men had been involved in the death of Dillinger but a few months earlier.

Though Nelson and Chase fled the scene, this time Baby Face Nelson did not escape justice. He died at 8:00 PM on the day of the shootout from the wounds inflicted by Hollis and Cowley.

In response to a tip, police later found Baby Face Nelson dead from wounds suffered in the shootout. Nelson's body had been laid out next to the Niles Center in Illinois Cemetery by his partner Chase.

Chase was later apprehended by Chief A.L. Roberts in Mount Shasta, California, in December 1934. He avoided the death penalty.

Baby Face Nelson was the third Public Enemy Number One killed by the FBI in 1934, but this time justice came at a heavy price.

SAMUEL P. COWLEY   HERMAN E. HOLLIS

The Barker-Karpis Gang: January 16, 1935

The Barkers were a family that stayed together by robbing and killing together. On January 8, 1935, after a prolific criminal career, Arthur "Doc" Barker, son of Ma Barker, was arrested in Chicago. He had a map containing cryptic clues which helped the Bureau of Investigation agents find Ma and her other son Fred Barker. The two were laying low in a two-story home at 13250 East County Highway 25 on the northern banks of Lake Weir near the town of Ocklawaha, Florida.

After setting up surveillance on the house, special agents on the scene determined that the people renting the house claiming to be the Blackburns were in reality Ma Barker and her son Fred.

Just before dawn on January 16, 1935, special agents from the Jacksonville office arrived with reinforcements from the Chicago and Cincinnati offices. They set up an air-tight perimeter and moved properly armed special agents into position. When it was determined that escape was impossible, they offered Ma and her son Fred an opportunity to surrender. Initially, there was no response. After a few minutes Special Agent Earl Connelly called out, "Unless you come out, we're going to start shooting."

Ma Barker, obviously unintimidated, answered matter-of-factly in her gruff, barely-female voice, "Go ahead."

Thus began the longest shootout in the Bureau's history.

During the next four to five hours, fifteen hundred rounds of ammunition were exchanged. It is difficult to determine how long into the shootout it was when the Barkers stopped shooting back. Finally, one of the Bureau commanders on scene noticed no return fire and ordered a cease fire.

A sweep of the house discovered both bodies located on the upper floor in the front left room (facing the house). Fred was dead, his body riddled with bullets. Ma had one wound, which could have been self-inflicted. A Thompson submachine gun was at her feet.

Hoover Arrests Alvin Karpis

With the death of Nelson and the Barkers, there was only one reasonable candidate for Public Enemy Number One, the remaining Barker-Karpis Gang co-leader Alvin Karpis. His criminal friends called him "Creepy" because of the strange persona he projected whenever he smiled.

Karpis had been robbing, killing, and kidnapping since 1931. Alvin had repeatedly shot his way out of tight spots. In 1931 he and Fred Barker shot and killed Howell County Sheriff C. Roy Kelley after the popular lawman had contacted them, believing them to be suspects in the burglary of a clothing store in West Plains, Missouri. Sadly, the sheriff was dead right.

Karpis was with the Barkers throughout their crime spree, but by chance he was not present at their bitter end. Alvin Karpis would be the last Public Enemy Number One. He managed to avoid apprehension for over a year after the death of Ma and Fred Barker.

Alvin's days were numbered, however, when in April of 1936 Senator Kenneth McKellar ridiculed J. Edgar Hoover in a Senate hearing. The Senator was complaining about the Bureau being run by a man who had never even made an arrest. Hoover was livid but could not respond effectively because the Senator spoke the truth. Even though he considered his primary mission was to lead the Bureau, Hoover would set out to remedy the oversight McKellar had pointed out.

Hoover declared that the arrest of Karpis was a high priority and he would be there to make the arrest when it happened. Information was received that Karpis was laying low in New Orleans.

Hoover flew to New Orleans to orchestrate the arrest. On May 1, 1936, Agents swarmed Karpis as he sat in a Plymouth coupe. From out of the swarm came the words, "You are under arrest," uttered by John Edgar Hoover himself.

Just days later, an editorial in the Merchantville, New Jersey, *Community News* entitled "The Gangster Doesn't Live Here Anymore" gave high praise to Hoover and his agents for the arrest of the last of the Depression Era gangsters. The editorial read, "The old spirit of bravado has disappeared; Karpis trembled like a coward when Hoover stood face to face with this murderer." The paper called Hoover "Chief of the G-Men."

Karpis would spend the next twenty-six years in Alcatraz. He was the only "Public Enemy Number One" to die of natural causes as a free man. He lived until 1979.

Birth of the FBI

Eventually, at the request of J. Edgar Hoover, the Bureau of Investigation's name was permanently changed to the Federal Bureau of Investigation. By this time, Hoover had established the FBI Crime Lab. He also set up the FBI National Academy, which he charged with offering local agencies high quality professional training. Throughout his fifty years at the helm, Hoover managed to absorb the political heat focused on the FBI while reflecting it back on politicians who tried to meddle with his agency. Hoover led the agency until his death in 1972.

Hoover's name has always been synonymous with the rise of the FBI, and it is reasonable to give him that credit. It is important, however, to put this into perspective. J. Edgar Hoover was an administrator and most certainly was not the only person responsible for the agency's rise. There may never have been a Federal Bureau of Investigation if the Bureau's special agents had lost their confrontations with Dillinger, Machine Gun Kelly, Pretty Boy Floyd, Baby Face Nelson, and the Barkers.

If medals were to be given for the painful birthing of the FBI, they would have to be given to a handful of special agents in 1934 who deliberately went head to head and gun to gun with some of the most heavily-armed killers in our country's history. Lives were taken in this deadly contest, and sadly, lives were lost.

Hoover's name is clearly remembered, but it would be good to also remember the hands-on heroes of this era who risked and sacrificed all in this struggle between good and evil: Winstead, Baum, Cowley, Hollis, Newman, Bryce, and Purvis.

History, however, does not remember these men individually since they sought neither personal fame nor recognition for their daring deeds. Each of the agents would have been satisfied knowing their combined reputation became a criminal's worst nightmare. The reason these criminals would be terrified of a bump in the night was a nameless, faceless, well-groomed man in a tailored suit wearing a fedora and carrying a Thompson submachine gun: the G-Man.

The author would like to thank the Little Bohemia Lodge for special access. There is nothing like a walk through at the scene of the crime that gives one a proper perspective.

CHAPTER 11

DELF A. "JELLY" BRYCE, THE FASTEST GUNFIGHTER EVER

In 1906 Jacob Adolphus "Delf" Bryce was born in Mountain View, Oklahoma. The boy grew to be such an incredible shot a story was circulated that as an infant he had "teethed" on his father's loaded pistol. The story was thought to be just a legend, but when his sister was asked about it in later years, she replied, "That's preposterous!" After a pause she added with a wry smile that her father always unloaded his pistol first. Then he propped it up in the crib, and Baby Bryce was allowed to "have at it."

As a youth, Delf always seemed to be heading somewhere with his .22 rifle in hand. Even then, he was described as a "perfect shot." Witnesses said he never missed.

The Contest

After graduating high school, Delf took a job as an Oklahoma State Game Ranger, but after six months he resigned and headed for college. While on his way, Bryce stopped at a shooting contest in Shawnee, Oklahoma. There was a $100 prize for the winner. Here he met the night chief of the Oklahoma City Police Department and future FBI Special Agent Clarence Hurt. Delf asked, "Can anyone enter?"

Chief Hurt in turn asked Bryce, "Can you shoot?"

Bryce answered, "I think I can."

Hurt set up target to see if the kid was any good and directed Bryce to show him what he could do.

Bryce asked, "Can I draw and shoot? I'm better if I draw first than if I stand still."

"Up to you," shrugged Hurt, as yet unimpressed by the young man's audacity. The distance was too far to expect much accuracy from someone shooting with a handgun after a quick draw.

Bryce astounded Chief Hurt by executing a flash draw after which he rapidly fired six times. Delf put the shots in a group one could cover with a silver dollar. Hurt had never seen such a display. He told Bryce, "Forget about college. You have a job with the Oklahoma City Police Department."

Although he hadn't considered it until that moment, the prospect of being a police officer intrigued Bryce greatly, and he agreed to take the job. He abandoned his college aspirations and never looked back. It turned out to be a smart move; the kid was a natural.

First Gunfight as an Oklahoma Police Department Officer

Bryce arrived in Oklahoma City and completed the paperwork required to be a police officer. He had neither a uniform nor a badge as he left the station on foot.

Minutes after leaving the station Bryce spotted a suspicious man in a vehicle. Since he was technically on the department, he felt he should do something about it.

Approaching, Bryce surmised the man resembled a person on one of the wanted posters he had seen at the police department. His instincts also told him the man was attempting to hotwire the car. His view was not so clear to be absolutely certain, so he moved in closer. The closer he got the more he knew he was correct.

Even though Bryce was a rookie, he realized he was now the only cop around and felt duty bound to take some action. Bryce walked up to the car, opened the car door, and asked the man, "What are you doing?" Bryce could now confirm the man was clearly in the middle of the hotwiring process and intent on stealing this car.

The man replied, "Who are you?"

Bryce, still in plain clothes with no badge, answered truthfully, "I am a police officer."

This revelation startled the criminal into immediate action. The car thief dropped his tools and jerked a pistol out from under his coat. He swung it toward the rookie and was about to shoot Delf dead his first day on the job.

Delf did not stand by and watch all of this transpire. He drew his pistol and fired once. A second shot would have been overkill; the suspect's lifeless body slid out of the car and onto the pavement. He had only been on the department a matter of hours, but Delf A. Bryce had stopped his first felony in progress. He also guaranteed this offender would not re-offend.

When his fellow Oklahoma City Police Officers arrived on the scene, however, they arrested Bryce for murder. Bryce explained to them that he was a police officer but no badge nor police identification had been issued to him yet. No one present at the station knew who Officer Delf A. Bryce was.

Delf told of his recent swearing in, which sounded plausible, so they called Night Chief Clarence Hurt to verify Bryce's claim. Chief Hurt said he would be down directly.

Chief Hurt arrived and confirmed that Bryce was indeed a member of the department. The investigating officers at the scene were also able to confirm Bryce's version of events. He was brand new on the job, yet he was able to interrupt a crime in progress being committed by an armed criminal. The gun was found fully loaded beside the body and was taken as evidence. Bryce was congratulated on a job well done and released from custody.

When Delf's father learned that his son had been involved in a shooting already, he traveled to the Oklahoma City Police Department and attempted to convince Delf to come back home with him. Police work was an especially dangerous profession in the 1930s, and his father's concerns were well grounded.

Delf told his father, "I've never disobeyed you before, but this is what I want to do. I want to be a policeman." His father acquiesced.

The Night Shift

Officer Bryce began his career as all officers do, working uniform patrol on the night shift. Bryce had always enjoyed hunting, and working the night shift was very much like hunting—hunting for trouble. He had a knack for finding it.

After a few months on the job, Bryce was on patrol in a squad car one quiet night, checking the security of businesses on his beat. He drove up on two men who were prying a door open. Bryce was alone, so he chose to quickly pull up on the men and light them up as he shouted for their surrender. He hoped to startle them into submission.

Faced with the options of flight, fight, or surrender, both suspects immediately chose to fight. The suspects opened fire on the lone patrol officer.

Delf A. Bryce did exactly what a police officer described as a "perfect shot" would do. Delf drew and fired twice, killing both suspects with one shot for each.

In another running gun battle, Bryce was credited for killing two of three suspects in a fleeing vehicle. His shots were made while standing on the running board of a squad.

"Jelly"

Early in his career, police prodigy Delf A. Bryce was promoted to detective, the youngest detective in the Oklahoma City Police Department. Plain clothes suited him to a T, not just because of the work but because Delf had always loved style. Delf went to work each day looking more like a movie star than a police officer.

One of Delf's earliest cases as a detective was a team effort to arrest a wanted gangster. These were the heydays of the robber gangs. Criminals were heavily armed and had no qualms about killing police officers. They often chose to fight rather than submit to a lawful arrest.

Delf located the subject of their search on the streets of Oklahoma City and called for the man's surrender. Instead, he produced a pistol and started shooting. The rounds flew wide, luckily missing Delf and the bystanders who were out and about.

Bryce returned fire, hitting the suspect. Although mortally wounded, the felon was able to escape into a nearby theater. The man staggered weakly into the seating area, dropped, and crawled into a dark corner.

Bryce directed the theater manager to turn up the house lights. With the theater evacuated of innocent bystanders and the house lights turned up, Bryce cautiously entered with gun at the ready. He slowly followed the trail of blood left by the severely wounded man. As Delf Bryce quick-peeked his way from row to row, he finally came upon the aftermath of his handiwork. At the far end of a row, he found the wounded gangster lying on the doorstep of death. There was no fight left in him, and he lay staring at the well-dressed man who had shot him.

The dying man gaped at Delf A. Bryce in his double-breasted suit, snap hat, and multi-colored loafers. Finally, he bemoaned his circumstance with his very last breath observing, "I can't believe I was killed by a Jelly Bean like you." With that, he expired. Of all the things a man in his death throes could be thinking, this man took notice of Delf's appearance.

Jelly Bean was a slang term for a well-dressed man during the twenties and thirties. When Delf's fellow detectives heard of the man's last words, they took to calling him Jelly, and the name stuck.

"Delf" was what his family called him, and "Jelly" was his cop nickname. Bryce embraced both.

J. Edgar Hoover's FBI is Outgunned and Outmatched

In the early 1930s the FBI, then known as the Bureau of Investigation, was struggling in its battle against the rise of bank robbers and gangsters. They were also trying to establish themselves as a credible law enforcement agency. Director J. Edgar Hoover's bookish cadre of special agents were not faring well in the battle against the robber-gangs.

J. Edgar Hoover was a realist as well as a pragmatist. The Bureau's early failures caused Hoover to re-examine his master plan. His agents were all well educated, well dressed, and physically fit, but they rarely possessed street smarts or firearm skills. Hoover recognized that conditions were so dire he would need to reach out to members of local law enforcement who possessed the right combination of these attributes.

Bryce Joins the FBI

One perfectly-timed incident brought Jelly Bryce to the attention of the Bureau of Investigation recruiters and would be the most celebrated of his career.

On July 18, 1934, Bryce was on the hunt for a partner of Clyde Barrow named Harvey Pugh, a bank robber, gangster, and cop killer. He was known to be on the run with two associates, J. Ray O'Donnell and Tom Walton.

Bryce received a tip that the O'Donnell, Walton, and Pugh triumvirate may be hiding out at the Wren Hotel in Oklahoma City. The information seemed promising, so Jelly chose to run it down.

At the hotel, Bryce made contact with Nora Bingaman, an older woman at the front desk. Her twenty-eight-year-old daughter Merle Bolen was the actual owner of the hotel, so Jelly asked to speak with Merle hoping to confirm the tip. Bingaman led Jelly to Merle's room. As Nora opened the door to her daughter's room, she looked startled and abruptly tried to slam the door.

Bryce blocked the door from closing then forced it back open. Inside he spotted J. Ray O'Donnell in bed alongside the scantily dressed Merle Bolen. O'Donnell had armed himself when he heard the door open, so it appeared Jelly was at a disadvantage. Ray had a Colt 1911 in each hand and was taking aim.

Bryce later described the action, "When I looked into the room there he was up on his elbows with a gun in both hands aimed right at me. He was lying on the near side of me and the woman was on the other side of him. I jumped to one side out of the line of fire, grabbed my gun, and tore him up."

Tore him up he did. Jelly Bryce fired six times on the move. The first shot hit O'Donnell just under the chin. The next four hit him in the head, and one round went into the mattress.

The women and Tom Walton, who were sufficiently cowed by what they had just witnessed, were taken into custody unharmed.

Surveillance was set up outside the hotel. Luck was with the OCPD this day, for the cop-killer Harvey Pugh was taken by officers a short time later when he returned to the hotel to pick up his car.

Underhill

It just so happened that another incident, which had taken place prior to the Pugh arrest, caught the attention of J. Edgar Hoover. Jelly Bryce and Clarence Hurt took part in the combined effort to apprehend Wilbur (born Wilber) Underhill with Bureau of Investigation Special Agent R.H. Covin. Underhill was a bank robber-killer-escape artist and every bit as dangerous as Dillinger and Nelson though he never captured the public's collective memory like Nelson, Floyd, Dillinger, Barrow and Parker did.

On December 26, 1933, the combined Bureau of Investigation and Oklahoma City Police Department team closed in on a rented cottage in Shawnee, Oklahoma, where Underhill and his new bride were honeymooning under an assumed name.

After Underhill saw the team from the window of his cottage, he armed himself with a fully loaded Thompson submachine gun. Officers saw this, so gas was sent into the house. As Underhill opened fire on the lawmen, the combined team answered with a ferocious barrage.

During the gunfight, Underhill burst out of the honeymoon haven in his night clothes and managed to break through the gauntlet of machine gun fire running hell bent for freedom. He did not, however, escape unscathed. Underhill was peppered with bullets, but even this did not initially slow him down.

In an almost super-human effort, Underhill ran, then walked, and finally stumbled approximately sixteen blocks from the cottage before he broke into a furniture store. He collapsed on a bed inside. The agents and officers were able to follow the copious blood trail and apprehended Underhill. He was still alive, but his wounds had bled him into a state of compliance.

It took several weeks for the notorious bank robber to succumb to his wounds from the five bullets he collected in his last futile but daring effort to escape justice.

During the interagency pursuit for Underhill, both Hurt and Bryce exhibited the ability to work as team for a unified goal. This was one of the traits that J. Edgar Hoover was looking for in his agents. He pictured the Bureau he was creating not only as a separate entity but working alongside local agencies all over the country as well.

What also caught Hoover's attention was their coolness under fire as well as their uncanny skill as gunfighters. Bryce's J. Ray O'Donnell shootout seven months later sealed the deal. The Bureau recruited both Bryce and Hurt.

There was, however, one obstacle. Jelly Bryce had no college degree. When this was discovered, J. Edgar Hoover himself waived the Bureau's college requirement to hire this man. This was only fair.

After all, the Bureau had come looking for Jelly, Bryce did not go looking for the Bureau.

Upon request, Bryce applied to the Bureau, and his application was expedited and accepted. Detective Jelly Bryce of the Oklahoma Police Department was now Special Agent Adolphus Bryce of the Bureau of Investigation. The time would come when even J. Edgar Hoover would call him Jelly.

A Natural Gunfighter

It was obvious by this point in his career that Jelly Bryce had extraordinary gun-fighting skills. Clearly this was attributed, at least in part, to excellent hand-eye coordination. Bryce also contended that if he was a "perfect shot," as some had said, it was because of frequent perfect practice.

Bryce was known to stand in front of a mirror practicing a fast draw for eight hours straight. As it turned out, Bryce was able to apply the skill he possessed in a positive manner considering the times in which he lived. Jelly Bryce was a man for his times.

During his thirty-two-year career as an officer of the law, Bryce became an indomitable law enforcement gunfighter as he battled through the Gangster Era. Bryce was as good when he shot instinctively as he was when he aimed. It could never be proven, but some are convinced that Jelly Bryce was the fastest and most deadly-accurate gunfighter in history.

Special Agent Jelly Bryce

In 1935 the Bureau of Investigation officially became the Federal Bureau of Investigation. While with the FBI, Bryce's specialty was ending the careers of criminals, quietly or dramatically. The decision was their choice.

In a time when the FBI had neither a hostage rescue team nor trained negotiators, they possessed a not-so-secret weapon. They had Jelly Bryce. In this era, his skill was widely known on both sides of the law. The FBI used his reputation to their advantage. Whenever an especially dangerous man was barricaded, Jelly would be called to the scene as the "Special Negotiator."

When Jelly arrived, he would "negotiate," eventually telling the man that he was Jelly Bryce. He explained that he wanted to bring them out alive rather than dead, but the situation was such that it had to be one or the other. Often, in a very short time, the criminal would come out and surrender. If they chose to fight, Jelly Bryce would oblige them.

After the untimely demise of a number of gangsters at the hands of Special Agent Jelly Bryce, a phenomenon developed called the "Bryce Effect." When suspects were told Jelly Bryce was on the way, they would surrender without another shot being fired.

On one occasion, a reporter took a shot at Special Agent Bryce asking, "Aren't you interested in bringing them back alive?"

Bryce returned fire, "I'm more interested in bringing me back alive."

A Happy Man

Bryce's career was most probably a factor in the demise of his first marriage. After his divorce he totally immersed himself in the job.

In 1944, when Jelly was working out of the El Paso Office he spotted a beautiful young lady crossing the street in Roswell, New Mexico. Bryce was so moved he approached her and told her, "I just thought you'd want to know. I'm going to marry you."

This was not just a line. Jacob Adolphus Bryce eventually took Shirley Bloodworth as his wife. Their thirty year union enhanced his life and produced great happiness as well as one son named Johnny.

Jelly's Guns

Jelly Bryce policed in an era when criminals traveled the country armed with military grade weapons. These men were not cautious about who was in the line of fire when they squeezed the trigger. Jelly always placed himself in the front line of the battle to end a killer's reign of terror.

Due to the place and time he policed, Bryce was involved in nineteen separate gunfights by some accountings. Jelly went into these fights armed with everything from a .38 caliber revolver to a Thompson submachine gun and was a master with all. His personal favorite was a Smith and Wesson .44 caliber revolver. It sported a pearl handled grip embossed with a black cat and the number 13, which only proved to be an unlucky number for the criminals who went up against him.

Bryce had something in common with Texas Ranger Frank Hamer, besides a knack for surviving gunfights. Bryce and Hamer both named their favorite handgun "Lucky."

Ironically, luck had very little to do with their success. They won armed encounters because of their preparation, alertness, and skill in the fight.

In 1945 *Life* magazine did a photographic study of Bryce dropping a coin from shoulder height, drawing, firing, and hitting the coin before it passed his waist. Experts who analyzed this incredible feat of marksmanship determined Bryce was able to draw and make that incredible shot in two-fifths of a second, which is almost inhuman.

Bryce was more than just a fast gun, however. He was also an effective investigator. Special Agent Weldon Gentry, who worked with Jelly Bryce, addressed this when he said, "All the time he was agent in charge we didn't have an unsolved bank robbery in the state."

Oklahoma City Police Chief L. Hilbert described the lawman in this way, "No doubt about it, he was the best."

Toward the end of his career, Bryce was utilized heavily, teaching agents gunfighting skills. To this day his point shooting philosophy is utilized by many firearms trainers. Bryce often gave incredible public displays of marksmanship, which he continued after retiring from the FBI in 1958.

Ultimate Victory

Jelly Bryce not only survived nineteen law enforcement gunfights, but he also trained an entire generation of gunfighters to survive their own. He became the standard of what an honorable gunfighter should be in that generation.

In May 1974 Jelly reminisced at a reunion dinner for retired FBI agents. As all old cops do, they laughed and told stories of what it was like "back in the day."

As he slept that night, the sixty-eight-year-old legend Jacob Adolphus Bryce, known to his family as "Delf" and his friends as "Jelly," achieved the honorable gunfighter's ultimate victory. He ended his tour of duty peacefully in his sleep.

CHAPTER 12

THE MOST DIFFICULT SHOTS EVER MADE

If a group of NRA members were asked, "Who made the most difficult shot in military history?" some would be able to make a few educated guesses. They might say Carlos Hathcock, Chris Kyle, or Timothy Murphy. There would be a knowledge base which would allow for discussion about the topic.

If the follow-up question were asked, "Who made the most difficult shot in *law enforcement* history?" the question would probably be met with silence. Few people are even aware of what law enforcement officers have to accomplish around the nation, past and present, in order to make it home at the end of a shift.

The shots taken by Officer Clarence Koblitz of Wisconsin's La Crosse Police Department would most certainly be in contention for the most difficult shots ever made in law enforcement history.

This is the story of a jail break. The criminals involved in the pursuit and gunfight may have become as famous as Dillinger or as deadly as the Barrow Gang if their escape had been successful. As it is, however, Orville Moore and Harold Chamberlain have been all but forgotten by history not because of one, or even two, but four well-placed shots taken by Officer Clarence Koblitz.

The Jail Break

It all started at 2:00 PM on July 20, 1935, when La Crosse County Jailer Robert Garrow was moving inmate Orville Moore from his cell to make a phone call. At the same moment, Trustee Dewey Meinertz was leading inmate Harold Chamberlain back to his cell after receiving a jail haircut.

The jailers did not know that these two men had planned for this very moment at length. Now the opportunity had arrived to put their escape plan into action. As the inmates passed, they signaled each other with simple eye contact.

On cue, the inmates exploded into the pre-planned attack simultaneously. Moore pulled a straight razor from his sleeve, spun Garrow around, and laid the sharpened edge of the razor against the jailer's throat.

At that same moment, Chamberlain produced a concealed wooden dowel used to wash prisoner's clothes and beat Jailer Meinertz to the floor with it while producing a pair of scissors as well. Meinertz ceased movement, prone on the floor with his hands up. He hoped by submitting he would live to see another day.

Moore, with the straight razor to Garrow's throat demanded, "Bob, you [expletive deleted]. I gotta have those keys!"

Garrow replied without hesitation, "Boy, you can have them." With that, Garrow tossed Moore the keys to the jail.

Before leaving the jail, the two escapees made good use of the keys. Moore and Chamberlain paid a visit to the La Crosse County Sheriff's Department Armory. They took possession of a Thompson submachine gun, a shot gun, and a pistol as well as the ammunition needed for each weapon.

Police Respond

Andrew Jungen, a gardener for the county, was working on the grounds outside the jail. He heard the considerable commotion caused by the jail break and quickly deduced an escape was in progress.

Jungen ran to a phone and made a call that triggered immediate response by the La Crosse City Police Department.

Officers Clarence Koblitz, Aaron Sanford, Joe McGrath, and Jack Fitzpatrick of the La Crosse Police Department formed a team and headed to the jail in one squad. Koblitz had the forethought to snatch a Remington 30-30 rifle from the gun rack and hopped onto the running board of the squad. Fitzpatrick, who was normally a motor-cop (motorcycle-cop) drove.

Rolling Gunfight

Back at the jail, the escapees' plan was progressing better than they could have hoped. They thought they would have to escape on foot through the marsh that lay directly to the north of the jail. Instead, as the two ran out the front door, they saw a Blue Cab sitting unattended at the front entrance that they couldn't pass up.

The two climbed into the cab and drove off. As they accelerated to flee the scene, they realized the cab was equipped with a "governor." A governor was a device installed in service vehicles to keep employees from driving unnecessarily fast. This cab's governor restricted the vehicle to a top speed of 35 miles per hour and absolutely no faster.

Moore and Chamberlain's soaring spirits plummeted when they saw police approaching; however, their odds of escape in a slow car was better than on foot. It was possible the officers would not even notice they were in the cab. Perhaps they could at least get clear of the scene then steal another faster vehicle.

As the squad pulled up to the jail, the gardener who had watched the men escape shouted and pointed at the cab as it passed the officers, "They're in the cab!!"

Fitzpatrick wheeled the squad car around with tires squealing and accelerated while Officer Koblitz and Officer Aaron Sandford held on for dear life. They were standing on the running boards on opposite sides of the squad. The high stakes race between the escapees and the police was on.

With the advantage of an unrestricted gas pedal, Fitzpatrick quickly gained ground between the squad and the cab. Within a few blocks, the space between them was minimal. It was here the first shots came from the cab, causing the police to duck instinctively.

After traveling only a half block more, Chamberlain, the cab's driver, pulled over to the side of the road. Even though shots had just been fired from the cab, Officer Sanford jumped from the running board of the squad and ran toward the cab. He thought the escapees were about to surrender.

As Sanford neared the cab, he saw a weapon pointed directly at him through the back window. Sanford instinctively flattened himself on the roadway as the muzzle of the shotgun belched, blowing out the back window of the cab. The deadly spray of unforgiving

---

buckshot passed mercifully over Sanford. He was alive thanks only to his quick reactions.

With this deadly ruse completed, Chamberlain accelerated, resuming their flight that somehow seemed to gain a greater degree of desperation, even though the speed remained a constant 35 mph.

Koblitz later said "Everything about this pursuit and gunfight had grown to feel as it was in slow motion." They had only been in pursuit for a few minutes and yet it seemed a lifetime had passed. For Sanford, it nearly had.

Sanford sprung up from the brick surface of the road and caught the door post of the car. He swung himself back onto the running board as Fitzpatrick drove past. Fitzpatrick continued his pursuit directly into the withering gunfire coming from the cab. Moore and Chamberlain continued firing, trying to either kill or discourage the cops on their tail. The officers would not be deterred. Sanford, McGrath, and Fitzpatrick returned fire, hitting the cab repeatedly.

Koblitz, however, held fire. He knew shooting at the cab would never get him off his precarious perch. He steadied his 30-30 as best as he could on the frame of the squad while wrapping his opposite arm around the post. Clarence, a crack competitive shooter, took careful aim at the driver and fired.

The round hit Chamberlain in the shoulder. With this warning shot, Koblitz hoped to take away Chamberlain's resolve rather than his life. Such was not the result. The pursuit continued, and rounds continued coming from the cab.

Koblitz aimed again and fired a second round which struck the driver in the neck; Chamberlain slumped to his side, dead. The vehicle slowed but did not stop.

Adrenalized, Moore quickly pulled his dead partner from behind the wheel of the rolling cab. He climbed into the driver's seat and accelerated away, once again reaching the top speed of 35 mph.

Orville Moore somehow continued to shoot back at the officers with one hand while he drove with the other. The freedom represented by the Minnesota border was in sight about a mile away as he crossed the "Wagon Bridge" over the Mississippi River.

The Drama Ends

The Minnesota border loomed large in front of Moore. He was convinced that the pursuit would end if he could just get across the border since Minnesota was out of his pursuer's jurisdiction. Moore could hear the 'thunk' of the bullets fired by Sanford, McGrath, and Fitzpatrick as the careening vehicles rolled steadily closer and closer to the border.

Meanwhile, Koblitz took careful aim while the two vehicles bowled steadily westward. He disregarded the almost incessant "Pop! Pop! Pop!" of his partners' fire as well as Moore's return fire. Koblitz concentrated on the task at hand.

Koblitz tightened his grip on the post. He steadied the sway of the fixed metal sights on his 30-30. Then he took in a deep breath, let part of it out, and fired. Instantaneously, the cab wavered as Moore was hit in the left shoulder. Again, Koblitz had delivered a less than lethal invitation for Moore to stop. Undeterred, Moore recovered and continued his flight.

Koblitz's re-gripped his 30-30 and took aim. Moore would not get another chance. Koblitz fired.

There was an immediate and dramatic reaction. The cab veered wildly, careening off ten guard rail posts before coming to a stop. The officers cautiously approached the cab and found both escapees dead. It was over.

Most Difficult Shot in Law Enforcement History?

In an interview in 1988, retired Captain Koblitz talked about that afternoon. He observed, "Those men were desperate to get away at all costs." Then as he lay in his bed at St. Francis Hospital his gaze seemed to drift from the present. It appeared as if he were watching the crystal clear memory of that day play out on a screen above him. The memory of a desperate afternoon he survived so long ago. After long moments of silence he added, "We're lucky we didn't get it instead of them."

Retired Captain Clarence Koblitz was too modest to tell the truth of the matter. Clarence Koblitz fired four shots from his 30-30 rifle, balanced precariously on the running board of a speeding squad while being shot at. He was holding onto the window frame with one hand while firing with the other. The weapon he was using had fixed iron sights.

In spite of these difficulties, Koblitz was able to accurately fire four times. Both of the first shots fired by Koblitz hit his target's shoulder giving him an opportunity to realize the folly of his actions and surrender. With Koblitz's unique "warning shot" ignored, he took a second shot that permanently stopped these individuals. The fourth shot fired by Officer Koblitz was a head shot.

These were arguably the most difficult aimed shots ever made in law enforcement history, giving credibility to advice passed on again and again from firearm instructors to novice shooters over the years, "Aim small, miss small."

In this case, Clarence aimed small and didn't miss at all.

PART THREE

PRESIDENTIAL SECURITY

CHAPTER 13

THEODORE ROOSEVELT
OF THE NYPD

On October 14, 1912 a mentally ill New York saloonkeeper was stalking former president and current presidential candidate Theodore Roosevelt. The two-term Republican President, now running as a candidate for a third term on the Bull Moose Party ticket, was being cheered by a crowd near the Gilpatrick Hotel in Milwaukee.

As President Roosevelt stood up in his open vehicle to acknowledge the crowd gathered outside the hotel, John Flammang Schrank aimed a revolver at Roosevelt. At the moment he fired, an alert stenographer for President Roosevelt, Elbert E. Martin leapt onto Schrank. Elbert, along with former Rough Rider A. O. Girard as well as several policemen, wrestled Schrank into custody.

The would-be assassin spent the rest of his life in Central State Mental Hospital in Waupun.

The bullet certainly would have killed Roosevelt except for a folded up fifty-page copy of his ninety-minute speech along with his spectacle case which slowed the bullet. Even so, the bullet lodged in Roosevelt's chest. Doctors eventually chose to leave the bullet in place as an operation to remove it would pose more of a threat to the Bull Moose candidate.

After Roosevelt had been shot in the chest, the adventurer, warrior, and president was not deterred. He waved off medical attention and delivered his speech to a wildly cheering crowd. He asked the crowd, "Friends, I shall ask you to be as quiet as possible." The cheers continued and then he added, "I don't know whether you fully understand that I have just been shot." He now had their undivided attention. Few knew that the very speech he was delivering had contributed to saving his life.

At the time of the attempted assassination, Roosevelt's résumé was already impressive. Before Theodore Roosevelt was the Bull Moose Party presidential candidate, he had already served two terms as President of the United States. Before that he had been Vice President. Prior to that, he was a dynamic leader serving as a colonel in the Spanish American War, known for leading the now famous "Rough Riders" and Buffalo Soldiers on charges that ultimately took San Juan Heights. This action greatly contributed to the winning of that war.

Roosevelt made the charge on foot fighting beside his troops, not on horse-back as the name "Rough Riders" would suggest. He earned the Congressional Medal of Honor for his valor. The honor was presented posthumously nearly one hundred years after the battle. He remains the only president to have ever earned this honor.

Prior to the Spanish American War he had been Secretary of the Navy. One must wonder why Theodore Roosevelt is included in a book about the great police officers in history. Theodore Roosevelt was a man of many talents. Before he was President, Vice President, or Secretary of the Navy, he served as a badge-carrying Police Commissioner for the City of New York. He was one of New York's finest and is revered to this day by the department for his time spent there.

Although President Roosevelt fired his weapon in Cuba and took a bullet in Milwaukee, he never fired his weapon while with the New York Police Department. Many in law enforcement history have made tremendous contributions without ever firing their weapons. The vast majority of officers who take the oath to serve and protect never fire their weapon during their long and sometimes quite distinguished careers, except in training.

Roosevelt is mentioned in this compilation of great Law Dogs because he said many things during his time on Earth which speak to the heart and mission of law enforcement. Many of his most cherished words as a world leader were forged and tempered during his time with the New York Police Department. He is included in these pages because of those timeless words as well as the exemplary example of principled leadership he displayed during every phase of his life.

Roosevelt's tenure as police commissioner was marked by his aggressive efforts to modernize the department as well as to remove the tentacles of corrupting political influences. Roosevelt wrote in his autobiography about the need to strike at the heart of corruption but noted there was little need for improvement in the area of courage on the NYPD. He said of New York police officers, *"They had always been brave in dealing with riotous and violent criminals."*

President Roosevelt's most memorable quote subtly reveals that his days in law enforcement had clearly left a mark on him. Roosevelt advised that as a nation the United States should, *"Speak softly and carry a big stick; you will go far."* Although Roosevelt was referring to U.S. foreign policy, these words are still passed on in some form by veteran beat officers to raw recruits. Roosevelt probably heard the words from some tough New York foot patrolman back in the day.

Roosevelt had this to say to the nineteenth century's soft-on-crime crowd. The quote could be used by any chief facing criticism for militarization. Roosevelt said, *"I have not the slightest sympathy with any policy which tends to put the policeman at the mercy of a tough, or which deprives him of efficient weapons."*

Roosevelt was able to put the enforcement aspect of ethical policing into perspective like no other when he concluded, *"No man is above the law and no man is below it; nor do we ask any man's permission when we require him to obey it. Obedience to the law is demanded as a right; not asked as a favor."*

While making arrests, officers often hear limp justifications for poor decisions miscreants have made. To wrong-doers trying to avoid taking responsibility for their actions, Roosevelt would say, *"No man is justified in doing evil on the ground of expediency."*

Every defensive tactics instructor spends hours trying to explain the concept and application of justifiable use of force. Roosevelt made the complex simple by using eight single-syllable words, *"Don't foul, don't flinch—hit the line hard!"*

Officers who have been compelled to act in a crisis only to later find themselves under attack by a "Monday Morning Quarterback" for the actions they took under extreme duress can take solace in Roosevelt's words, *"In any moment of decision the best thing you can do is the right thing, the next best thing is the wrong thing, and the worst thing you can do is nothing."*

Roosevelt's guidance to leaders still ring true today. He declared, *"The best executive is the one who has sense enough to pick good men to do what he wants done and self-restraint enough to keep from meddling with them while they do it."* This is one of the simplest rules of leadership to follow and at the same time one of the most violated.

Every man and woman in law enforcement as well as the military should feel proud of their career choice for in this great man's assessment every cop hitting the highways and streets of this country would be worthy of his respect. Roosevelt once observed, *"No man is worth his salt who is not ready at all times to risk his body, to risk his well-being, to risk his life, in a great cause."*

Policing with honor in the United States of America is a great cause. Policing in compliance with the wishes of our founding fathers pays homage to the million souls who have died fighting for our freedoms. This country can't be free unless the police in this country respect the constitution, which limits their powers for a reason.

For those striving valiantly each day to do their best Roosevelt also said, *"Far and away the best prize that life offers is the chance to work hard at work worth doing."*

Although Roosevelt certainly did not have to, he was often seen walking a beat when he was serving as a police commissioner. He served the police department for a short time, but the New York Police Department remains proud of his affiliation with the NYPD.

One particular quote by Teddy Roosevelt has been framed by many in the law enforcement profession and put on the walls of police gymnasiums, command rooms, locker rooms, firing ranges, and line-up rooms nationwide. These words speak straight to the heart of those who are placed in a position to be physically attacked on behalf of others.

Theodore Roosevelt proclaimed, *"The credit belongs to the man who is actually in the arena; whose face is marred by dust, sweat, and blood; who strives valiantly; who errs and comes short again and again; who knows great enthusiasms, the great devotions, and spends himself in a worthy cause; who at best knows in the end triumph of high achievement; and at worst, if he fails, at least fails while daring greatly."*

Thank you, Mr. President.

CHAPTER 14

THE OFFICERS WHO SAVED PRESIDENT TRUMAN

By 1950, the country had lost President Lincoln, President Garfield, and President McKinley to assassins. Attempts were made on the lives of Andrew Jackson, Teddy Roosevelt, and Franklin D. Roosevelt. These tragedies and two World Wars had inspired round-the-clock protection for the President of the United States.

The Secret Service, which was started by President Lincoln, had its original mission expanded to include presidential protection duties. Additionally, a contingent of officers were developed to police the presidential grounds. They were simply called the White House Police.

The Secret Service Police and White House Police were designed to be a formidable barrier between unseen enemies and the president and his family. In 1950 the on-duty professionals tasked with guarding President Truman and his family would face the ultimate test, a test all United States Secret Service and White House Police details hope they are prepared for.

The effort made in the president's defense would be great and the sacrifice greater.

Planned Attack

During the fall of 1950, President Harry Truman and his wife Bess were not living in the White House. The White House was undergoing extensive renovations, so the First Family was living at Blair House, across the street from the White House. They were being protected by a combination detail of White House Police as well as United States Secret Service Officers.

On October 31, 1950, Oscar Collazo and Griselio Torresola arrived in Washington from the Bronx, New York. They were radicalized members of the Puerto Rican Nationalist Party. They wanted Puerto Rico to break away from the United States and become an independent nation. They hoped to achieve attention for their cause by killing the President of the United States.

There had been an uprising in Puerto Rico on October 30, and these two men were outraged by how President Truman, in their minds, had minimized their movement. President Truman had made a statement about the violence and described it as, "an incident among Puerto Ricans."

Torresola and Collazo conspired together and decided that even though it would probably be suicidal, they would launch an attack on the President Truman's residence and attempt to kill the man. They arrived in Washington on October 31 and reconnoitered Blair House. During additional preparations, Torresola, who was skilled with firearms, quickly taught Collazo how to load and fire his weapon. There was little time to train, so this simple instruction would have to suffice.

The Attack

At the onset of the assault, Torresola approached Blair House from the West on Pennsylvania Avenue. Collazo approached from the East. They would simultaneously attack two separate access points in the hope that one of them could gain entry into Blair House to kill the president.

Collazo quietly came up behind White House Police Officer Donald Birdzell, put his gun near the officer's head, and fired, "Click!"

Collazo had failed to chamber a round. He began fumbling with the weapon to charge it. Meanwhile Birdzell turned to face the threat and drew his weapon, but Collazo recovered and shot the officer in the right knee.

Secret Service Agent Vincent Mroz heard the gunfire and instinctively ran toward it. Mroz had been a Marine Corps Combat Lieutenant during World War Two. He exited Blair House and quickly assessed what was happening. He spotted Collazo, aimed, and fired hitting him in the chest. This well-placed shot eliminated Collazo as a threat to the president.

Prior to the attack, President Truman had been taking a nap. He awoke when the gunfire erupted and went to the window at the front of the residence to see what was happening. Secret Service Agents shouted for him to get down, and he immediately did so.

Simultaneous to Collazo's attack, Torresola, the more experienced of the gunmen, arrived armed with a 9mm German Luger at another access point to Blair House. He approached the booth where Officer Leslie Coffelt of the White House Police stood guard, and without warning, shot him three times. Coffelt fell mortally wounded.

Torresola turned and fired again at Officer Joseph Downs, hitting him in the hip before Downs could even draw his weapon. The badly wounded Downs turned and was shot in the neck and back by Torresola as he courageously dragged himself to the entrance to Blair House and secured the door, denying access to Torresola. The actions of this wounded officer effectively thwarted the assassins. No matter what happened next, President Truman and his family were safe.

Torresola was not finished though. He directed his fire at Officer Birdzell, who was still standing. There was now return fire coming from all officers and agents present. Torresola hit Birdzell in the left knee, and this second wound put Birdzell down.

Torresola took cover and began to reload. He thought he had killed Coffelt in the guard booth, so he did not see the gravely wounded officer perform a truly magnificent last act of defiance. Coffelt pulled himself out of the booth and propped himself up against the booth's wall for stability. He took careful aim with his 38 caliber revolver and fired, hitting Torresola two inches above the ear and killing him instantly. The assault on Present Truman and his family was over.

Although it was the fiercest gunfight in Secret Service history, both attacks were thwarted in less time than it takes to read this account. To be exact, Collazo's attack was over in 20 seconds and Torresola's assault was complete in just 38 seconds.

The self-sacrificing White House Police Officer, Leslie Coffelt, was taken to the hospital, but his courageous heart stopped beating four hours after he had sustained multiple gunshot wounds.

Justice?

Collazo was tried, convicted, and sentenced to death. Just days before his scheduled execution in 1952, President Harry S. Truman showed the would-be assassin more mercy than Collazo would have shown the president and his family by commuting his sentence to life in prison.

In 1979 President Jimmy Carter commuted Collazo's life sentence to time served. The terrorist walked out of prison a free man; however, the benevolence of this country's criminal justice system could not remove the label of terrorist, no matter how repentant he was.

On the other hand, Leslie Coffelt, who had already distinguished himself during World War II, added another laurel to his crown of service. This modern knight remains the only law enforcement officer to prevent a presidential assassination by sacrificing his life to kill the man who would kill the president.

If heroes exist, Officer Coffelt was one. If glory can be realized, Leslie Coffelt achieved it. In the end Officer Coffelt gave his life in combat so that our nation's president and first family might live.

A grateful nation gave Officer Coffelt a hero's farewell; he was buried with honors at Arlington National Cemetery. President Truman himself attended the ceremony to say goodbye to the fallen American hero.

CHAPTER 15

J.D. TIPPIT, THE FORGOTTEN HERO OF THE DAY EVERYONE REMEMBERS

For those who were alive, November 22, 1963, is a day that no one would ever forget. Every man, woman, and child remembers where they were and what they were doing when they first heard the news of the assassination of John F. Kennedy. However, few remember the name of one remarkable man who also died on that tragic day while wearing the uniform of the Dallas Police Department, Officer J.D. Tippit.

Early Years

J.D. Tippit was raised the son of a cotton farmer in the Red River Valley area of Eastern Texas. The letters J and D do not stand for anything; J.D. was Tippit's given name.

He probably would have remained a farmer all of his life except his, like so many others, was a life interrupted by World War II. Initially, his parents' wishes that he be exempted from service because he was needed on the farm were granted. In respect of their wishes, Tippit stayed on the farm for a time.

J.D., however, did not want to miss the opportunity to serve his country during this trying time. J.D. apologized to his parents and left the farm. He joined the army, and after completing his basic training, he volunteered for Airborne Infantry. He saw heavy combat and earned a purple heart and a bronze star with the vaunted 17th Airborne Division, whose motto was "Thunder from Heaven." J.D. was engaged in the brutal combat during the Battle of the Bulge.

In March of 1945, J.D. dropped out of the sky, landing across the Rhine into Germany to help deliver the death blow to the Third Reich. Germany surrendered in April thanks to J.D. Tippit and a few hundred thousand of his buddies.

Life in Texas after the War

After the war, J.D. returned home and married the love of his life, Marie Frances Gasway. Their union would be blessed with three children.

In 1952 Tippit gave up cotton farming for good. During the war, Tippit realized he had a different calling. J.D. was what some would call a sheepdog, a protector of the flock. That calling eventually inspired him to join the Dallas Police Department. He was sworn in and issued badge number 848.

On Officer Tippit's first night on the job, he was assigned to work a local fair. J.D. made his "first arrest" when he spotted his brother with friends enjoying the fair. J.D., a notorious practical joker, came up behind his brother, swept him to the ground, and handcuffed him. He quickly whisked him away telling the crowd that they could go about their business because there was, "nothing to see here, folks."

As J.D. reached his squad, he and his brother shared a good laugh and J.D. released him. J.D. loved police work immediately, and in spite of such a lighthearted start, he took it very seriously.

The Iceman Cometh

On April 28, 1956 J.D. and his partner Officer Daniel Smith responded to a Violent Domestic in Progress. As the two Dallas officers arrived on scene, a crying, battered and abused wife ran screaming from the house. The husband was in hot pursuit but turned and ran back into the house when he saw Tippit and Smith.

The officers rushed the front door as the abuser slammed it in their faces. J.D. and Smith were undeterred. They did not even slow down, and their momentum carried them crashing through the door.

Once inside, the officers were set upon by a madman. The husband, who they later described as "demented," armed himself with an ice pick.

As soon as he acquired the horrific weapon, the belligerent psychotic began slashing it at the officers; the fight over the weapon was on. The three slammed, rolled, thrashed, and crashed about the kitchen until all three combatants lay sweating, panting, and bleeding on the floor. The mad man was in handcuffs headed for jail. Though Smith and Tippit won the contest, they would be headed to the hospital emergency room. Smith suffered a deep wound to his shoulder, while J.D. was struck in the stomach and the knee.

After a few days, the knee wound worsened and became infected. Officer Tippit underwent surgery where doctors discovered a tip of the ice pick had broken off and became embedded in Tippit's knee cap. The tip of the ice pick was removed during the surgery, and in a short time Officer Tippit was able to return to duty.

Shots Fired

On September 2, 1956, a fully recovered J.D. and his partner Dale Hankins were doing a "routine" walk through at the Club-80 in Dallas. Tippit spotted a man in one of the booths who looked like the face on a wanted bulletin the department had received from Denver. The two officers contacted the man and asked him to step outside with them so they could investigate further. The man initially feigned cooperation but suddenly shoved a concealed 25 caliber semi-automatic into J.D.'s face and squeezed the trigger. Luckily, the would-be cop-killer had left the weapon set in the safe position. Nothing happened.

J.D. did not try to disarm the suspect this time. He and his partner both drew their service weapons and fired. Together, they put seven rounds into the suspect, killing him before the wanted man could recover from his mental misstep and resume his assault.

Tippit later confided to a fellow officer what it looked like to have even a small caliber gun shoved into his face. J.D. said the muzzle, "looked like a stove pipe!"

Even though J.D. possessed clear leadership skills and could have pursued a promotion, he preferred the job of patrol officer. He found it satisfying to make a difference in people's lives one call at a time. He especially enjoyed the excitement of not knowing what lay ahead for him around the next corner.

Officer J.D. Tippit finally made day shift, and his favorite part about this shift was being able to be with his wife and children every night. The day shift in Dallas was plenty busy enough to keep life interesting for J.D.

Last Kiss

On November 22, 1963, the entire city of Dallas was buzzing about the visit of President John F. Kennedy. J.D. checked in at 7:30 AM at the Oak Hill substation to begin his patrol shift. J.D. was a little disappointed that he would not see the young president because his assigned patrol area, Section 78, was five miles from downtown Dallas where the President would be making his rounds.

J.D.'s shift was initially uneventful. Everybody in Dallas seemed to have gravitated toward the presidential motorcade route. Officer Tippit was even able to stop home for lunch. His wife Marie was home from work because his their son Allen had come down sick and she had brought him home from school.

Marie made tuna sandwiches and fried potatoes, and the three enjoyed lunch together. J.D. discussed the potential problems related to the presidential visit. He said, "When you get a lot of people together, you can never tell what's going to happen. The crowd could get out of hand, or someone might try something." This thought may have weighed heavily on J.D.'s mind because he cut his lunch break short.

After enjoying this simple yet blissful half hour, he ruffled his son's hair and kissed his beautiful Marie goodbye. Neither of these people, who were so deeply in love, realized that they had just shared their last kiss in this world.

With that done, J. D climbed into patrol car number 10 and drove off to make history.

President Kennedy Has Been Shot

At 12:30 PM President Kennedy was shot. J.D., who was far from the chaos, was unable to help in any way other than to diligently begin a search of his own area after a description of the assassin was broadcast. Eventually his dispatcher advised him to move toward the central area and aid in the search for the suspect.

As J.D. swung central, he must have experienced the rush of adrenaline that every cop gets when they join a search for a wanted man. This search was the most important man-hunt in United States history since the United States Cavalry spread out across Virginia looking for John Wilkes Booth. There was a major difference, however. No one knew, as yet, who had shot the president.

At 1:14 PM just 44 minutes after shots rang out in Dealey Plaza, the veteran Dallas Police Officer J.D. Tippit spotted a young man who was visibly nervous near 10th and Patton in the Oak Cliff section of Dallas. The man's eyes darted about and looked away as he saw the patrol car. He matched the description of the suspect in the shooting of President Kennedy right down to his toes.

With the uncertainty shared by every officer that has ever glanced at a suspect walking down the street and thought to himself, "Is that the guy we're looking for?" Officer J.D. Tippit pulled alongside the man to take a closer look. Witnesses later said that after talking to him briefly at the window of the patrol car the man was directed to the front of the squad and J.D. exited to continue his investigation.

As the still clearly uncertain Officer Tippit approached, the man suddenly drew a .38 caliber revolver and shot J.D. three times in the chest at close range. J.D. fell, wounded, but still alive. As this American hero lay helpless on the ground, Lee Harvey Oswald walked over to him, bent down, placed the cold steel muzzle of his weapon next to Officer J.D. Tippit's temple, and fired.

After executing this husband and father of three, the killer fled.

A citizen who had witnessed the murder climbed into squad number 10 and immediately called in the shooting by using J.D.'s radio.

Minutes later Dallas officers converged on a theater. Witnesses had seen the killer duck into the movie house as he saw the approaching officers. When officers converged on Oswald, he drew his weapon, again intent on murder, but he was subdued and disarmed by officers after a fierce struggle.

Oswald was taken into custody for the murder of Officer Tippit. J.D.'s instincts were proven to be correct, for Lee Harvey Oswald was the man who shot President John F. Kennedy.

More Than a Footnote to History

Officer J.D. Tippit should be much more than a footnote in history. J.D. Tippit repeatedly put himself in harm's way to defend his country and his community.

From 1941 through 1945 he entered a war that killed millions, even though he had been exempted from service to stay home and take care of the family farm. During that war he could have attempted to get a less dangerous assignment state side. Instead, he chose to be one of the best, a member of the airborne infantry, knowing he would most likely be placed at the tip of the proverbial spear.

As a police officer he continued that pattern of trying to make a difference every day even though he put himself at great risk. Ultimately he did make a difference. Officer Tippit initiated the action that ultimately led to the apprehension of a presidential assassin at the cost of his own life.

J.D. was the total package. He was a great father, great husband, great soldier, great American, and the last action he took during his life is proof that he was a great cop.

Officer J.D. Tippit was a perfect example of the Greatest Generation, a generation whose epic stories of victory, valor, and sacrifice are destined to echo throughout history like "Thunder from Heaven."

PART FOUR

DOING THE RIGHT THING

CHAPTER 16

FRANK SERPICO. UNCOMPROMISING INTEGRITY AND COURAGE

To this day, Frank Serpico's name is synonymous with two words in police training all over the nation: Police Ethics. In the old days before "Verbal Judo" and "Professional Communications," cops would say to resisting miscreants, "Now fella' there's the easy way and the hard way. It's your choice. Which will it be?" Frank never was offered the choice for which way he wanted to become famous. The hard way chose him.

When Frank Serpico was a little boy, he had no dream of becoming famous. His dream was to grow up, be a cop, and catch bad guys. Frank was able to realize that dream. He became a cop and caught many bad guys. If life were simple, that would be the happy ending to Frank's life story; however, Frank lived in a complex world. He discovered that some of the "bad guys" were fellow officers.

This is Frank's story.

The Beginning

Frank Serpico was born April 14, 1936, to two proud but poor Italian immigrants, Vincenzo and Maria Giovanna Serpico. Their lives demonstrated hard work and integrity to their children. Vincenzo repaired and made shoes while Maria worked wrapping candy in a factory to make ends meet. Things were so tight at times that, during the winter, Frank's dad would bring home leather trimmings from his shop to burn in the stove in order to help heat their home.

As a child, Frank loved detective stories on the radio and was one of those kids who dreamed of becoming one of New York's finest. Even in his youth, Frank had an inclination to pursue justice. Frank told a story in one interview of a time when he had a toy pistol. He was proud of that pistol, but one day as he played with it, a larger kid snatched it from him and ran. Even though Frank was much smaller than the thief, he still pursued the stranger through the streets of New York until he lost him.

One interaction he had with a police officer as a young boy took a bit of the shine off the badge for Frank. At the time Frank was making money shining shoes. He was thrilled when one of his heroes, a policeman, approached him and asked Frank for a shine. Frank diligently and with great excitement shined the police officer's shoes.

When Frank could see his reflection in the spit shine of those shoes, he was shocked when the officer stood up and walked off without paying. Frank would never forget how that felt. He decided then and there, when he became a police officer he would never be that kind of cop—a cop who felt entitled.

At eighteen, Frank enlisted in the Army and served in Korea. After he was honorably discharged from the Army, he proudly donned the uniform of the New York City Police Department in 1959.

Frank excelled as a patrol officer. In an era, when one arrest a shift was an acceptable night's work, Frank would make multiple arrests each night. Why not? He was living his dream.

Plain Clothes

Frank had one burning ambition in law enforcement. He wanted to achieve the gold shield of a detective. Frank's incredible work ethic got him one step closer to that goal when he was promoted to the plain clothes division. Serpico showed the same enthusiasm toward plain clothes enforcement as patrol, making many arrests each shift.

To catch criminals, Frank blended into the city by disguising himself. It also helped that he had mastered the multiple languages and dialects spoken in the melting pot that was New York. Frank added a dramatic flair for acting and used all of these talents together to make criminals believe he was not a police officer.

One day he might be a butcher, another a Rabbi. In one instance he took a limo out of impound, dressed as a sheik, and made many prostitution arrests. His personas allowed him to blend into the surroundings and watch criminals break the law right in front of him. If all Frank had to worry about was enforcing the law, he would have thrived until it was time for him to retire. Shortly after arriving in plain clothes, however, Frank was introduced to The Pad, which would make Frank Serpico's life a boiling cauldron of turmoil. If life for a New York City Police Officer wasn't dangerous and stressful enough, The Pad would make Frank's life uniquely more dangerous and infinitely more stressful.

The Pad was a system of payments made by gamblers to the precinct plain clothes officers, which amounted to arrest insurance. No one knows how long it had been in place, but it was a complex system which consisted of the criminals making payments to a Bag Man. The money was then distributed to the plain clothes officers so they would be aware whose illegal enterprise was to continue unmolested by the plain clothes men of the precinct. When Frank received his first payment, he was shocked and confused.

Frank's parents had raised him to recognize the difference between right and wrong and to do the right thing even when it was the most difficult of the choices. Frank would make them proud, but it would not be easy.

Frank knew taking bribe money from criminals was wrong and refused to take his share. Initially, Frank's partner concealed the fact that Frank had refused his share from the others in the unit. Frank's partner collected Frank's share as well as his own and told Frank that if he changed his mind he could have every penny of it. It would not be good if the others in the unit discovered Frank was not taking the money.

When Frank was given a new partner, the other members of his unit inevitably discovered Frank was refusing money. This enraged the members of his unit because Frank's partner had been receiving double payments for over a year and was pocketing the extra money.

This was not the only thing that upset them, however. Ironically, because Frank was an honest cop and would not take any money, he was deemed to be untrustworthy to those that did. The members of his unit conspired to convince him to accept his share of the bribes.

After Frank was unsuccessfully cajoled, pressured, and finally even threatened into taking money, Frank reported the corruption to his superiors. Instead of appreciating Frank's dedication to honorable policing, commander after commander treated Frank as if he was the problem. Frank took his complaint eventually to the highest level of the department. Nothing discernible was done except for the fact that more pressure was brought to bear on Serpico. Pressure was taking the form of serious threats.

One of the most pointed threats directed at Serpico was, "Frank, no one has to do anything. They just have to not be there for you."

Refusing to provide back-up for a fellow police officer could be tantamount to a death penalty for an officer in any city, but this was especially true in New York. Death by withholding back-up would be the perfect crime, and Frank knew it. In spite of this, Frank strapped on his gun and went to work each day.

Serpico Goes Public

The pressure was ever present and wore on Frank. When he received no relief from the departmental command staff, Frank went to the mayor's office. This achieved nothing except another level of city administration who viewed Frank as a problem.

After working for years under these conditions, Frank finally concluded he was in imminent danger of death and decided he did not want to die in vain. He also believed that the change needed could not happen from the inside. Frank decided to go public. He was not alone in this endeavor.

Frank, Sergeant David Durk, and Lieutenant Paul Delise told their story of corruption to David Burnham of the *New York Times*. Burnham in turn wrote a Pulitzer Prize Winning exposé that revealed the existence of institutionalized corruption in the plain clothes division of the New York Police Department referred to as The Pad. As a result of the story, the Knapp Commission was convened in April 1970 to investigate the alleged corruption. This investigation proved to be an institutional turning point for the New York Police Department.

Frank would discover what most whistle blowers realize even today. People who expose corruption rarely receive awards for their efforts since the people who give awards are generally the same people who ignored the corruption in the first place. Frank's award was not a gold detective's badge but a transfer to plain clothes narcotics.

Narcotics was a dangerous place to do police work. Every cop working in narcotics needs back-up ready at all times. Every door a narcotics officer goes through could potentially be their last. It was hard to view the transfer as anything but a bad omen.

Frank Loses the Career He Loved

On February 3, 1971, at 778 Driggs Avenue in the Williamsburg Section of Brooklyn, New York, Frank was part of a four-man drug investigation team following up on a tip. They had just arrested two suspects who had bought drugs at an apartment there. What transpired is provided in Frank's own words:

> ...we were moving in on a drug dealer on the fourth floor of a walk-up tenement in a Hispanic section of Brooklyn. The police officer backing me up instructed me (since I spoke Spanish) to just get the apartment door open and leave the rest to them.
>
> One officer was standing to my left on the landing no more than eight feet away with his gun drawn; the other officer was to my right rear on the stairwell, also with his gun drawn. When the door opened, I pushed my way in and snapped the chain. The suspect slammed the door closed on me, wedging in my head and right shoulder and arm. I couldn't move, but I aimed my snub-nose Smith & Wesson revolver at the perp...
>
> ...From behind me no help came. At that moment, my anger got the better of me. I made the almost fatal mistake of taking my eye off the perp and screaming to the officer on my left: 'What the hell you waiting for? Give me a hand!' I turned back to face a gun blast in my face. I had cocked my weapon and fired back at him almost in the same instant, probably as reflex action, striking him. (He was later captured.)
>
> When I regained consciousness, I was on my back in a pool of blood trying to assess the damage from the gunshot wound in my cheek. Was this a case of small entry, big exit, as often happens with bullets?

Was the back of my head missing? I heard a voice saying, "Don' worry, you be all right, you be all right," and when I opened my eyes I saw an old Hispanic man looking down at me like Carlos Castaneda's Don Juan. My "backup" was nowhere in sight. They hadn't even called for assistance—I never heard the famed "Code 1013," meaning "Officer Down." They didn't call an ambulance either, I later learned; the old man did. One patrol car responded to investigate, and realizing I was a narcotics officer rushed me to a nearby hospital...[1]

Frank Serpico's life was saved, but his recovery was long and arduous. He was left permanently deaf in his left ear while bullet fragments would be forever lodged just below his brain.

Aftermath

As a result of Serpico's revelations, others came forward and testified along with Frank in front of the Knapp commission. The revelations led to sweeping reforms in the NYPD, finally enabling honest officers to wrest control of their department from the dishonest.

Frank eventually received his detective's gold shield and the department's Medal of Honor. Receiving his department's highest honor was bitter-sweet for Frank. There was never a formal ceremony for him. He would never stand before his family, friends, and peers wearing the iconic double breasted blue tunic of the NYPD while receiving the honor. Frank would later say the medal was handed to him "like a pack of cigarettes."

Frank retired from the career he loved in 1972 as a result of his wounds. A best-selling novel was written on his life. The book was made into the movie *Serpico*. Frank became instantly famous but was just as instantly uncomfortable with his celebrity status. Detective Frank Serpico (Retired) moved to Switzerland to leave the notoriety and threats behind him. He bought a small farm.

---

1   From an essay by Frank Serpico which appeared in *Politico*, October 23, 2014.

Frank found love, married, and happily lived the life of a farmer. Tragedy visited him once again when his wife died at a young age, stricken by cancer.

Frank eventually returned to the United States and now lives a quiet life in upstate New York. For many years he was available to give presentations to law enforcement groups and academy classes. Frank Serpico has become the standard for police ethics for the ages.

Frank's life is a testament to the fact that the right thing is rarely, if ever, the easiest thing. In spite of great difficulties and even placing his own life at risk, Frank did the right thing. In doing so, he barely survived, but he lived to facilitate a positive change in the New York City Police Department.

Frank Serpico's legacy to law enforcement is timeless. He serves as an example of honor and integrity that police officers can, should, and do aspire to. Frank Serpico has left words, backed up by deeds, that are so profound they should be carved in granite and displayed at every police academy in the nation. As profound as these words are, they are equally simple, *"Police work is an honorable profession... if you do it with honor."*

CHAPTER 17

JOHN DODSON & BRIAN TERRY. FAST AND FURIOUS

S pecial Agent John Dodson of the Bureau of Alcohol Tobacco and Firearms (ATF) went to the border fully aware of how dangerous policing the border between the United States and Mexico could be. The Mexican drug cartels were as well armed as some military units and operated on both sides of the border.

John Dodson knew that stemming the flow of arms between the criminal elements in both countries would be dangerous work, but ultimately, by bringing bad people to justice, it would make life better for good people on both sides of the border. He was excited to join a special unit he believed was tasked at interdicting the flow of arms.

Sadly, John would discover that whatever the purposes of the program called "Fast and Furious" were, the interdiction of arms was not one of them. John's efforts to sound an alarm about the program would put him at odds with not only supervisors in his own agency but also the Attorney General and the White House.

Who is John Dodson?

John Dodson served in military intelligence while in the United States Army. After he was honorably discharged, he entered law enforcement as a night shift "road dog" with the Orange County, Virginia, Sheriff's Department. Dodson loved being part of a team whose members made their own decisions and investigated their own cases. "We did it all," he explained.

As his career progressed, he became an investigator with the Loudon County Sheriff's Department working undercover as a part of the High Intensity Drug Trafficking Area Task Force. His job was to buy drugs often, and if possible, work his way up the ladder. "Make the case and get the hell out," was what Dodson said undercover work was all about. He excelled at it.

While working in this capacity, John Dodson became acquainted with tactics and techniques to legally arrest people and make that arrest pay dividends. Dodson could flip the small time dealer and start their team on the climb up the ladder to eventually reach the suppliers—locally, nationally, and sometimes even internationally.

During this period he also had an opportunity to take part in two historic law enforcement cases. He was one of many police officers who assisted in the D.C. Sniper case. He also provided assistance at the scene of the horrific September 11, 2001, Pentagon attack.

What John Dodson liked most about his early career was the feeling of being part of a team. He perceived that if he were able to join a Federal Agency, he would be part of an even larger team and the work would make an even bigger impact.

Hired By ATF

Dodson applied for and was hired by the ATF. In 2004 he was assigned to the Harrisonburg, Virginia, office. His state and local connections proved to be valuable in doing his work with the ATF.

In 2007 Dodson was sent with many other law enforcement officers to assist at the scene of the Virginia Tech Massacre. During an interview much later, he said the one thing he would never forget was the sound of cell phones ringing in the victims' backpacks.

John realized the calls were from frantic family members and friends who were trying to verify that their loved ones were OK. As the ringing continued, John became acutely aware of the fact that these still figures lying scattered before him weren't OK, and nothing could make them OK ever again.

This shadow from the past haunts him still.

Bank Robber

While in Harrisonburg, Agent Dodson's most satisfying case was his pursuit of a serial bank robbery suspect. By chance, his investigation led him to the suspect's house at exactly the moment the suspect was returning from robbing a bank. He was in exactly the right place at the right time.

The problem was that Dodson was alone, and taking a serial bank robbery suspect into custody alone is not the recommended standard police protocol. As the suspect entered the house, Dodson called for backup and waited. Before his backup could arrive, however, the suspect exited the house and headed for his vehicle.

Dodson knew that if he didn't act immediately the suspect would be long gone the minute he got into his vehicle. No sooner had the thought crossed his mind than Special Agent John Dodson was out of his unmarked car. He drew his weapon, identified himself, and shouted for the suspect's surrender. The bank robber threw his hands up and hit the ground. He was taken into custody without any resistance.

Minutes later, backup was swarming, but all that was left to do was collect the evidence and write the reports. The bad guy was in handcuffs. Dodson had to chuckle the next day when a witness was quoted in the newspaper saying, "Thank God for the FBI."

Phoenix and Fast and Furious

In September 2009 Special Agent John Dodson was selected to join Strike Force Special Group VII. He was moved to Phoenix by the ATF to join what he believed to be an elite team.

Upon arriving in Phoenix, he was immersed into a program called Fast and Furious. John was excited to be a part of what he felt would be an innovative weapons interdiction program. He initially felt he was where the action was and making a difference.

John's enthusiasm deflated when he discovered that Fast and Furious was not an innovative weapons interdiction program. It was a program which facilitated the sale of weapons to agents of dangerous criminals.

Fast and Furious allowed people with no significant criminal records to buy a variety of weapons. These people were called "straw buyers" since they were hired by the Mexican cartels to walk the weapons across the border for resale to the cartels. These straw buyers were allowed to repeatedly purchase weapons under the watchful eye of the ATF and then leave, while under surveillance.

The weapons the straw buyers purchased were many and varied, but these middle men especially liked the AK and AR knockoffs. They also preferred the firearms to have folding stocks, which enhanced their conceal-ability. This made the weapons more user friendly for someone intending to commit a crime.

Even though the ATF knew these buyers were being paid by criminal organizations in Mexico, no effort was made to stop and arrest them. John immediately recognized that although strong cases were built against the straw buyers, nothing was being done to arrest them and flip them to move up the ladder. The ATF was only documenting who bought the weapons and where they were sold. When the weapons turned up at a crime scene, the weapon's "last crime" was documented.

Special Agent John Dodson was deeply troubled by this protocol because he could not see where the investigation was leading. There was no discernible big picture vision as to what they were trying to accomplish beyond the arming of criminals.

Many gun shop owners expressed concern to John's supervisors about who were getting these weapons. The owners emphasized they would not be selling to these people if the gun shop owners had not been asked to cooperate with the ATF. Dodson's supervisors told them not to worry because they said, "We're on it."

Dodson found himself continually sounding the alarm to his supervisors that they were not "on it." He had worked enough undercover cases to know the procedures in this program were limited to the straw buyers. Even so, none of these people were being arrested.

At one point Dodson became so frustrated he told his supervisor in the presence of other members of his unit, "We're walking guns. How many guns have we flooded the border with? How much crime down there are we responsible for? We are just as culpable as if we had sold them ourselves. We're never going to get anywhere with this case. We're never going to climb the ladder."

Dodson asked his superiors, "Are you ready to explain to the family of a Border Patrol Agent or Cochise County Sheriff's Deputy at a funeral for their loved one that the weapon used to kill them was a gun provided to the criminal as a result of an ATF program?"

For his efforts Dodson was repeatedly chastised until he was finally transferred out of Special Group VII. John Dodson was gone from the Fast and Furious program, but the program was hardly forgotten by him. Dodson got into law enforcement to do some good, and he dreaded what kind of bad would come out of this ill-conceived operation. He felt the black cloud of inevitability hanging over the Phoenix Office.

He would not have to wait long to find out that his concerns were well founded.

Brian Terry

Brian Terry was five years old riding in the back seat of the family car when suddenly the lights of a patrol car came on summoning his father to pull to the side of the road. Brian could hardly control himself; he was so excited.

As his father anxiously awaited the approaching state trooper, Brian rolled the window down in the back seat. When the Michigan State Trooper reached the window, he was met by Brian Terry's smiling face proclaiming, "I'm going to be just like you when I grow up." The trooper returned the smile and gave Brian's father a warning.

Brian Terry grew up knowing exactly what he wanted to do when he grew up. In the meantime, he competed in sports while attending Flat Rock High School. After graduation, he joined the United States Marine Corps and became a Military Police Officer. After the Marines, there was college. After completing college, his life-long dream of becoming a police officer came true. He joined the Ecorse, Michigan, Police Department. Law Enforcement was his passion.

Lincoln Park Police Department

On April 17, 2000, Brian Terry was hired by the Lincoln Park, Michigan, Police Department in his home town.

On April 18, his second day on the job, Brian and several other officers responded to an in-progress active shooter at the Lincoln Park Senior Tower. Kenneth Miller had already shot and killed three and was determined to continue killing.

Upon arrival, Brian advanced on the shooter, who fired toward him. Brian found a superior position and called for Miller's surrender. Due to Brian's commanding presence and aggressive response, Miller complied, and Brian was able to take him into custody without further loss of life.

For his actions on that day, Officer Terry was awarded a Certificate of Merit by the Lincoln Park Public Safety Commission for displaying "true courage" during this critical incident.

Border Patrol

Brian believed he could achieve anything he put his mind to in life as long as he followed his own motto, "Put in the Work!" Brian had set his sights on Federal Law Enforcement. After establishing a reputation in Lincoln Park as a professional other officers could count on, Brian Terry applied for and was hired by the United States Border Patrol.

Brian's record of excellence continued as a Border Patrol Agent which helped him achieve his next goal, to be accepted on the BORTAC Unit.

As the Border Patrol puts it, "The Border Patrol Tactical Unit (BORTAC) was originally created to fulfill a civil disturbance role in 1984, but quickly evolved and acquired additional skill sets in high-risk warrant service, intelligence reconnaissance and surveillance, foreign internal defense training, air mobile operations, maritime operations, and precise/marksmanship."

At thirty-eight years of age, Brian became the oldest member in his BORTAC class to partake in the one month of grueling training designed after the United States Military's Special Forces training. Brian lived up to the moniker he had been given—Superman—during this life challenge.

As training progressed, one of the instructors thought Brian had mistakenly taken another man's helmet. As punishment, Brian was directed to fireman-carry his partner three times around the course they were on. Halfway through the ordeal, they discovered another officer had taken Brian's helmet, forcing him to take the only

one left. Therefore, Brian was not the one deserving punishment and was told he could put his partner down.

Brian always felt training should be real, and he was troubled with the idea of putting his buddy down now. The reason he was able to perform the task at all was his mental focus that he really was carrying a downed buddy. Setting him down at this point would be like leaving a man behind. Brian asked for and received permission to finish the simulated rescue, and he completed the task in full gear. In doing so, Brian achieved total exhaustion as well as the admiration of everyone who witnessed this event.

Brian graduated first in his BORTAC Training. He was chosen to be the president of his class.

Brian's Last Shift

On the night of December 14, 2010, Brian was part of a four-man team which moved into position on a slight rise in a rugged area on the Arizona-Mexican Border north of Rio Rico called Peck Canyon. The team was on the American side watching the trails aided by night vision. They were trying to interdict heavily armed Mexican criminals called "Rip Teams" who roamed the border region intercepting drug mules—people who transport drugs and sometimes cash across the border. These ruthless killers have been known to leave no witnesses behind.

Brian went into the darkness that night with William Castano, Gabriel Fragoza, and Timothy Keller. Approximately fifteen minutes before the end of their shift, the four agents spotted five suspects armed with rifles. The BORTAC team shouted for their surrender.

Without hesitation, the Rip Team opened fire on the officers. There was a sharp fire fight during which Brian said, "I'm hit. I can't feel my legs."

After quiet returned to the desert night, Manuel Osorio-Arellanes, a wounded Rip Team member, was left behind. Near him were two Romanian WASR 7.62X39 AK47 knock-offs.

Brian had been hit once during the gunfight and died shortly after midnight on December 15.

Within 24 hours of this tragedy, the AFT's Special Team VII would be aware that the weapons left at the scene had been "walked" across the border by Straw Buyer Jaime Avila Jr. as a part of the Fast and Furious Program. The ATF had supervised the transfer of the weapons which eventually made it into the hands of the men who killed Brian Terry.

Christmas in the Terry Household

Brian Terry's family was preparing for Christmas with great anticipation. Brian would be coming home for Christmas. The family was so proud of their son, brother, and uncle—their very own "Superman."

On December 15, the family received notification that Brian had been killed in the line of duty in a gunfight near the border. Instead of celebrating the joy of Christmas, the family would gather to mourn a devastating loss.

After receiving the news, the family experienced an incredibly bittersweet moment when a package was delivered to them. After opening the large box, they discovered that Brian had shopped, purchased, wrapped, marked, and mailed all his Christmas presents to the family just before attending his last line-up. Each family member would receive one last personal Christmas gift from their dearly loved Brian.

Each gift had been thoughtfully picked out. It was as if Brian had found a way to send his love from Heaven. No one even attempted to hold back their tears.

Dodson Becomes Clairvoyant

Within twenty-four hours of the border shootout that killed Brian Terry, a friend from the Bureau of Alcohol Tobacco and Firearms contacted John Dodson and confirmed that the weapons left on the scene of Brian Terry's killing had been weapons walked across the border by a Straw Buyer under the supervision of ATF. John's greatest fear had become a reality.

John Dodson outlined how the ensuing cover-up unfolded right before his eyes in great detail in his book *The Unarmed Truth, My Fight to Blow The Whistle and Expose Fast and Furious*.

Agent Dodson realized that it would be easier for him to do nothing, but he felt compelled to do what he knew was the right thing. John appeared in front of a Congressional hearing and told the unvarnished truth, the whole truth, and nothing but the truth about the program.

This investigation brought an official end to Fast and Furious. For the first time in history, an attorney general of the United States was cited for Contempt of Congress. The investigation was stymied, however, when the President of the United States himself interceded and sealed subpoenaed documents claiming Executive Privilege.

Many have theorized why weapons were being placed into the hands of the cartel, but those will continue to be speculation until files that are now closed are someday opened. The president and the attorney general's reactions do not explain the reason for Fast and Furious, but they show the dizzying heights reached when John Dodson took that courageous step out of the shadows and into the limelight to tell the public he serves the truth.

That unadulterated truth was the Bureau of Alcohol Tobacco and Firearms facilitated the delivery of the weapons that killed Border Patrol Agent Brian Terry to the people who killed him. Many other police and civilians south of the border were also killed by the weapons of Fast and Furious.

Heroes

Why was the ATF directed to facilitate gun trafficking to the cartels and whose idea was it? Someday, hopefully, this will be answered. Maybe it will come in a time when people like Frank Serpico and John Dodson will be rewarded instead of punished for telling the truth. Sadly such a time has not yet arrived in this country.

During an interview, John Dodson was asked, "Why did you choose to do the right thing, even though you knew it would be much easier to go along?"

John explained, "I did it for Brian Terry's family. They deserved to know the truth." He added, "I did it for my family as well. I want to always be the man my son believes me to be." John Dodson is still with the ATF, and he is an American hero for doing so.

On the Mexican-U.S. border, which by lack of resolve has been made notably porous, Brian Terry also took a stand when it would have been easier to stand down. For that he is also a hero, a hero gone too soon.

PART FIVE

GREAT PREVAILING

CHAPTER 18

OFFICER KATIE CONWAY AND THE NIGHT UNLIKE ANY OTHER

Sometimes a police officer earns a place in history because of an incredible career. Others deserve to be remembered because of one unimaginable moment. Officer Katie Conway's name should forever be linked to police courage and fighting spirit. Her story happened on one night unlike any other...

On February 2, 1998, twenty-three-year-old Officer Katie Conway was working a beat in one of Cincinnati's toughest neighborhoods, "Over-the-Rhine." She had just completed a "prison run" and was slowing for a traffic light at an intersection, near the Cincinnati Police Division. Katie had the driver's side window of her patrol car open so she could hear the sounds of the night. This act of awareness, usually indicative of an excellent officer, would be disadvantageous this night.

Out of the blue, a man carrying a boom box stepped out in front of her squad. This unexpected movement caused Katie to slam on her brakes to avoid hitting what she initially thought was a wayward pedestrian.

The man was forty-one-year-old Daniel Williams who had been arrested seventeen times in the past and had a history of being dangerously mentally ill. Earlier in the evening, his family had called the police to report that Daniel had stopped taking his medication and threatened his seventy-one-year-old mother's life. The family took Daniel's threats seriously and felt he was in a murderous mood.

Katie was unaware of Williams' personally history as he stepped out in front of her squad.

After Katie stopped her squad to avoid hitting Williams, the man moved quickly to the open driver's side window and without warning slammed the boom box into Officer Conway's face. Katie was knocked to her right side, and before she could recover from the vicious physical assault, Williams produced a .357 magnum handgun and began squeezing the trigger.

The repeated muzzle flashes lit up the interior of the squad. A witness later reported that while Williams was shooting Katie he was, "Yelling like a demon from hell, 'I'm going to get you!'" Williams hit Officer Conway four times in the legs and hip area. Katie felt an intense burning pain in her legs, but she could not move them.

Katie slumped to her right and was initially stunned by the trauma of the devastating attack. She sensed she was losing blood rapidly. Katie fought to stay conscious and focused.

Williams opened the driver's door, pushed Katie's limp body farther into the squad and climbed in behind the wheel. Williams clearly believed Officer Conway must be dead after he had shot her so many times with a .357 at close range. Williams slammed the door and began accelerating the squad car down Central Parkway in Cincinnati.

The suspect drove northbound at high speed seemingly intent upon driving into oblivion. Meanwhile Katie managed to maintain that tenuous hold on consciousness. She heard the voice of one of her academy instructors as if he was next to her in that speeding squad. Her instructor shouted, "Get your gun out! Get your gun out! Finish the fight!"

Katie was energized immediately. She knew from her training that pain was good. Pain meant she was alive and still in the fight. Renewed by these thoughts, she told herself, "Someone's going to die tonight, and it's not going to be me."

Thus began her intense struggle to remove the 9mm Smith and Wesson semi-automatic handgun from her holster, which she was lying on top of. She overcame excruciating pain to make this monumental effort. The holster's security features designed to keep assailants from being able to snatch her weapon from her were now an impediment to her success. Although slowed by the holster, she would not be deterred. She managed to free her firearm.

Katie could tell by the movement of the squad and the lights passing in the windows that they were traveling at a very high rate of speed. She had only one chance to live. As she lay painfully jammed between Williams and the passenger door of the squad, she took careful aim. It was difficult to hold steady on the suspect while the car was careening through the streets of Cincinnati.

How could anyone in such a circumstance—given the suddenness of the assault, the severity of her injuries, and the total absurdity of this man's actions—be so focused? Katie was. Her trainer shouted loudly in her thoughts once again, "Finish the fight!"

Her 9mm flashed, recoiled, and without pause flashed again. Williams instantly slumped forward against the steering wheel.

Katie did not need to check the man's pulse. She knew there was a dead man driving as the squad began to swerve wildly out of control. All she could do was pray and wait to see if she was still alive when the car stopped. In what seemed like an eternity of moments, the car drifted off-line, jumped a curb, went airborne, and slammed into a wall at the Sam Adams Brewery. The car went from 50 mph to 0 mph in a violent millisecond.

Katie flew forward and slammed into the lower dash then bounced back onto the seat. There was a pause to assess whether she was in Heaven or still on Earth. The pain was intense so she knew she was still among the living. She lay broken and bleeding, but she was still alive and undefeated.

Calm in the Eye of the Storm

At the start of the assault, Katie Conway managed to send a transmission which was broken up because the suspect was shooting her at the time. Only forty seconds after the shooting of Officer Conway, the theft of the patrol car, a midnight drive to nowhere, her struggle to access her weapon, return fire and a car crash, Katie made one of the most amazing radio transmissions in the history of law enforcement.

Like a seasoned veteran, the seriously wounded Katie Conway, in unimaginable pain, keyed the mic and calmly reported, "Distress.

I've been involved in a shooting on Central Parkway, North of Liberty. I need some help."

The dispatcher asked, "Are you hurt?"

Katie, who had a total of eight entrance and exit wounds in her body, answered just above a whisper, as if she was revealing a secret to a friend, "Affirmative."

The Aftermath

Investigators piecing together statements and physical evidence discovered that Katie had fired her 9mm duty weapon at the suspect twice. They recovered the two brass cartridges. These investigators also noticed that there was but one hole in the right side of the deceased suspect's head.

The detectives determined, under the circumstances, that Katie only hit him once and missed him once. It seemed to be perfectly reasonable that someone so suddenly and violently attacked who was so severely injured could possibly miss one out of two shots.

The autopsy, however, revealed something these investigators had neither suspected nor even imagined. Officer Katie Conway, while lying prone next to a raging lunatic, in a speeding squad car, her life blood spilling from multiple gunshot wounds had fired twice. The autopsy revealed that she had not missed at all.

The two bullets entered through the same hole.

Life After

Officer Conway's injuries were serious, but she was able to survive. Sadly, for medical reasons, she would have to retire from the career she loved and had only just begun.

Before Katie left law enforcement, she provided an in-depth analysis of her survival. She not only told her story but gave advice worthy of a seasoned veteran. Sometimes becoming a seasoned veteran takes years, but in this case, it only took forty seconds.

Her Words

During an interview, Officer Conway shared some valuable insights with officers whose life-threatening challenges still lay ahead. Katie made it clear that her trainers had prepared her to prevail. She said she actually heard her trainer's voice in her head during the assault urging her to, "Call on the radio, let them know where you are. Get your gun out! Get your gun out! Get your gun out!"

She also emphasized that if a potential police officer thinks they can't strike someone with a baton or shoot someone when they have to, then they are choosing the wrong career.

Officer Conway stressed to any officer who finds they have to fire their weapon to save their life, "Don't think twice, because if you think twice about it, maybe that was the round that killed you."

Katie is as tenacious and courageous as any modern knight who has survived personal combat. People who find themselves standing at that dangerous precipice between life and death have her example to inspire them to victory, even when the fight is desperate. Katie's fighting spirit was breathed into the fictional character Madison "Maddy" Brown in *S.W.A.T.: Blue Knights in Black Armor*.

Katie Conway's story is one of great courage and tenacity. She prevailed on the night unlike any other.

CHAPTER 19

OFFICER MARCUS YOUNG
MEETS THE DEVIL

One of the most unique gunfights in law enforcement history took place on March 7, 2003, in California. The fight involved a mixture of hand to hand combat, a knife, and multiple firearms.

It started at the beginning of a shift when Sergeant Marcus Young found himself with seventeen-year-old Explorer Scout Julian Covella as a ride-along. All four of the squads on his shift were already doubled up, so he scheduled Covella in his own squad. This decision would have fate changing consequences for Marcus Young as well as Julian Covella.

It was a busy shift. When security at the local Wal-Mart reported that they had a shoplifter in custody, Sergeant Young took the call since all the other units were already responding to calls. This was not unusual as Sergeant Young was what police officers call a "working sergeant," a sergeant who leads from the front by helping patrol officers with his share of the load. Arriving at the Wal-Mart, Sergeant Young and his ride-along discovered what appeared to be a run-of-the-mill shoplifting case.

A husband and wife security team had seen the boyfriend of an eighteen-year-old female suspect remove a $29 duffel bag from the rack and then the girlfriend took it to the service counter. She produced an old purchase receipt and attempted to return the duffel bag for cash. The girlfriend was detained, but the boyfriend had already exited the store.

When the security officers described the man and his tattoos, Marcus thought they sounded like the type of tattoos a criminal in prison might possess. When Marcus ran a check on the female suspect, he discovered she was wanted on a $10,000 burglary warrant.

Monumental Battle

Marcus handcuffed the female and placed her into his squad car. Just as Marcus was clicking the seatbelt on the suspect, the female security guard shouted a warning to him.

Marcus turned to discover the boyfriend approaching with his hands shoved into the pockets of his brown bomber jacket and wearing a ball cap. Marcus instinctively shouted, "Take your hands out of your pockets!"

The response to Marcus' command was an angry, "Why is she in your car?" The man's hands remained in his pockets and he continued his approach.

With more urgency Marcus ordered, "Take your hands out!"

The tattooed man indignantly asked, "Why?"

"Because I'm concerned for my safety," came the reasonable response.

At the time, Marcus did not know that this man was Neal Beckman, a thirty-five-year-old career felon with outstanding felony warrants for his arrest. If Beckman had not been wearing a ball cap, Marcus would have been able to see the two devil's horns tattooed on Beckman's forehead.

Neal, still closing ground quickly, started taking his left hand out of his pocket. He admitted, "Just so you know, I've got a knife." He now was within arm's reach of Marcus.

Marcus could not help but notice the intense, something's-about-to-happen look on Beckman's face. They were too close to be having a discussion about a knife, so Marcus closed the distance and put a control hold on Neal's left arm.

As Marcus was focused on controlling the left arm, which he perceived was the immediate threat, Beckman suddenly pulled a stolen 38 caliber Smith and Wesson revolver out of his right pocket.

He brought the revolver around over his left shoulder. At the same moment Marcus saw the firearm, there was flash. Beckman sent a round through Young's cheek and out the back of his neck. Marcus felt a burning sensation but, oddly, no pain. Luckily, the bullet's path missed his spine by mere millimeters.

NEAL BECKMAN

The bullet did great damage, but at that moment it may as well have been a starter's pistol for Marcus. The fight was definitely on!

Marcus Young had trained in martial arts. He overcame his wound and used Beckman's momentum to spin him and slam him against a nearby parked car. Beckman had prepared for this fight quite differently than Marcus. Beckman was on meth at the time of the assault. He appeared unfazed after the impact and merely scooted away doing a reverse crab crawl across the car.

Marcus managed to maintain his grip, however, and physically directed Beckman off the car onto the pavement. Marcus attempted to deliver a full power strike to the suspect's face, but Beckman ducked the blow. Young's fist missed Beckman and connected with a concrete parking curb, severely cutting his hand.

Beckman, still squirming, freed himself enough from Marcus' grip to fire two more rounds, hitting him in the chest and back. Luckily, Marcus had put on his Second Chance vest at the beginning of his shift, but he still felt the blunt force impact of the rounds.

As the struggle continued, Beckman fired two more rounds that by-passed the vest's coverage. One round entered Young's armpit, took out two inches of his scapula, and exited near the spine. The last round in the five-shot revolver tore through Marcus's bicep disabling his right arm.

A courageous, unarmed security guard rushed Beckman and slammed him to the pavement wrestling the gun away from him. The guard put the revolver to the Beckman's head and squeezed the trigger twice. Nothing happened. The hammer fell on spent cartridges.

As it turns out, Beckman did indeed have a knife. He pulled out an ugly looking hunting knife from his coat pocket and buried it into the security guard's shoulder so deep that it hit the guard's lung. The guard slumped over and rolled off Beckman. The serious wound took him out of the fight but would not prove fatal.

Marcus used the time the security guard's actions had bought him and drew his weapon and fired it, but nothing happened. He immediately realized that even though his mind perceived that his right arm was doing what his brain was commanding it to do, his right arm was actually hanging limply at his side. The round that severed his bicep rendered his right arm totally disabled. Even though Marcus vividly pictured himself drawing and firing his duty weapon, the weapon was still secured in his holster.

Marcus now felt himself weakening from loss of blood. While on his knees in the parking lot at Wal-Mart, he noticed customers running about. He looked down and saw his badge and uniform covered with his own blood. Marcus recognized that he may very well be bleeding to death, and he had to do something to turn the tide in this struggle. Beckman still posed a danger to Marcus's ride-along cadet and all these citizens.

Marcus concluded he was badly broken, but if he could get his firearm out he could still stop Beckman. Marcus crawled between two parked cars and desperately tried to remove his sidearm from his holster, but due to his disabled right arm and injured left arm he just couldn't manage it. Beckman's shift in tactics gave Marcus a few moments to think.

Beckman, as yet uninjured in the fray, scampered away from the wounded officer. Beckman made a direct-line to Marcus's squad. If Beckman's intent was to free his girlfriend and get away, he could have accomplished it, but this was not his intent.

Beckman climbed into the front seat of the patrol car and frantically tried to access the H & K that was locked in the rack located there. Marcus realized Beckman was attempting to get either his fully automatic Heckler Koch .223 police carbine out of the car or his Remington Model 870 12 gauge shotgun. Marcus knew this man would kill if he acquired those weapons. Marcus later said, "If I didn't stop the suspect, he'd kill us or anyone else in the parking lot."

Marcus did not know that Beckman also possessed five homemade explosive devices in his own vehicle. If not stopped, Beckman would have the means to kill many.

Once again, Marcus fruitlessly tried to remove his weapon from its holster. Something caused his eyes to make contact with Cadet Covella's as the ride-along was peeking out from behind cover. Covella had a look on his face which seemed to ask, "What should I do?"

Marcus called him over; Covella came immediately. Marcus said, "Take my gun out and put it in my left hand."

The cadet eyed the weapon and the security holster. Marcus added urgently, "Do it!"

It took a few moments for Marcus to talk him through it, but in short order Covella had the weapon out and placed in Marcus's injured but functional left hand. Marcus brought up the weapon as Beckman was still working furiously at the police long gun in the rack. Marcus did not have a clear shot, so he aimed and fired twice through the front door of the squad. Neither of the rounds penetrated through to hit Beckman.

Instinctively, Beckman's head popped up in response to the shots, and Marcus saw he had a startled expression. Beckman looked toward Marcus, his hands still wrapped around the long gun. With Beckman's head up, Marcus had a target. He took deliberate aim and fired, concentrating with all the effort he could muster.

Marcus fired. With a bang, the round left the muzzle spinning toward Beckman. It struck him in the forehead, directly between the tattooed horns. Beckman slumped forward, and the next round Marcus fired struck Beckman in the buttocks. The fight and Beckman's life of crime were at an end.

Marcus directed Covella to radio "Officer Down" and take his flashlight to summon emergency personnel to his location. With that done, Marcus began survival breathing exercises to slow down his heart rate.

Marcus Young's Aftermath

Marcus Young's story illustrates how a police officer's life can drastically change or dramatically end without warning in just ninety seconds. Marcus Young's monumental struggle shows the supreme determination a police officer needs at times simply to make it to the end of a shift.

After that difficult night, Marcus recovered enough to return to light duty. He could have ridden a desk to the end of his career, but that was too hard on him. Marcus Young was a street cop through and through. You can no more permanently shackle a street cop to a desk than you can hitch a thoroughbred race horse to a plow.

Marcus returned to school and earned a master's degree. He continues to serve by teaching police officers. Marcus travels around the country teaching officer survival classes. His story emphasizes that the struggles officers encounter will not be easy, and may even be very painful, but they can and must prevail.

Marcus has shared not only his story but also crucial street survival information and tactics to over 50,000 police officers all over the nation since his retirement. He continues to be a priceless asset to law enforcement because of his positive attitude and his willingness to share his compelling story of survival.

Julian Covella received the Carnegie Hero Award for the courage he displayed on the night of the struggle. Eventually his dream came true, and he became a police officer.

The security guard recovered from his wounds and was recognized for his courage. He also returned to work.

Marcus Young received many awards for his courageous struggle, including the Presidential Medal of Valor for Public Safety Officers delivered by President George W. Bush in the oval office.

Marcus's story is a reminder to American police officers that anything can happen anywhere and when you least expect it. Marcus answered a "routine" shoplifting call and found himself in a bloody fight for his life.

During that fight, Marcus Young refused to give in to surprise, fear, pain, disabling injury, and exhaustion. He fought through them all. His epic struggle should serve as an inspiration to every cop in the nation. Marcus was able to survive this challenge not only physically but emotionally. Marcus greets everyone with a smile. It is the genuine smile of a man who will forever appreciate how valuable life is.

His injuries would lead him to retire from law enforcement, but due to Marcus Young's indomitable spirit, he was able to retire undefeated.

A special thanks to Marcus Young for his continued inspiration.

CHAPTER 20

GUNFIGHT AT THE SIKH TEMPLE

Brian Murphy and Sam Lenda are two officers who engaged and ultimately defeated the highly trained Neo-Nazi Wade Michael Page. This is the story of how they overcame their encounter with the man who lived and died hating.

Shots Fired

On or about 10:28 AM on the morning of August 5, 2012, Lt. Brian Murphy of the Oak Creek Police Department received information that there was a disturbance at the Sikh Temple in Oak Creek, Wisconsin. There were reports of "shots fired."

Multiple units were dispatched besides Lt. Murphy, but the lieutenant was the first to arrive on the scene. He drove down the long blind driveway to the temple and entered the parking lot area. Initially, all was quiet. Murphy radioed for his approaching back-up, Officer Sam Lenda, to enter via the same driveway.

Unknown to Murphy at the time, Wade Michael Page had already killed six of the temple faithful who had come to the gathering place that morning for a blessed and peaceful service. Instead, they died at the hands of a hater.

Page was one of those especially disturbed human beings who have become a modern phenomenon called the "Active Shooter." They appear to kill for no other reason other than to pile up the score of dead. Unchecked, Page would continue to kill.

One of the people lying dead inside the temple was the sixty-five-year-old temple founder Satwant Singh Kaleka. This brave man placed himself between the gunman and his congregation. He stood and fought with the killer, who was armed with a Springfield XD (M) 9mm semi-automatic handgun. Kaleka delayed the shooter long enough to allow others to hide and lock down fifteen children inside a pantry in the kitchen of the temple. All were saved.

According to witnesses this valiant Sikh priest bravely battled Page armed only with his Kirpan. The Kirpan is a curved ceremonial knife given to baptized Sikh men as a symbol of their faith. Its name comes from the word *Kirpa*, which means mercy, grace, compassion, and kindness as well as the word *aan*, which means honor, grace, and dignity. It is a religious symbol of his personal commitment to protect his nation while doing noble deeds.

Kaleka's commitment was proved in deeds rather than mere words, and his Kirpan was more than symbolic this day. No one survived who witnessed Kaleka's courageous last stand, but there was physical evidence of a fierce struggle, during which Page was required to shoot Kaleka several times to stop his determined defense of his spiritual flock. Kaleka's bloody Kirpan lay next to his body.

Kaleka's ultimate sacrifice was not in vain. The delay Kaleka created gave Murphy time to arrive and further distract Page from his murderous mission.

As Murphy exited his squad and drew his weapon, he located two deceased victims lying next to some parked cars. Scanning the lot, he saw a man walk out the front doors of the temple. Murphy keyed his mic and reported, "I have someone walking out the driveway towards me."

Suddenly, the heavily tattooed Wade Michael Page, wearing a white T-shirt and black BDU's, started running laterally across the parking lot. He was not trying to escape but making himself a harder target to hit by running laterally in relation to Murphy's position. Murphy saw a firearm in Page's right hand, but not until he was bringing it up to fire at Lt. Murphy.

Murphy made his last transmission, "Man with a gun. White T-shirt!" Simultaneously, he engaged the suspect. The initial gunshots were heard over the radio. This transmission provided a last minute warning to Sam Lenda as he approached.

At the very same moment Murphy fired, the suspect fired at Murphy. Murphy later declared, "I missed; he didn't." Though the round struck his chin and throat, it was, "not as devastating as you might think." Murphy moved quickly to cover then peeked out to acquire a sight on Page's position, but in that instant Page had somehow disappeared.

Later investigation revealed that Page was highly trained in combat tactics while in the United States Military. Page had changed directions after firing, and he executed a flanking movement on Lt. Murphy. Page emerged behind Murphy and opened fire. The first round in this volley blew part of Murphy's thumb off his right hand, knocking the gun out of his hand.

Murphy later acknowledged, "Now that one hurt!"

Lt. Murphy, who had been disarmed by that shot, scooted tightly beneath the parked car he was next to and covered his vitals as best as he could while Page rained down bullets upon the lieutenant.

Lenda Arrives

Just as this gunfire was erupting, Sam Lenda entered the temple parking lot. As Lenda pulled up on the scene, he saw Page firing, but due to of the lay of the land could not see Lieutenant Murphy. Page turned immediately and fired toward Lenda. There was a short pause in his fire as Page dropped the magazine in his weapon and reloaded another magazine.

Murphy used the reload to make a dash for his squad, which contained another weapon. After hitting Murphy repeatedly, it must have shaken Page to have that same officer suddenly spring up and run toward his squad. Page now had to contend with two officers.

As Lenda exited his squad with his carbine in hand, one of Page's rounds smashed through the windshield into his headrest, just missing Lenda. The exploding safety glass slapped Lenda hard, embedding glass fragments into the right side of his face. Lenda paid no more attention to this than he would have to a gentle breeze. There would be time to feel pain later.

Lenda positioned himself in the "V" between the open door and the frame of his squad while aiming at Page. Now running laterally again, Page continued firing at Lenda. Lenda placed his sights on Page following his movement. While Page's rounds zipped passed him, Lenda fired twice, striking the killer once.

As Lenda's second round hit the suspect, Page went down instantaneously but still managed to roll into some shrubs. As he laid concealed in the shrubbery, bleeding to death, he realized his murderous rampage was over. Page turned his Springfield pistol on himself and pulled the trigger. It was over.

Murphy was shot fifteen times, but he absolutely refused to die.

Thanks to Lt. Brian Murphy's and Officer Sam Lenda's immediate response, no one died except Page after they arrived on the scene. This is one of the best results one can hope for in assessing the police response to an in progress "Active Shooter." Such is the gritty reality of these horrific crimes.

Shared Message From Lt. Murphy

Lieutenant Murphy ultimately would return to work but has since retired. He continues to train law enforcement officers to survive their careers. Murphy attributes his own survival to two factors:

1. He consciously decided, while being shot at, that he was not going to die in that parking lot.
2. His motto, which got him through that horrible day and its aftermath, "Never give up!"

BRIAN MURPHY

SAM LENDA

Conclusion

Both Officer Sam Lenda and Lt. Brian Murphy earned the Congressional Badge of Courage for their selfless actions in front of the Sikh Temple. They also received the Police Medal of Valor from Vice President Biden.

Satwant Singh Kaleka undoubtedly received a much loftier award for giving his life in defense of the children of his congregation.

Sadly, six innocent people who gathered in a place of peace and love died at the hands of a person who was moved to violence because he was consumed by an irrational hate. There would have been more casualties except for the heroic actions of this flock's spiritual shepherd, Satwant Singh Kaleka, and two dedicated sheepdogs, Officer Sam Lenda and Lt. Brian Murphy of the Oak Creek, Wisconsin, Police Department. They risked all to save many.

CHAPTER 21

THAT DAY
IN SEPTEMBER

ach year as September 11 rolls around, it becomes more and more like every other tragedy in the course of human history. Individuals who suffered become shadowed by the event itself like a silhouetted line of soldiers on a far-away horizon backlit by the setting sun. We can see them marching off but can barely make them out. Somehow they have lost their identities. The farther we move away, the less likely we are to look back.

Our nation finds it easier to process great human sacrifice as a date that "will live on in infamy" rather than confront the loss the date represents. It is right that we remember December 7, June 6, and September 11, but we should also take time to remember those human beings whose sacrifice each date memorializes.

Since this is a book about law enforcement officers, here are the names of those police officers who died on September 11, 2001, the most deadly day in United States law enforcement history:

Christopher Amoroso	Kevin A. Czartoryski	Clyde Frazier
Alex W. Baez	John D'Allara	Greg Froehner
Frank Balusi	Vincent Danz	Barry Galfano
Maurice Barry	Garrett Danza	Fred Ghussin
Cesar A. Borja	Clinton Davis	Rodney Gillis
Thomas G. Brophy	Corey Diaz	Captain Edward
Liam Callahan	Jerome Dominguez	C. Gilpin
Madeline Carol	Stephen Driscoll	James J. Godbee
Robert Cirri	Renee Dunbar	John E. Goggin
Charles J. Clark	Robert M. Ehmer	Thomas Gorman
Charles D. Cole Jr.	Mark Ellis	Robert C. Grossman
Daniel C. Conroy	Robert Fazio	Richard Jerry
John Mark Cortazzo	Edward M. Ferraro	Guadagno
John Coughlin	Donald G. Feser	Claire T. Hanrahan
Michael Curtin	Donald Foreman	Leonard Hatton

Kevin Hawkins
Robert B. Helmke
Aleck W. Herrmann
William J. Holfester
Uhuru Gonja Houston
George Howard
Steven Huczko Jr.
Anthony Infante
Richard Jackubowsky
Louise M. Johnston
Paul Jurgens
Thomas Jurgins
Robert Kaulfers
Ronald Kloepfer
Thomas Langone
Paul Laszczynski
James Leahy
David LeMagne
John Lennon
John Levi
James Lynch
Frank Macri
David Mahmoud
Fred Marrone
Vito Mauro
Gary Mausberg
Kathy Mazza
Jacqueline McCarthy
Brian McDonnell
Donald McIntyre

Denis McLarney
Christopher McMurry
Walter McNeil
Craig J. Miller
Charles Mills
Brian S. Mohamed
Richard Moore
Michael Morales
Dennis Morales
Joseph Navas
James Nelson
Robert Nicosia
Alfonse Niedermeyer
Carlos Ocasio
Edwin Ortiz
Robert V. Oswain
Patrice M. Ott
Salvatore Papasso
James Param
Angelo Peluso
John Perry
Glen Pettit
Domnick Pezzulo
William Pouhlmann
Christopher Pupo
Gerald Rex
Bruce Reynolds
Claude Richards
Roberto Rivera
Antonio Rodrigues

Richard Rodriguez
James Romito
Timothy Roy
Michael Ryan
Joseph Seabrook
John Skala
Moira Smith
Harold Smith
Walwyn Stuart
Ramon Suarez
Paul Talty
Ned Thompson
William Thompson
Kenneth Tietjen
Martin Tom
Santos Valntin
Joseph Vigiano
Mitchel Scott Wallace
Charles Wassil
Walter Weaver
Nathaniel Webb
Ronald E. Weintraub
Michael Wholey
Robert W. Williamson
Richard D. Winter
George M. Wong
John T. Young
James Zadroga
Robert A. Zane

The story of September 11 is still too recent and personal to feel like history to an entire nation and to individuals who watched the events unfold in real time at the scene or on television.

Rather than make a feeble attempt to tell, explain, or analyze what happened on that day in story form, I have attempted to summarize the events within the framework of a poem:

That Day in September
by Lt. Dan Marcou

My fellow Americans, you shall hear
A story whose retelling may inspire a tear,
A story of a day we all must remember.
It all started on the eleventh...
That day in September.

The story is filled with thousands of faces;
The tragedy played out in a variety of places.
On New York then D.C. the world's eyes were peeled.
Then in a blink, all were drawn to a smoldering field.

The day started as passengers took seats on four planes.
Each flight interrupted by the murderers' refrain.
They cried "Allah Akbar!" as they slashed and they killed.
Those left alive, to the bone, must have been chilled.

The whole story unfolded in but a few hours
As planes were flown into the Pentagon and World Towers.
In burning towers thousands struggled to get out.
Some leapt as they prayed their last prayer in a shout.

Our enemies danced, thinking evil had won.
But this fight had not ended; it had only begun.
All tales of treachery have Osamas and Neros.
On this day the battle was joined by our heroes.

Those first responders arrived on September eleven
Not knowing they were climbing their stairway to heaven.
Courage carried them up toward that burning hell,
And their souls met St. Michael when two towers fell.

The day was not over and the fight was not lost.
For terrorists had vowed to strike D.C. at all cost.
The heroes of Flight 93 formed a plan.
In Pennsylvania skies they took one final stand.

Millions mourned thousands, our country was weeping,
But the giant awoke who so long had been sleeping.
As firefighters and police paused to bury their friends,
The standard was passed to those on whom freedom depends.

From the rubble came a shout, "Our enemies will hears us,"
American soldiers gave evil a reason to fear us.
Our soldiers fought bravely and won every battle,
In spite of the incessant political prattle.

Thanks to those in uniform with guns at their hips,
With a fire in their hearts and a prayer on their lips.
They fought far from home so we can live free,
They brought Osama his justice—a grave in the sea.

The fight is not over, neither lost nor yet won
They continue the struggle and with courage carry on.
They sweat, they bleed and for us they remember,
Ever vigilant, they prevent another day like…
That day in September.

22

OFFICER JUSTIN GARNER. THE STANDING HERO OF CARTHAGE

March 29, 2009, was a warm sunny Sunday in Carthage, North Carolina. The sky was clear in this southern town of 2,000 people. A lone on-duty police officer, twenty-five-year-old Justin Garner sat in the Glass Plus lot peacefully watching traffic trickle lazily toward church. At about 10:00 AM, the Moore County 911 dispatcher disturbed the Norman Rockwell-like setting with a report, "Shot's fired at 801 Pinehurst Avenue."

Justin, a four-and-a-half-year veteran of the Carthage Police Department steered his Dodge Charger patrol car toward the Pine Lake Health and Rehab Center for the elderly. His mind had not yet considered the possibility that someone might be shooting inside the facility.

Calls of this type were usually hunters in the wood-line near the facility mistakenly getting too close. When Officer Garner rolled into the lot, however, a red Ford Ranger caught his attention. The driver's side window had been shot out, and he knew something more serious was in store.

As Justin exited his squad, he cautiously, but quickly, approached the front door of the Rehabilitation Center. It suddenly burst open and a frantic health care worker exclaimed almost in disbelief, "There's a man inside, and he is shooting people!"

Stay Calm

Justin had recently attended a class training officers to respond to an active shooter. After the class he asked himself what he would do if this call were ever given to him. He decided he should stay calm.

Justin Garner, who was the only officer on duty in Carthage, entered the rehab center. He was met with dead silence. He later said, "You could have heard a pin drop." As he moved farther into the facility, he could see no one near the front door other than a blameless victim in a wheelchair who had been shot to death for no discernible reason.

In a later interview Justin would recall, "I saw there were elderly residents wandering about the facility who did not have a clue what was happening. I knew that someone was shooting them and could not figure out why anyone would shoot them. They were like children... defenseless. I thought, I had to find this guy,"

Justin advanced alone into the facility to the nurse's station, which was located in the center of the complex. Other than disoriented elderly patients, he saw nothing and heard nothing to indicate where the gunman was at this moment. He instinctively stepped into one hallway and paused. Then he heard shots after which the gunman stepped out of a room and appeared straight down the hallway from where Justin was standing.

Gunfight at Pine Lake Health and Rehab

The suspect, Robert Stewart, was carrying a 12-gauge shotgun and had a bag filled with ammunition strapped over his shoulder. He possessed a revolver in a holster slipped in the middle of his back, and he was hunting for his ex-wife, who was working in a locked down facility at the rehab center. She was the reason he was there.

Stewart's wife was separated from Robert because she could no longer tolerate his abuse. Robert Stewart was now killing innocent patients for no other reason except to ruin his wife's life. He hoped to kill her also but had satisfied his blood lust in the meantime by killing people who she was charged to take care of. Even if she lived, he reasoned that she would not be able to go to work every day in this place. Such is the vindictive nature of Domestic Violence.

At this moment Stewart reloaded his shotgun as he turned to face Officer Garner. Eight innocents were already dead and two more were wounded. The only person standing between Robert Stewart and more victims was Justin Garner. This was the most desperate moment of the young officer's life. Many lives hung in the balance.

Justin raised and aimed his .40 caliber Glock 22. Stewart was loading shells into his shotgun, and Justin shouted for him to "Drop the weapon! Drop the weapon! Drop the weapon!" Justin shouted three times, because even under these dire circumstances, Justin hoped he would not have to shoot another human being.

Stewart turned, shouldered his weapon, and brought it to bear on Justin. Assessing the movement as posing a deadly threat, Justin fired once. Simultaneously, Stewart also fired.

Justin felt a sharp sudden burning in his leg and foot but instinctively moved into a doorway for cover. He was concerned Stewart might be advancing on him, so he leaned out and saw Stewart was down and not moving. Justin had fired once and hit Stewart in the chest. The bullet hit his spine incapacitating Stewart immediately.

Justin later remembered, "I felt the burning in my leg, but it did not really, really hurt. I was still able to walk up and cuff the man." Justin added, "I thought it would hurt more to be shot."

In the initial scan of the area, it appeared the suspect was alone, down, and conscious, but not moving. Stewart had dropped the shotgun, but Justin found a revolver in the small of his back and removed it from Stewart's holster then slid it out of Stewart's reach.

From the time of the call to the time Justin calmly reported that shots had been fired and the suspect was down, four minutes had elapsed. He radioed to his dispatcher that he was also wounded.

The Aftermath

Justin had been hit with pellets in the leg and one in the foot. He returned to duty after one month of recovery.

Justin was recognized for his bravery by his High School Alma Mater, the Union Pine High School. Officer Garner received the "Standing Hero Award." The award is given in the memory of Officer Tye Pratt of the Omaha Police Department who was killed in the line of duty.

Justin Shares His Insight

Justin suggests that to prepare for such an incident officers need to train. During Justin's training for the active shooter, he had wondered about whether such an incident could possibly happen to him. He observed, "I can say to everyone, it can." The training prepared him to think calmly about what needed to be done and then do it. "I knew I had to remain calm, and I did. I didn't rush."

He also said he has been around firearms, "since I was a pup, and I felt comfortable with my skills." Having confidence in his firearms skills helped when it counted.

A "Standing Hero"

It is fitting that Justin Garner, one of Carthage North Carolina's finest, was given the Standing Hero Award. The citation on the award declares, "America is the home of the free, because of the brave."

Justin Garner, the lone officer on duty, could not have imagined on that sleepy Sunday morning that he was going to be called upon to handle an in-progress active shooter call. He did receive the call and handled it with undeniable courage and unmistakable skill.

Justin was not fighting just for his own life. Many lives were depending on the outcome of this gunfight. Most of these residents were members of the "Greatest Generation," who had saved the world and now at their advanced age they needed someone to save them.

Thanks to decisiveness and skill, when the gun smoke cleared, there was Justin, the Standing Hero of Carthage.

PART SIX

GREAT DETECTIVES

JAMES HUME, WILD WEST SHERLOCK HOLMES

James Hume was the Sherlock Holmes of the Wild West years before Sir Arthur Conan Doyle created the iconic literary sleuth. In the nineteenth century, when western law enforcement's main tool was direct pursuit by a local posse, Hume would establish himself proficient in three areas that Sherlock was known for.

1. Hume would work in conjunction with law enforcement partners to accomplish goals.
2. Hume would establish himself as an expert in the gathering and the utilization of physical evidence for the successful prosecution of criminals.
3. Hume could get a confession from suspects time and time again with a conversational rather than accusatory style of interrogation.

Hume not only would gather and analyze evidence, but he would also explain the significance of each piece of physical evidence to the satisfaction of juries. Witnesses could be mistaken, or even lying, but then as now physical evidence, when understood, told the unadulterated truth.

Hume would survive forty years in his varied career pursuing murderers, brigands, and bandits.

Law Enforcement During The Civil War

Hume became a law man in 1862, after his appointment as city marshal of Placerville, California. Shortly thereafter he became under-sheriff for all of El Dorado, California, the county where Placerville was located.

In 1864 one of Quantrill's Raiders, Captain Rufus "The Red Fox" Ingram brought the Civil War to El Dorado County. Captain Ingram traveled west after taking part in the Lawrence, Kansas,

Massacre, where 150 men and boys were brutally murdered. Ingram's intention was to use his commission as a captain in the Confederate Army to raise and equip his own company of raiders after which he would return east to continue his fight for the Confederacy.

Ingram successfully recruited as many as fifty members of an already existing organization, the Knights of the Golden Circle. This secret San Jose society were "Copperheads," whose sympathies aligned with the Confederate States of America. Ingram concluded the best way to quickly acquire the kind of money needed to fully supply and equip Ingram's partisan raiders was to steal gold and silver shipments, which were regularly hauled on the treacherous roads of California and Nevada.

On June 30, 1864, just after dusk, Ingram and his heavily armed and masked Confederate raiders robbed two stages about eleven miles outside of Placerville, simultaneously. The robbery occurred at a curve in the road which would forever be called Bullion Bend. The raiders escaped with 250 pounds of gold bullion from each stage as well as a substantial amount of gold dust.

Two of Hume's deputies, Joseph Staples and George Ranney, trailed the raiders and found them at Sommerset House, an inn. Staples would have been wise to remain out of sight until the rest of Sheriff Hume's posse caught up with them.

Staples, however, had something to prove. He had been with Under-sheriff Hume's posse recently when they had a bitter shoot-out with members of the McCollum Gang. During the opening volley of this encounter, an outlaw's bullet hit Staples' horse, causing it to bolt and flee the fight with Staples still in the saddle. Staples was unable to control the runaway horse, and some had accused Staples of cowardice. Staples was humiliated by the suggestion and had said, "Next time I'll be brought back dead, or I'll bring back my man."

Probably driven forward by this indignity, Staples rashly burst into a room containing Ingram and several members of his gang and called out, "You are my prisoners. Surrender!" Sadly, Staples' courage would not sustain him.

Initially, Ingram began to slowly raise his hands as if surrender was his intent. This distracted the deputy for a moment, and the other members opened fire. Deputy Staples fired one blast of his shotgun into the face of raider Thomas Poole before he was cut down.

Deputy Ranney, just outside the room, ran for cover, firing as he retreated, but he was also shot and seriously wounded in the exchange. Ingram's men looted the body of Staples and robbed Ranney as they fled, leaving Poole and Ranney for dead.

As Sheriff Hume arrived on scene, he was deeply moved by the death of El Dorado Deputy Staples, who was his close friend. Due to the size and mobility of Ingram's raider band, Hume combined forces with legendary law man John Hicks Adams. Adams was sheriff of the adjacent Santa Clara County. This collaboration would pay off.

On July 15, 1864, after receiving information that Ingram planned to rob the Almaden Mine just outside San Jose, Sheriff Adams' waited for the raiders with a posse. When Ingram and his men arrived as predicted, a skirmish ensued. During the sharp fight, Adams was spun around by a bullet but stayed in the fight.

The sheriff later discovered the bullet had ricocheted off his pocket watch. Although it badly bruised his ribs, Adams was saved not *in* the nick of time but *by* the nick of time.

After the fight, Sheriff Adams and his Deputy Brownlee were wounded. Ingram and one of his raiders escaped, while two other raiders were killed. One raider named Glasby surrendered.

Sheriff Adams and Hume convinced Glasby to save himself and give state's evidence. In doing so Glasby identified Poole as one of the leaders of the raiders and implicated the secret organization, the Knights of the Golden Circle. He revealed that the Knights not only had members who were raiders but had grandiose visions of turning California into a southern slave state that would eventually annex Mexico as a Confederate state as well.

Based on the information Glasby provided, Sheriff Adams and James Hume obtained warrants. Then, on July 29, 1864, Hume and Adams rode into San Jose with posse members re-enforced by four companies of infantry. They interrupted an in progress meeting of the Knights of the Golden Circle and arrested all members present.

By the end of the Civil War, all the Knights had been released and forgiven their treason. Rufus Ingram escaped by returning to Missouri and literally disappearing into history. Thomas Poole was not so lucky.

Poole had asked to be treated as a prisoner of war, but California was so far from the battlefields of the east that few could perceive his robbery and the death of Deputy Staples as anything but a heinous crime. There was a petition for leniency sent to the governor pleading for Poole's life since, prior to the war, Poole had actually served as sheriff of Monterrey County. This did not sway the governor.

At 12:00 noon September 29, 1865, Poole took thirteen steps to the top of a scaffold and shook hands with his executioners, assuring them he bore them no ill will. After the rope was properly affixed to ensure efficiency, Poole took the quick drop to a sudden stop ending his secessionist struggle less than six months after Lee's surrender.

Some considered Poole a criminal, others considered him the last martyr of a lost cause.

Collecting Evidence

In 1869 Hume was elected Sheriff of El Dorado County.

The pursuit of stage coach robbers was regularly on Sheriff Hume's to do list. Many of the shipments by Wells Fargo and others began in or traversed through El Dorado County. The rugged terrain favored the robbers.

Sheriff Hume and his posses excelled in the pursuit and capture of bandits. The jurisdictional difficulties were overcome by establishing working relationships among Sheriff Adams and other adjoining counties. Criminals were not able to avoid the pursuit of lawmen simply by crossing jurisdictional lines in the El Dorado-Santa Clara area. Adams and Hume repeatedly worked together.

After robbers were captured, Hume added a new twist to the prosecution of these cases. He discovered it helpful to gather physical evidence of the crimes to bolster testimonial evidence and obtain convictions.

Sheriff Hume took the time to meticulously dig buckshot out of the sides of stagecoaches and even dead horses. He would save this shot for comparison with the shot he would later find on the suspects he arrested.

Hume found criminals might discard a mask, a hat, a bandana, or a duster, but they rarely changed their boots. Hume would sketch boot impressions at the crime scene to compare with the footwear of suspects at the time of their capture.

He also became an expert at analyzing the handwriting on notes left at the scene of robberies. Hume realized handwriting as well as the way a criminal misspelled words were both unique identifiers.

Using physical evidence to bolster eye-witness identification helped in the adjudication of these cases. In addition to collecting this evidence, Hume developed a way of convincing even the hardest of criminals to confess their misdeeds to him.

Hume Joins Wells Fargo

Wells Fargo took notice of the investigative skills of Sheriff Hume since they were being plagued by robberies. They recruited Hume for the position of Wells Fargo Detective. Wells Fargo could have found any number of lawmen, but they wanted someone special. Richard Dillon, Hume's modern biographer, said, "When Wells Fargo hired Hume, a skilled detective out west was as rare as a sober lawyer."

No sooner was he hired by Wells Fargo than his assistance was also requested by the Bureau of Prisons in the State of Nevada. They were in desperate need of Hume's talents. Wells Fargo granted Detective Hume a year's leave to become deputy warden for the Bureau of Nevada Prisons. The prison system in Nevada was in a shambles after a mass escape of prisoners.

Wells Fargo decided Hume was worth waiting for. They held his position for him.

The Problem in Nevada

On September 17, 1871, approximately twenty-nine prisoners escaped from the Nevada State Prison in Carson City. During the escape, prisoners attacked the residence of the prison's warden, Frank Denver. Denver lived in an apartment within the prison with his family.

Denver defended his family with the only weapon he had, a derringer. He shot one of his attackers before he was overpowered and shot with his own weapon. A prison lifer kept the group from killing the warden by fending them off with a heavy wooden chair. This action was all that saved the warden's life.

Other escapees raided the prison armory, commandeering pistols, rifles, shotguns, and ammunition. These criminals waged a vicious battle with the prison guards, who were badly out-numbered but managed to shoot a number of the escapees before two guards, F.M. Isaacs and John Newhouse, were shot. Isaacs later died from his wounds.

Warms Springs Hotel owner Matt Pixley even joined the fray firing with his pistol, but his reward for this act of public service was death at the hands of these desperate men.

The escapees equipped themselves by stealing horses, guns, money, and supplies wherever they could. A number of them were led into Eastern California by Charlie Jones.

In Mono County, California, the escapees encountered an eighteen-year-old Pony Express Rider named Billy Poor. They stole Billy's horse, and Charlie Jones shot and killed Poor needlessly. Billy was a well-liked lad, and the senseless killing of this Pony Express rider known for his ever-present smile incensed citizens of Mono County. A vigilante group pursued the escapees and rode down two of their number. These two were hung without a trial in the name of justice for poor Billy Poor.

Hume had been contracted to not only help reform the Nevada State Prison but also help organize the search and apprehension of the Nevada escapees, who had participated in a prolonged crime spree since their escape. Hume personally took part in the pursuit and apprehension of a number of these escapees; however, the record is unclear as to how effective he was as a reformer.

Eventually, he and many other lawmen either captured or killed twenty-eight of the twenty-nine escapees. (The exact number of escapees varies in the historical accounts.)

Charlie Jones, the murderer of Billy Poor, was never found; however, according to some of his fellow escapees, Charlie had been gunned down by his fellow criminals and left dead in the wilderness immediately after his unnecessary killing of the Poor boy.

After one year doing what he could for the Nevada Prison System, Hume resumed his work as a detective for Wells Fargo.

Black Bart

Shortly thereafter, Hume took up an investigation which would be his most famous case. He concentrated his investigative team's efforts and directed assistant detectives in the pursuit of the gentleman bandit, Black Bart. This robber not only lined his pockets with gold but also deeply embarrassed Wells Fargo.

Modern biographer George Hoeper would say that this criminal was not famous for the quantity of his crimes but for the quality of his crimes. Black Bart would capture the public's imagination for his style and flair for the dramatic.

In 1875 this gentleman bandit committed his first of twenty-eight stagecoach robberies dressed in a linen duster, black bowler hat, wearing a flour sack with holes cut in it. He re-enforced his frightening persona with a double barrel shotgun. In contrast with his look, the suspect had a British accent and was quite polite.

Black Bart targeted Wells Fargo stages exclusively. He left this poem at the scene of his fourth robbery, which secured his legendary status. He wrote:

> I've labored long and hard for bread
> For honor and for riches
> But on my corns too long you've tread,
> You fine-haired sons of bitches.

Another was left at his fifth robbery:
Here I lay me down to sleep
To wait the coming morrow,
Perhaps success, perhaps defeat,
And everlasting sorrow.
Let come what will, I'll try it on,
My condition can't be worse;
And if there's money in that box
'Tis munny in my purse.

He signed these poems "Black Bart."

Ironically, this criminal Black Bart had chosen the moniker given to a contemporary fictional character who had been patterned after Confederate Raider Rufus Henry Ingram. It was his raiders which had been decimated by the combined efforts of Sheriff Hume and Sheriff Adams during the Civil War.

Master of Deduction

Hume and his team would arrive at the scene after Bart was long gone, so it fell to them to approach his apprehension as detectives. They reviewed all the information already accumulated, but Hume also went back to the scene of the robberies.

Hume made a number of deductions from the evidence at hand. Many witnesses had seen a man on foot before and after the robbery who seemed to be in great physical condition and out for a long walk. The man quite noticeably had the front part of his boots slit open.

The description reminded Hume of the line from the poem, "But on my corns too long you've tread." He deduced the long distance walker was Black Bart. The cuts in the boots were to relieve the pressure on his corns.

Hume discovered that Black Bart had claimed to have accomplices hidden in the bushes prepared to fire a volley if anyone resisted during one robbery. Witnesses said rifle barrels had been pointed at them from the very bushes Bart had called out to. Hume discovered the barrels were actually wooden sticks carved to look like rifles.

Hume also deduced that the man they were looking for was an English immigrant who had fought in the Civil War. He was accustomed to marching long distances and in fact came in on foot. The use of wooden weapons, "Quaker Guns," to give the appearance of more troops was a tactic used during the war.

Hume concluded with certainty that Bart resembled Hume himself because those who had seen the long walker would often say, "He looked like you." Another common observation was, "He could have been your brother."

The Last Robbery

In 1883 Black Bart committed his last robbery on Funk Hill, located on the road between Copperopolis and Milton. It just so happened that it was also the scene of his first robbery.

After stopping the stage, Bart ordered its driver, Reason McConnell to unhitch the team of horses and walk them out of sight around the hill. McConnell complied.

Hume, also a pioneer in crime prevention, had advised Wells Fargo to bolt all strong boxes to the floor of the coaches to make them more difficult to steal. The strong box Bart was attempting to steal had been bolted to the floor. This significantly slowed Bart's escape from the scene.

As Black Bart finally managed to open the strong box, Jimmy Rolleri, the nineteen-year-old son of a local Ferry operator, happened upon the scene while out hunting with his rifle. The stagecoach driver, Reason McConnell, and Jimmy Rolleri both used Jimmy's rifle to fire at Black Bart. One of them hit Black Bart, who judiciously fled the scene.

Black Bart ran a quarter mile from the scene and, due to injury and exhaustion, stopped to lighten his load. The bandit kept $500 in gold coins but hid some gold amalgam in a rotten log, probably hoping to return for it. The wounded outlaw ditched his shotgun in a hollow tree and dropped some bloody mail and a pair of glasses. The most significant item he cast off, however, was a bloody handkerchief he had used as a bandage.

An Arrest

Hume believed the handkerchief offered the most hopeful of possibilities. It bore a unique laundry mark, "F.X.O.7." He was certain this mark was the clue to locating the real Black Bart.

Neatly dressed in his tweed suit, Hume and his team spread out across San Francisco. Finally, one team member, Harry N. Morse arrived at Ferguson and Biggs on Bush Street. Laundry personnel there declared that the handkerchief belonged to a customer who lived in a modest boarding house not far from the laundry.

The man identified himself as T. Z. Spalding. When Hume finally met Spalding he knew he was looking at Black Bart because the man claiming to be Spalding could have been Hume's brother.

Spalding initially denied being Black Bart, but Hume uncovered his deception by locating a Bible which had an inscription identifying its owner as Charles Earl Boles (also sometimes spelled Bowles).

Boles' Story Revealed

Hume had an effective conversational style of interrogation which worked often. He believed people had more of a need to explain their actions rather than admit their actions. The confession he needed was always a part of the explanation. Hume used this with Boles and allowed him to tell his interesting story.

Charles E. Boles was born in England, but his family came to the United States when he was young. During the American Civil War, Boles fought with the 116th Illinois Infantry. He was wounded in the battle of Vicksburg and mustered out in 1865 as a lieutenant after having been brevetted twice for bravery in battle. (Brevet is a warrant giving a soldier a promotion for gallantry in battle.)

After the war Boles left his family in search of gold in California. Boles was approached one day as he was working his claim. Some men asked to buy him out, but he declined the offer because the claim was paying off for Boles. The men proceeded to use the land they had purchased near Boles to redirect the water cutting through Boles' claim. This effectively put Boles out of business since he needed moving water in his search for gold. He believed the men were representatives of Wells Fargo.

After perceiving this as a grievous offense committed upon him by Wells Fargo, Boles took to prospecting for gold the easy way, by robbing the stages which carried it. Boles proudly described to Hume how he walked many miles to and from the scenes of his crimes. This made him invisible to a world accustomed to criminals on horseback. He did indeed cut slits in his boots to relieve the pressure on his corns, which he had on both feet.

Boles carried the feared shotgun to achieve compliance. He claimed his shotgun was always unloaded, but this could neither be proved nor disproved.

Even though Boles admitted to other robberies, Wells Fargo only pursued a conviction on his last, for which they had the most and best evidence. Boles was convicted and sentenced to San Quentin for six years but was released after four years for good behavior. He was an exceptional prisoner who had accumulated no demerits.

After his release, Boles was asked by newspaper reporters if he would return to his life of crime. Boles answered he would, "commit no more crimes."

After this response, another reporter asked if he would write anymore poetry?

Boles responded tongue in cheek, "Young man, didn't you hear me? I said I would commit no more crimes."

On November 14, 1888, another Wells Fargo stage was robbed at gunpoint by a masked poet who left this note:

> So here I've stood while wind and rain
> Have set the trees a-sobbin'.
> And risked my life for that box,
> That wasn't worth the robbin'.

Hume was called in and determined that the man who committed the robbery was a "copycat." He declared that the handwriting was markedly different.

His Passing

Hume relentlessly pursued criminals as a marshal, deputy sheriff, under-sheriff, sheriff, deputy warden and finally as a detective for Wells Fargo for a total of forty-two long years. His ground-breaking techniques helped solve countless cases, but he was so ahead of his time they would not be generally accepted in law enforcement for decades.

CHAPTER 24 PIERCE BROOKS, MOST INFLUENTIAL DETECTIVE OF OUR TIMES

ossibly the most influential detective in American law enforcement history was the legendary Los Angeles Police Detective Pierce Brooks. He was a great cop, and many of the concepts he developed are accepted doctrine by officers to this day.

Pierce Brooks dreamed about being a police officer his whole life. In a unique move for his time, Pierce felt he should acquire a college degree before becoming a police officer, so he entered UCLA in 1941. His college studies were interrupted by the Japanese attack at Pearl Harbor. Brooks enlisted in the United States Navy and became a navy pilot with a unique specialty; he piloted blimps.

After the war he went back to college to complete his studies, and in 1948 he joined the Los Angeles Police Department. Pierce began his career as a patrolman and quickly worked his way through Vice, Narcotics, and Plain Clothes Investigations. Since he excelled at everything he did in law enforcement, he was eventually promoted to the storied Los Angeles Police Department Robbery/Homicide Division.

As a detective, Pierce Brooks had a phenomenal clearance rate. His powers of analysis and deduction were uncanny. His ability to elicit a confession once he was certain he was dealing with the perpetrator of the crime was astounding.

A Drink of Water Leaves Murderer High and Dry

Brooks was assigned to investigate the rape and murder of a woman in her own home. This kind of crime demands quick results because it threatens the feeling of safety in a community, even one as large as Los Angeles.

While investigating the scene of the crime, Pierce noticed the victim had been a meticulous housekeeper. The only thing out of place in the home, except for the murdered victim, was an ice cube tray which had been taken out of the freezer and left on the counter. The ice cubes still in the tray were left to melt.

Brooks was certain this detail would have been impossible for the woman to overlook. Detective Brooks decided that whoever she took the ice cubes out for must have raped and murdered her before she had the opportunity to return them to the freezer.

After examining the scene, Brooks personally canvassed the neighborhood. When he asked neighbors if anyone new or suspicious had been noticed in the area, many mentioned that a door-to-door salesman had stopped by on the day of the murder. Most added, "But it couldn't have been him because he was such a nice man."

Brooks chose to pursue this lead and tracked down the salesman. Upon locating him, Brooks confirmed the man did indeed seem like a nice man. The salesman was cooperative and openly admitted he had stopped at the victim's house to attempt a sale. He went on to say he did not make a sale, but he was saddened to hear what happened to her because she was so friendly. The man said the day was very hot, and she was thoughtful enough to offer him a cold drink of water. Once his thirst was quenched, he left.

Armed with that simple admission, Detective Brooks knew he was looking at the killer.

Certain he was seated across from the murderer, Brooks began to work his magic. He was an interrogator who rarely failed to get a statement when he knew he was looking at a guilty suspect. The salesman described as such a nice man had a dark side. As in so many other cases, Brooks was able to convince the salesman to tell him about this dark side which he had kept a secret from everyone he knew.

Pierce Brooks' son Dan Brooks was a police officer for the West Covina Police Department. He shared one of his dad's philosophies which Pierce often put into practice to get statements. Dan explained, "You've heard of the good cop/bad cop technique? Dad taught me that you never use 'bad cop.' The way you get people to confess is not to scare them into a confession, which rarely works. Instead you are nice to people and show them respect, no matter how heinous their crime is."

"They Asked Me to Kill Them"

The Glatman Case was an opportunity to test the limits of Pierce Brooks' philosophy. Glatman's crimes were heinous indeed.

As a youth Harvey Murray Glatman was caught by his parents achieving sexual gratification by masturbating while strangling himself with a noose around his neck. As a teenager he exhibited a tendency toward being, what is called today, a habitual sex offender and served time for his crimes in Sing Sing Prison. Psychiatrists diagnosed Glatman as a psychopath, but nevertheless, he was a model prisoner and therefore eligible for early release.

After he was released, he moved to California and disappeared from the radar. In 1957 he could contain himself no longer. Glatman convinced nineteen-year-old Judy Ann Dull that he was a photographer for a crime magazine and paid her $50 to pose. While he posed her as a victim, he photographed her scantily dressed and tied up. Glatman made the entire affair look like a professional photo shoot and photographed her in multiple poses and costumes but always as a victim.

As it came toward the end of the shoot and Glatman decided he had enough photographs, he posed her one last time while immobilized and helpless. At this point he put down his camera, raped, and strangled Judy Ann. Judy Ann probably did not know she was going to die until the very end. By then it was too late.

After he finished with her, Glatman abandoned the body of the poor woman in the desert like the burned out shell of an old Studebaker.

Glatman repeated his murderous performance for twenty-four-year-old Ruth Mercado, and once again for twenty-four-year-old Shirley Ann Bridgeford. It has since been determined that he was probably involved in the fatal hit-and-run of eighteen-year-old Dorothy Ray Howard.

Glatman's string of killings ended on October 31, 1958, when he attempted to kidnap Lorraine Vigil. During his encounter with Ms. Vigil, he pulled out a gun to gain her compliance. Lorraine fought back like her life depended on it because she sensed that it did.

During the struggle, she was shot by Glatman in the thigh. Lorraine shook off her wound and still managed to wrestle the gun away from Glatman.

Tom Mulligan, an alert highway patrolman, came across the fight in progress. He intervened and arrested Glatman on an armed assault charge.

Brooks Enters the Case

Mulligan suspected Glatman was involved in other cases because of his criminal history of sexual assault. He called in assistance, and Pierce Brooks was assigned to the case. With little to go on other than the in-progress crime, Brooks went into action.

Brooks had done research on perpetrators he later identified as "serial criminals." He sensed that Glatman was one. In all cases Brooks had studied, these unique criminals had kept souvenirs, so he was convinced that Glatman had souvenirs of his victims. He subtly suggested to Glatman that Brooks had found this evidence. Glatman seemed to believe it and began referring to the "tool box."

Brooks praised Glatman's ingenuity on his hiding of the tool box and asked Glatman how he thought to hide the tool box in the place that he did? Glatman, accepting this feigned praise as sincere, unwittingly gave away the tool box's location.

Pierce nonchalantly broke away from the interview and located the tool box. When he recovered it, he found the chilling photographs of all of the victims Glatman had killed. Pierce discovered Glatman had posed the young ladies before and even, quite gruesomely, after he killed them. It appeared in some of the photos that the ladies knew their death was imminent.

Glatman confessed to three homicides, and there would be no more releases for good behavior. On September 18, 1959, Glatman was executed in the gas chamber at San Quentin. His body was immediately cremated and buried in the cemetery there.

Dragnet

This case was depicted "with names changed to protect the innocent" in the original movie *Dragnet* (1966) starring Jack Webb as Joe Friday. The ending of the movie contains this actual dialog from the Pierce Brooks' interview of Glatman.

> *The Killer:* "The reason I killed those girls is because they asked me to." (Pause) "They did, all of them."

Joe Friday: "They asked you to." *(Not a question. A statement by Friday.)*

The Killer: "Sure. They said they'd rather be dead than be with me." *(Music Plays as killer takes bite of his favorite candy bar provided by Friday.)*

Pierce Brooks was the technical adviser on this film which gave it a realistic feel.

Second Movie Depicts Brooks Pierce

Another book and movie were made of an actual event which depicted the investigatory style of Pierce Brooks. The book and screen play were written by a detective who knew Pierce Brooks because he had the privilege of working with him. The author was Detective Joseph Wambaugh; the book was *The Onion Field.*

In the actual event, two career criminals, Greg Powell and Jimmy "Youngblood" Smith, teamed up to commit a series of armed robberies. Late in the evening on March 9, 1963, they were driving about plotting their next robbery when they were spotted by Officers Karl Hettinger and Ian Campbell. The two officers came to the conclusion that Powell and Smith were involved in criminal activity, so the plain clothes officers effected a stop on the vehicle.

As the officers contacted the two men, Powell pulled a revolver on Campbell and took him hostage. After some tense negotiation, Karl Hettinger was convinced to give up both cover and his weapon and submitted himself to the mercy of Powell and Smith. It would be a miscalculation that anguished Hettinger for the rest of his life.

The two officers were taken hostage, and Campbell was made to drive at gunpoint to an onion field in the area of rural Bakersfield. Both officers were ordered out of the car with the assurance that they would not be harmed and that they would be left to walk back from the remote site allowing Powell and Smith time to escape.

Hettinger would recall in the tense moments after exiting the car smelling the onions and listening to Powell and Smith talking about the Lindbergh Law. (They had the false impression that because they had kidnapped someone they would get the death penalty if captured.)

Without warning, they executed the disarmed Campbell. They also shot at Hettinger, but he was able to escape by running into the darkness of the onion field. Hettinger ran for four miles until he reached help. Powell stayed out on foot and directed Smith to parallel him in an attempt to flush Hettinger out. Smith feigned agreement but then drove off leaving Powell alone.

Powell, abandoned by Smith, stole a car and tried to make his escape. He was stopped in the stolen car and arrested by officers from the California Highway Patrol shortly after the murder. Jimmy Smith was arrested the next day.

Sergeant Brooks was called in to interview the two suspects. This case is an example of Brooks' ability to do so much more than interview and interrogate suspects. He established a bond between himself and each suspect. He had the ability to make them trust him more than their own partner.

Detective Brooks believed major crimes, to criminals, were "an extraordinary event." He proceeded under the premise that everyone wanted to tell someone their story when they did something extraordinary. This belief proved true in most cases for Brooks.

Detective Brooks believed criminals had another motivation to talk: their need to lay blame on someone else. Sometimes that was the victim, sometimes it was society, and sometimes it was a partner. In this case, Brooks was able to establish rapport with both Powell and Smith, get them talking, and eventually get them to admit culpability. Each of them admitted some involvement, but both of them accused the other of the actual shooting.

The physical evidence would bring the whole truth out. It showed that both suspects were equally culpable in the shooting death of Officer Campbell.

Since Pierce Brooks had established a relationship with both criminals, it led to a high degree of cooperation during the investigative stage. This led to admissions that yielded a conviction, and both criminals were sentenced to death.

These partners avoided death when the Supreme Court struck down California's Death Penalty. This allowed Smith to eventually go free, only to reoffend and return to prison where he died. Powell, however, would never see the outside of a prison again.

Brooks' Legacy

Pierce Brooks had an uncanny ability to be able to go to some of the most gruesome homicide cases and not be negatively impacted by them. He was able to work the cases as a professional and still, as he put it, never have a sleepless night. These two cases, however, made an impression on Brooks that would inspire his legacy.

Brook's Legacy Shared from the Glatman Case

The Glatman case triggered something in Detective Brooks. As a homicide detective, he realized that there was a particular kind of killer who was hard to find. Working homicide cases required the investigator to establish MOM: Motive, Opportunity, and Means. Once the investigator identified the suspects and determined which one had MOM, the case was on its way to being cleared.

Brooks realized Glatman was a different sort of killer. Pierce Brooks was a voracious researcher, which is one of the reasons he would clear this and countless other cases during his career. As he took up the task of researching this type of killer, he realized Glatman was not unique. There were many killers whose only motive in the killing was some inner satisfaction or gratification.

Some individuals developed within themselves an almost uncontrollable compulsion to kill. Once they killed, their urge to kill was not satisfied, but magnified, leading them to kill over and over again. In each homicide, the killers had no traditional motive to kill. Their reason to kill was their desire to gratify themselves. Brooks coined the term "serial killers" in describing this kind of killer.

Serial killers each had their own psychotic reasons for killing again, and again, and again. The only things that could stop these killers were death or capture. Brooks' study made him realize he could link these homicides with what he would call a "signature" present at each crime scene. He also noticed that most serial killers were also sex offenders.

In 1958, Pierce Brooks recognized the need for the Los Angeles Police Department to purchase a computer in which information on violent killers could be stored. This information could be analyzed and quickly accessed to solve crimes and eventually prevent crimes. He was chastised at the time because as someone said, "A computer is not practical because they are as big as a city and just as expensive as one."

Brooks would not be deterred. He would remain persistent on achieving a central location to store, analyze, and access information on violent criminals. The idea was sound, but it was so far ahead of its time his law enforcement supervisors could not contemplate it as being a practical option.

Finally, in 1985, Pierce Brooks became the first VICAP (Violent Criminal Apprehension Program) Director. The program, his brain child, was located at the site of the FBI Academy in Quantico, Virginia. In 2008, the information became available to local agencies.

Brooks' Legacy from the Onion Field Case.

The Glatman case set Brooks off on a life-long pursuit to establish a system of information which would aid investigators in identifying and apprehending serial killers. His dream was finally realized in the development of VICAP. In the Onion Field killing, Pierce Brooks was moved to pursue what would become his second legacy to law enforcement.

Brooks decided he had attended too many police funerals. He came to the conclusion that in every killing of a police officer, the subsequent investigative reports answered the questions who, what, when, and where. The investigations failed to honestly look at the reason *why* the suspect was able to kill an armed and highly trained officer.

Brooks began his research on the whole stories behind line-of-duty deaths. He documented not only how these deaths happened, but how they could have been prevented. Without naming the officers involved, Brooks compiled these stories in the book, "... *Officer Down, Code Three.*"

The book was released in 1975 and instantly became a must-read, nation-wide, for all street level police officers.

The message of the book is that police officers must be ever vigilant and avoid committing what Pierce Brooks referred to as the "Ten Deadly Errors" that open police officers up to deadly assaults.

Brooks' Ten Deadly Errors have been circulated by nearly every police trainer in the nation from then until now, making Pierce Brooks

---

one of the most quoted police survival trainers in the nation. The Ten Deadly Errors as written in *"...Officer Down, Code Three"*[1] are:

1. Failure to maintain proficiency and care of weapon, vehicle, and equipment. If you have learned to shoot, will your gun fire when you pull the trigger? Will your car respond when you need it?
2. Improper search and use of handcuffs. Many fatalities here.
3. Sleepy or asleep. How can you react, when you are sleepy?
4. Relaxing too soon. Usually at those "phony" alarm calls.
5. Missing the danger signs. Miss or don't recognize them. They can be fatal either way.
6. Taking a bad position. Write a citation or field interrogation card with your back turned to the subject. Or, while confronting the barricaded gunman, be casual or curious from your place of concealment rather than careful and cautious from a place of cover.
7. Failure to watch the hands. Where else can the subject hold a gun, or knife, or a club?
8. Tombstone Courage? Why wait for back-up?
9. Preoccupation. Worrying about personal problems while on duty may be the hard way to solve the problem.
10. Apathy. A deadly disease for the cynical veteran officer.

Pierce Brooks' son attributed his father's success to the fact that, "He was fascinated by police work. He felt like he was a good guy and wanted to put the bad guys in jail. That was the best way he could serve his country and his community."

While looking back on Pierce Brooks' career as a detective, one of his former partners, Dan Bowser, observed that his success in investigations was owed to conducting all of his investigations with "precision and dedication."

Including Detective Pierce Brooks in this list of great Law Dogs was, to use an old law enforcement term, "reasonable and necessary." Any investigation into Pierce Brooks' life would lead one to conclude that he left a signature of excellence.

Pierce Brooks was not only a great investigator but a gifted innovator. Dan Bowser, Brooks' former partner, was correct, when he said, "There was nobody better at this type of work."

---

1   Reprinted with permission from *"...Officer Down, Code Three"*

PART SEVEN

REAL COMMUNITY POLICING

CHAPTER 25

DOC HOLLIDAY

oc Holliday was the embodiment of community policing.

"Community policing" is a term bandied about by many people who don't know what it is but like the sound of it. Too often, community policing is practiced as a funded program. When the program's funding disappears, so does community policing.

Community policing, however, is not a program but a philosophy. It is firmly rooted in the vision of the father of modern day law enforcement, Sir Robert Peel. Peel established modern policing in England, and his vision of policing is still revered as the standard to follow. One of Peel's *Principles of Policing* key to the community policing concept states,

> To maintain at all times a relationship with the public that gives reality to the historic tradition that the police are the public and that the public are the police, the police being only members of the public who are paid to give full-time attention to duties which are incumbent on every citizen in the interests of community welfare and existence.

In today's world, it is rare for a citizen to step forward to help an officer in need of assistance beyond digitally recording the event for the six o'clock news. Too many have forgotten that they, too, can play an important role as caretakers of their communities.

There was a time, however, when if a lawman needed help, all he needed to do was sound the alarm and the town's people would gather on their horses with weapons at the ready. The posse was sworn in, and they rode off together, sharing the excitement and dangers of the pursuit.

Most of these brave men's names have been lost to history. One citizen, however, had no desire to become a lawman himself even though he was a friend of lawmen. In their time of need, this posse-man was always there for them.

He was a man of considerable skills, a sharp intellect, and possessing no detectable fear of death. He was clearly the most famous posse-man in history, bar none. His name was Doc Holliday. (See chapter on the Earps of Tombstone.)

Doc Holliday's Early Years

August 14, 1851, John Henry Holliday was born to Henry and Alice Holliday in Griffin, Georgia. At the age of fifteen, his beloved mother died of consumption, which today is called tuberculosis. This was a devastating loss to John, who was very close to his mother, but he managed to carry on.

John was an extremely bright young man and he entered dental college, graduating at the age of twenty. John joined a practice in Atlanta and was so skilled in dentistry he actually won a dental competition.

His future success in dentistry seemed assured when he was dealt a devastating, life changing blow. He was told he had contracted the same disease that took his mother's life and had but a short number of years to live. John's doctor suggested he might prolong his life by moving to a dryer climate.

Although he was still a skilled dentist, few people wished to be treated by a dentist with an incessant cough. Doc stewed on his options, becoming moody and irritable.

In 1873 Holliday became embroiled in an argument at a swimming hole which resulted in his first gunfight. Reliable details are unavailable. Shots were exchanged in the argument, and it is most probable that no one was killed. This incident may have been the final catalyst for his move. Doctor John Holliday boarded a train and headed to Dallas, Texas.

Dentist to Gambler

After initially hanging out a shingle in Dallas, Doc came face to face with the realization that he had to find another way to make a living. As talented as he was, patients absolutely did not want a dentist coughing in their face. His practice became all but non-existent.

Doc was a naturally gifted card player, a sharp dresser, and, when he wanted, Doc simply oozed southern charm. He decided he was perfectly suited for gambling.

Gambling was a respectable trade in the nineteenth century as long as you were not a cheat. It was dangerous, however, because the biggest losers had a tendency to drink too much and become unreasonable. The combination of losing money and alcohol made dangerous men even more so.

To prepare for every eventuality, Doc honed his skills with his pistols and the large knife he carried. When he played cards, he brought his knife as well as a pistol in a shoulder holster and another at his hip. Although there were stories of Doc ending the life of many who dared to face him, closer historical examination reveals little evidence to confirm most of them.

One story that persists is an actual, documented event. On July 19, 1879, while Doc was in the saloon business in Las Vegas, New Mexico, an intoxicated man named Mike Gordon went out into the street and began shooting randomly. According to the tale, Doc met the armed man in the street and told him to cease and desist. He didn't, and Doc shot him.

Even though the anecdotal evidence credits Doc Holliday with the shooting death, an inquest at the time ruled that Gordon was shot by an unknown man.

It's possible that many of the stories about Doc were just that, stories. Doc was undoubtedly talented with his pistols. It's also quite probable that he may have encouraged or even spread some of the stories himself to discourage confrontations.

Even though historical records do not support the myth that Doc was a cold-blooded killer, he probably did kill Mike Gordon.

Doc left Las Vegas, New Mexico, after Mike Gordon's death and eventually made his way to Griffin, Texas.

Griffin, Texas

Three important incidents took place in John Shanssey's Saloon in Griffin, Texas, while Holliday was playing cards there. He met an attractive dance hall girl named Mary Catherine Elder, who was educated and in possession of many eye catching features—including a prominent proboscis. This nose earned her the moniker "Big Nose Kate." Their relationship was the closest thing to a long term love-based relationship Holliday would find in his short, difficult life.

The second and most important moment was when a lawman named Wyatt Earp was referred to Doc by John Shanssey. Wyatt was on the hunt for a bad man named Dave Rudabaugh. Doc provided Wyatt with information leading to Rudabaugh's capture.

A third incident, embellished and distorted to a great degree by word of mouth, happened when Doc was playing cards with a man named Ed Bailey. Bailey was sifting through the discard pile, which was definitely against the rules of the game. Holliday warned him several times to cease and desist; however, the disagreeable Bailey disregarded the warning. Finally, Doc took the pot, which by rights he could do under the circumstances. According to the story, Bailey drew his pistol, and in a flash, before Bailey could get a shot off, Doc produced his knife and cut him long and deep.

Doc was arrested and confined to the hotel. Ed Bailey's friends were talking about finding a path to justice that did not include the courts. Even though Doc's actions were justified, he did not want to end his life on the end of a rope when all he had done was defend himself. Kate set a shed on fire as a diversion, then she and Doc saddled up and bid adieu to Griffin, Texas, for good.

Doc Saves Wyatt Earp

Doc and Wyatt crossed paths again in Dodge City. It was here Wyatt claimed Doc saved his life. The story has been passed down in several versions. If the least dramatic version is the closest to the truth, this would be it.

Wyatt was arresting a cowhand in a crowded saloon when a number of the cowhand's friends trained their guns on Wyatt from behind. Doc stepped between Wyatt and the cowhands with guns drawn, smiled, and asked them if they had the nerve to kill a man while he was looking them in the eye. He invited them to try him on because he would shoot back. He may have even used his favorite line, "Go ahead and shoot. You'll be a daisy if you do."

The least dramatic ending of this event has the cowhands backing down when they realized they were facing the feared Doc Holliday. This is probably closer to the truth than other versions ending in gunfights and mass arrests, which can't be confirmed by the historical record. Regardless of what happened, Wyatt always credited Doc with saving his life in Dodge City while he was a lawman there.

Since Wyatt felt he owed his life to Doc, this was probably enough to establish a friendship. This was not all that kept the friendship intact, however. Wyatt was known to be a serious man, but Doc made him laugh.

Tombstone

Countless volumes have been written about the historic events that occurred in Tombstone, Arizona. The details of what led up to the gunfight in Tombstone and its aftermath are related in Chapter Six: The Earps of Tombstone in this narrative.

For the sake of this chapter, suffice it to say that Doc Holliday could have opted out of the gunfight, but he didn't. Doc could have left his friends, who happened to be lawmen, to fend for themselves, but he chose to put himself in harm's way. Doc did not have to shed tears when Morgan Earp was murdered. Nor did he have to donate his best suit for his friend Morgan to be buried in just because Morgan had admired it while he was alive.

Holliday was just a card player and, as some would cruelly say, a "lunger." He did not have to join Wyatt on what would be called the Vendetta Ride, but there he was, right beside his friend at the campfire and in the gunfights on that dangerous ride.

Holliday's Last Days

At the conclusion of the Vendetta Ride, Doc and Wyatt shook hands and bid each other farewell. Doc left the state of Arizona for good and returned to card playing. He never pinned on the badge of a deputy again.

Doc would ultimately make his way to Glenwood Springs, Colorado. On November 8, 1887, Doc was being attended to by a nurse. He knew he was near death. He asked his nurse for one last shot of whiskey. The historical record is conflicted on whether or not Doc's request was met. Some say he got his drink; others say it was denied.

After he did or did not drink this last shot of whiskey, Doc looked down at his bare feet, smiled, and said, "This is funny." With that, consumption claimed John H. "Doc" Holliday.

Like Doc's life, his last words are open to interpretation. Doc probably found it funny that after all the dangerous predicaments he had survived, here he was dying in his bed with his boots off.

Compelled neither by law nor money, Doc was one of the most intriguing characters drawn into the Tombstone gunfight. Without absolute historical confirmation, one has to conclude that the only reason Doc was induced to pin on a deputy's badge was because his friends happened to be lawmen and they desperately needed him. If Doc had not been at that gunfight, the story may have played out much differently. Wyatt, Virgil, and Morgan always knew that.

Years after Doc's death, Wyatt shared his view of Holliday, "I found him a loyal friend and good company. He was a dentist whom necessity had made a gambler; a gentleman whom disease had made a vagabond; a philosopher whom life had made a caustic wit; a long lean blonde fellow nearly dead with consumption and at the same time the most skillful gambler and nerviest, speediest, deadliest man with a six-gun I ever knew."

In taking Doc with them on that pivotal day in the history of Tombstone, Virgil hoped that his mere presence and reputation might prevent the fight. Ever present in Virgil's tactical mind was the belief that having Doc with them markedly improved their chances of winning if the fight could not be avoided. History proved him right on the second count.

To this day, Doc Holliday is the most famous posse-man in the history of the United States. Historians can argue about whether or not that made Holliday a good man; however, no one could make a case that Holliday was not a good friend—a good friend to the bitter end.

CHAPTER 26

THE CITIZENS OF NORTHFIELD AND MADELIA – MINNESOTA

One of the most famous and courageous actions taken by any townspeople in history occurred in the Midwestern city of Northfield, Minnesota. Their spontaneous stand against the most infamous criminals of their time was so effective that it shut down the criminal activity of a gang that had been committing robbery and murder for ten years.

When the gang rode into Northfield on September 7, 1876, they were supremely confident that they would leave town whooping and shooting and carrying thousands of dollars in cash that belonged to the hardworking citizens of Northfield. The citizens of Northfield, however, would most definitely have their say in the matter.

Some effort must be taken to explain who exactly rode into Northfield that day. What was the James-Younger Gang? The James-Younger Gang undoubtedly was and still is the most famous criminal gang in the Old West. They were not Robin Hood and his merry men. They were thieves and killers.

The Beginning

The gang's story started in Missouri during the Civil War. Frank and Jesse James were as pro-slavery, anti-union as any southerner in the Confederate States of America. Passions on these issues possibly ran even hotter in Missouri because both pro- and anti-slavery factions had been fighting a low grade war in Missouri for years before the Civil War began.

When the Civil War began in 1861, Frank, the older of the two brothers, initially joined the Confederate Army and fought with General Sterling Price. Jesse was too young to go off to war with Frank in the beginning and stayed home on the family farm with his mother Zerelda, a rabid southern democrat, and his step-father

Rueben Samuel. Their farm was in the "Little Dixie" section of Missouri in Clay County.

After fighting in the battle of Wilson Creek, Frank came down with the measles and was left behind by his unit when it moved out. Frank was captured by Union troops. They mercifully allowed Frank to swear an oath of allegiance to the Union and left the measles-infected rebel behind. It may not have been a gesture of pure mercy, leaving Frank behind with the measles, since the measles killed more soldiers than bayonets during the Civil War on both sides.

After Frank recovered, he joined a group of Confederate irregulars led by William Quantrill. While riding with these Confederate guerillas, Frank James took part in the murderous raid on Lawrence, Kansas. The rebel bushwhackers rode into the town, rounded up more than 150 unarmed men and boys, and shot them dead.

The Union militia in Missouri scoured the state for the bushwhackers and visited the James-Samuel farm looking for Frank James, who they knew was one of Quantrill's men. In an effort to extract information from Frank's stepfather Rueben Samuel, they put a rope around his neck and repeatedly hung him just short of death and then lowered him until he gave them information on the whereabouts of Frank. This information turned out to be useless.

The militia didn't stop there, however. While Mr. Samuel was being interrogated, another soldier beat and horse-whipped Jesse James while trying extract information from him. Jesse was just an innocent teenager doing chores for his mother at the time. As the story goes, Jesse did not shed a tear and gave them no information. All their cruelty did was turn a teenage boy into a bushwhacker.

Jesse immediately donned a colorful shirt, put a pistol on each hip, and joined the Confederate guerilla Bill Anderson. Jesse was there when Bill earned the moniker "Bloody Bill" after the actions he took in and around Centralia, Missouri. Bill and his men, including Jesse, stopped a train and had the twenty-three unarmed Union soldiers on furlough step off. Bill ordered them to strip off their uniforms. Once they were compliant, defenseless, and naked, he and his men gunned downed the surrendered prisoners. They deliberately left one alive.

The Battle of Centralia

After the massacre at the train station, a Union unit which outnumbered Anderson and his men pursued them. Instead of fleeing, however, Bill ordered his men to turn, and they charged. The Union soldiers formed a line and on command fired a volley into the oncoming guerillas, killing and wounding some, but Bloody Bill's hard riding bushwhackers were on them in an instant, among them and behind them. The Confederates were heavily armed with multiple pistols, carbines, and huge deadly Bowie knives. On this day they used them all.

The bushwhackers achieved victory immediately since the Union troops had no opportunity to reload their single shot muskets after the first volley. Many Union soldiers tried to surrender, but no quarter was given. They were shot down with their hands up. The ones who died immediately were the lucky ones. Others were tortured, scalped, disemboweled, and mutilated in a most horrible manner. Even in a war that would see 600,000 Americans die, this was deemed an unforgivable war crime.

On that day the seventeen-year-old Jesse James was credited with killing the unit's commander, Major A.V.E. Johnston.

After the war, Confederate troops were universally pardoned and offered the opportunity to say an oath of allegiance to the United States of America allowing the country to be whole again. Jesse, however, was considered a war criminal because of his affiliation with Bill Anderson. If Jesse planned to ask for a pardon, it would never happen. He was shot through the lung at the war's end. The young bushwhacker was allowed to return home only because he was thought to be dying.

The James-Younger Gang Rides

The Youngers, who were also from Clay County, rode with Quantrill as well. The James and the Youngers held an attitude after the war which was immortalized in a contemporary song:
> "I'm a good old Rebel, yes that is what I am,
> And for your land of freedom I do not give a damn.
> I'm glad I fought against it, I only wish we'd won,
> And I don't want no pardon for anything I done."

In the mind of the James and Youngers, they were still at war with those "Damned Yankees."

In 1866 the first peacetime daylight robbery of a bank took place in Liberty, Missouri. It was robbed by one of Bill Anderson's lieutenants, Archie Clements, and he was most probably accompanied by Frank James. Jesse was likely still at home on the mend from his debilitating lung-shot.

That would be the start of a long string of robberies perpetrated by what would eventually be called the James-Younger Gang. They would terrorize many towns robbing trains and banks on a regular basis.

In Gallatin, they mistook an innocent cashier named John Sheets for the Major Cox who killed Bloody Bill Anderson. Even though Sheets was perfectly cooperative and had nothing to do with the death of Bloody Bill, Frank and Jesse shot the innocent man dead.

In Iowa, the gang caused a train to derail during one robbery; the engineer was crushed to death. During the Kansas City Exposition robbery, one of the multiple shots fired by the gang seriously wounded an eight-year-old girl.

The Pinkertons bungled an attempt to capture Frank and Jesse when they threw a smoke bomb into the Samuel farmhouse. Zerelda swept the smoke bomb into the fire place turning the volatile components in the smoking canister into a real bomb. It exploded, killing Jesse's younger half-brother and blowing Zerelda's arm off.

The James gang determined who was responsible for giving Pinkerton's investigators information and killed an unarmed neighbor they suspected.

The core members of the gang were Jesse and Frank James along with Cole, Bob, Jim and sometimes John Younger. A variety of former Confederate bushwhackers rode with them at different times. Due to the bond they shared, having been to war together, they possessed a loyalty that could not be compromised. They also had skills and tactics they utilized in their robberies which were executed in the same fashion as their guerilla raids during the war.

It was common for the gang to ride up and down the streets wildly firing their weapons to terrorize the citizens so they wouldn't dare to resist. Then they would gallop out of town bidding their victims farewell with a rebel yell.

This dangerously effective gang was lionized by the press as Robin Hoods, robbing from the rich and giving to the poor. This image created a false narrative on the gang. They robbed from everyone who had money in those banks, and they spent it on themselves.

When the James-Younger Gang rode into Northfield, Minnesota, they were the most wanted criminals in the nation. Depending on a person's loyalties during the War Between the States, the gang was either revered or reviled.

On that memorable day, the citizens of Northfield had no inkling of what was about to transpire. They were good people who thought the war had ended years ago. They were about to be set upon by ruthless killers who were still at war. Even though they were surprised, outgunned, and at a distinct disadvantage, the citizens of Northfield, Minnesota, would rise to the occasion.

Northfield Raid

Northfield was a long ride for the gang, but as a group they decided it was a worthy target. The gang perceived, incorrectly, that two union generals, Adelbert Ames and Benjamin Butler, owned the bank. Although both men had money in the bank, neither held a controlling interest.

On September 7, 1876, at 2:00 PM, three groups of riders converged slowly and nonchalantly on the First National Bank of Northfield, Minnesota. Their nonchalance was for naught. Suspicions were aroused in many citizens around the bank and near the Lee and Hitchcock Dry Goods Store next door.

What caught the townspeople's attention was the fact that the three groups were all riding horses and converging from three different directions at once. This was peculiar in itself since most people in this farming community traveled by wagon or buggies. In addition to this, the riders were all dressed identically in white linen dusters and Western-style hats. Apparently, the gang hoped the dusters would conceal their weapons, but it was clear that all of these men were heavily armed wearing holstered pistols on their hips and Winchesters in the scabbards on their horses.

Having so many pistols was also unusual. Even though most citizens had a firearm close by, the weapon of choice in Northfield was a long gun. This gun was primarily used to put food on the table.

Those on the streets of Northfield, as well as some from second and third story windows that lined the street, watched the gang's approach with great interest. There was a tension in the air as many eyes followed the gang members.

A Robbery in Progress

When three of the robbers entered the bank, J.S. Allen, a citizen whose suspicions were aroused, walked up to the window of the bank and looked inside to assess the situation. Inside the bank, the robbers confronted assistant cashier Joseph Lee Heywood, a Civil War veteran. They demanded that he open the safe. Even though the safe was unlocked and could have been pulled open easily, he bluffed the robbers and told them, "I can't open it. It has a timed lock."

Two of the robbers inside the bank were most certainly Bob Younger and Charlie Pitts. The identity of the third bank robber is a historical mystery, still open to speculation. It was either Frank or Jesse James, but no one knows for sure.

Heywood was threatened at gunpoint by the third robber, and during this commotion Alonzo Bunker, another banker, bolted out the back door of the bank. Charlie Pitts turned and shot Bunker in the right shoulder. Bunker was wounded but undeterred; he made it out of the bank.

J.S. Allen watched this all happen then turned and ran. As he did, he sounded the alarm in a manner that energized the townspeople to action in defense of their money in their bank. Allen's shout was as much a call to arms as a drum roll on the battlefield. Allen shouted in a booming voice, "Get your guns, boys! They're robbing the bank."

There was an instantaneous flurry of activity. The citizens of Northfield armed themselves.

The Shooting Begins

With the alarm sounded, Cole Younger began riding up and down the street shooting with the intent to frighten the residents into submission, but that tactic had run its course. The citizens of Northfield would not submit today.

Inside the bank, Heywood maintained that he could not open the safe. One of the bank robbers threatened to kill Heywood, but the Civil War combat veteran's response was to shout loudly, "Murder! Murder! Murder!"

One of the armed men stepped into the safe area through the large outer door, and Heywood slammed the door on the robber, most certainly injuring him. This action infuriated the robber, and Heywood's continued act of defiance was rewarded with a brutal pistol whipping. Heywood was also cut slightly with a knife on the neck as a warning of impending death if he wouldn't cooperate. A robber then fired a warning shot into the floor near his head to further convince him to open the safe. Nothing would compel the faithful cashier to walk over to the safe and open its unlocked door for these men.

Outside the bank, Cole Younger, Jim Younger, and Clell Miller were riding back and forth firing to terrorize citizens and make them flee. Instead of cowering until the gang could ride out of town with their money in hand, the citizens of Northfield poured stinging fire down upon the gang.

With the return fire of the gang, the street lined with businesses was instantly turned into a battleground. Citizens of all walks of life took up weapons of every make and caliber imaginable and showered hell-fire down upon the James-Younger Gang.

Some citizens who were not armed reported to the hardware store where they borrowed guns and ammunition after which they also joined the fight. The famous James-Younger Gang had ridden into a wide-awake nightmare. They had to sense that some of their number would never ride out.

When Charlie Pitts heard the heavy fire, he exited the bank and was almost immediately shot in the face by a brave citizen named Elias Stacy. The only thing that momentarily saved Pitts was Elias' shotgun was loaded with bird shot. Even so, Pitts was disoriented by the sharp burning pain the blast caused.

Another Northfield resident, A.R. Manning, joined the fight from his place of cover at the corner of the Scriver Building. Manning was armed with a Remington rifle, and he fired a round into the horse in front of Pitts, intent on preventing his escape. The horse dropped dead where it stood in the street.

The exchange of gunfire had become more regular when a recent Swedish immigrant, Nicholas Gustafson, arrived in town with his cousin on a wagon filled with vegetables which they intended to sell. Nicholas heard the shooting and out of pure curiosity ran to the scene to see what all the excitement was about. Nicholas had not yet learned how to speak English.

Cole Younger turned in his saddle and saw Gustafson. The new immigrant was a totally innocent, unarmed farmer who traveled across an ocean to live the American Dream. Instead, the voyage did nothing but put him in the wrong place at the wrong time. Younger took direct aim at Gustafson and gunned him down in the street without a scintilla of justification.

As Gustafson fell, the gunfire rose to a crescendo. Bullets and buckshot rattled down upon the Missouri raiders like hail in a summer thunderstorm. Cole Younger rode up to the door of the bank and shouted, "For God's sake, come out! They are shooting us all to pieces!" Every gang member outside had been hit with birdshot.

With the pressure on, Bob Younger abandoned the idea of getting into the vault, collected $26.00 from the cash drawer, and joined Pitts on the outside of the bank. The citizens immediately engaged Bob in a deadly gunfight.

The third robber (Frank or Jesse) apparently noticed Heywood slowly lifting himself off the floor, still dazed from the pistol whipping. This third robber took careful aim shooting down the brave and defenseless cashier who risked his life to successfully protect all but $26.00 of the Northfield citizens' money. Heywood, still the good soldier, crumpled to the floor and died honorably at his post.

Outside, citizen Henry Wheeler extended his rifle out the third floor window of the Dampier House Hotel across and down the street. He picked his target, took careful aim, and fired. In response Clell Miller rolled out of the saddle and fell to the dusty street dead.

In spite of the fact that A.R. Manning had become a focus of the robbers' gunfire, he stood his ground and determinedly returned fire. The bank robber Bill Chadwell (A.K.A. William Stiles) was hit by one of Manning's rounds, and Chadwell joined Miller in the dust. The war was finally over for both of them.

As Bob Younger stepped out of the bank into the maelstrom, he realized he had no horse. His horse was the one shot dead by Manning earlier. He paused to look for another option, and in that moment he was hit and wounded. Bob opened fire in all directions in response. He was at a loss to come up with any other options.

Seeing his younger brother on foot, Cole galloped up. He brought his horse to a stop and hoisted Bob up behind him. In one motion, Bob was up and Cole spurred his horse out of town.

Things were desperate for the surviving members of the gang. They followed Cole and Bob riding out of town at a thunderous gallop. They left two of their dead in the middle of the street. As they departed, they manage to muster a feeble rebel yell that had a sickly sound to it. Every member of the gang was wounded. All would have been dead in the streets if more residents had been loaded with something more lethal than bird shot.

In making their escape, the gang took an irregular route across the state of Minnesota trying to avoid the posses and pickets that were mobilized to capture them. The gang's progress was slowed not only by pursuers but also by their wounds, which made riding painful to all. Much of the time they walked and led their horses. Bob Younger had the most trouble staying in his saddle.

The Battle of Hanska Slough

The gang worked their way south and west trying desperately just to get out of the state of Minnesota. Every one of the gang members had been hit by buckshot, and most also had been hit with slugs from the Northfield residents' long guns. They longed to be back in Missouri on the mend in their beds.

As they reached the outskirts of Mankato two weeks after the Northfield raid, the gang had a conference. It was clear that those who were less wounded—Frank James, Jesse James, and Charlie Pitts—had a chance of escaping if they separated from those who were more wounded. The gang agreed on this point, and Frank and Jesse immediately went off on their own. Charlie Pitts, though less wounded, decided to stay with the Youngers. He felt the wounded had a better chance at escape and survival if he were along.

Ultimately, Frank and Jesse made their way back to Missouri. The other members would fall victim, in dramatic fashion, to citizen volunteers within Minnesota.

On September 21, the wounded members of the gang were spotted just north and west of Madelia. The farmer who spotted them rode hard to find Sheriff James Glispin and report the sighting.

As soon as Sheriff Glispin received the report, he contacted former Union Army Captain William W. Murphy as well as Corporal Thomas L. Vought and filled them in. The three formed a posse of approximately thirty-five volunteers and began searching for the gang in the area where they were last sighted, about seven miles outside Madelia.

The remnants of the gang were spotted on foot just outside a scrub-covered area called Hanska Slough. The posse called for their surrender from a distance, but the gang limped as fast as they could into Hanska Slough while firing at the posse.

Sheriff Glispin positioned some of his posse strategically around the slough to prevent escape and again called for their surrender, but the gang refused. Volunteers were asked to form a skirmish line to approach the slough and flush out the gang, allowing other posse members to cut off their escape.

Ben M. Rice, Charles A. Pomeroy, Corporal Thomas L. Vought, George A. Bradford, James Severson, Captain Murphy, and Sheriff Glispin formed the skirmish line and advanced at a walk toward this deadly gang of bandits. True to form and defiant to the end, the gang fired on the skirmish line.

Captain Murphy was hit in the side. One of the rounds struck and doubled over Corporal Vought, who had survived the Civil War fighting with the 14th Wisconsin. He straightened back up after he was hit and returned fire. He later discovered the round had been stopped by his cartridge belt.

The gang's belligerence would mark the end to the real life drama of the infamous James-Younger Gang. When the desperados opened fire, it pinpointed their position for the rest of the posse which poured convergent fire into the deadfall the gang was concealed in.

Charlie Pitts initially suggested surrender to Cole, but Cole shook off the suggestion saying, "We can die right here."

Pitts shrugged his shoulders as he seconded Cole's emotion declaring, "I can die as well as you can." As soon as those words were spoken, Pitts rose up to fire at the skirmish line. These words became Pitts' dying declaration. He was hit repeatedly; the final shot to his heart was fired by Sheriff Glispin. Pitts fell face first into the mud, dead.

At nearly the same time, Cole was hit three more times. One shot fired by Corporal Vought hit him in the head, knocking him out of the fight.

Jim Younger rose up to fire, but posse member Bowen G. Yates fired a shot that hit him between the nose and upper lip.

This left Bob Younger alone as bullets zipped and zinged all around him. Bob had already been diminished by the Northfield citizens' gunfire. The only role he could perform in this fight was to reload the guns for the others, but now there was no one left. The tattered remnants of the notorious James-Younger Gang were either dead or defenseless.

Sensing the fight was over, Sheriff Glispin called to his men, "Cease Fire!"

After the posse's fire ceased, Sheriff listened to the silence emanating from the dead fall. He called out to the robbers, "Do you men surrender?"

Bob Younger responded by waving a bloody white rag as he shouted, "I surrender! They're all down but me. For God's sake, don't shoot me too."

Bob Younger was ordered to come out with his hands up. Bob tried to comply, but one of his arms was broken and therefore hung at his side. Posse member Willis Bundy spotted Bob Younger exiting the deadfall with one arm raised and the other down. He perceived that Bob was still a threat and was advancing rather than surrendering. Bundy aimed and fired at Bob. The round tore through Bob Younger's lung, dropping him instantly.

Sheriff Glispin shouted to his posse, "The next man to fire will be shot by me!" The fight was officially at an end.

As Sheriff Glispin's posse drove their wagon loaded with the infamous James-Younger Gang into town, the grievously wounded Cole Younger would quite famously muster up enough strength to pull himself into a standing position. Once upright again, he smiled while tipping his hat to the ladies. This last flamboyant act served as an example of the dash that made the James-Younger Gang so appealing to the public.

The deadly fire from the citizens first in Northfield and then outside of Madelia all but delegated the James-Younger Gang to the history books. Jesse and Frank James had escaped, but they would never again be able to raise a gang as criminally effective without the Youngers.

Chadwell, Miller, and Pitts were dead. Bob, Jim, and Cole were shot to pieces as Bob had described. Cole alone had eleven wounds in his body. The captured survivors would all serve time in Stillwater Prison to pay for their crimes.

The Destruction of the James-Younger Gang

This was community policing. For it to work there had to be a partnership between the police and the community. The citizens who rallied to defend their bank and those who advanced on Hanska Slough alongside their law enforcement officers demonstrated true partnership.

The good citizens of Northfield, Minnesota, refused to submit to threats and intimidation. They met criminal violence with a justifiable and effective armed response. They stood beside their law enforcement brothers and engaged in a heroic battle against armed intruders. When ordered to submit and capitulate to armed thugs, these citizens could have easily done so. Instead, a call to arms was sent out, "Get your guns, boys! They're robbing the bank."

Later, the men of Madelia volunteered to advance along-side their sheriff toward Hanska Slough, absolutely sure a portion of the notorious James-Younger Gang was armed and waiting for them. When they were fired upon, they held their ground, fired back, and won the day.

The James-Younger Gang's decade-long reign of terror was ended by this community partnership. Men came forward and risked their lives in defense of their communities to face the most feared robber-gang in their time, and remarkably, they won a decisive victory.

PART EIGHT

MILITARIZATION OF CRIMINALS

THE FBI MIAMI SHOOTOUT

On April 11, 1986, one of the most famous shootouts in modern times took place between the FBI and two serial bank robbers. In law enforcement, it is simply referred to as the FBI Miami Shootout. Before delving into the shootout, it is important to have a proper perspective of law enforcement at the time.

During the 1980s, many law enforcement administrators seemed to possess an almost Pollyanna-style view as they equipped their officers. This attitude existed in an era where the numbers of officers killed in the line of duty were startlingly high.

You saw the traditional black and white squad cars disappear as agency administrators began using soft pastels for their squads. Even the trusty Model 870 Shotgun was being delegated to the trunk of squads because administrators thought these weapons were too aggressive looking. Even though semi-automatic handguns had been around for 90 years, transitioning to these weapons was strongly resisted by most law enforcement agencies. Soft body armor was available, but only a few agencies were purchasing them for their officers, and virtually none required that they be worn. Criminals, on the other hand, had been ahead of law enforcement in the weapons race since Machine Gun Kelly earned his nickname.

Some officers took it upon themselves to purchase their own vests and equip themselves with semi-automatic handguns. These officers had to equip and train themselves "on their own time, on their own dime."

Department qualification courses for police officers in this era of policing often resembled a merit badge course for Boy Scouts rather than professional law enforcement training to prepare officers for gunfights. Targets were often bulls-eyes or simple black silhouettes which did little to prepare officers for facing human threats.

SWAT (Special Weapons and Tactics) teams were showing up occasionally, but officers in SWAT found resistance from within law enforcement agencies. First, officers fought for SWAT to exist. Then, they fought to get approval for equipment and training. They even fought to deploy when a SWAT response was clearly called for.

On April 11, 1986, many detectives still carried two-inch snub-nose revolvers. The heaviest fire power at an officer's disposal was a Remington model 870 12 gauge shotgun loaded with four rounds of double ought buckshot. Such was the case for local, state, and federal law enforcement, which illustrates de-militarized law enforcement.

Platt and Matix, Militarized Criminals

Michael Platt and William Matix had a different approach to preparing for gunfights than many of their potential adversaries in law enforcement. They agreed they would not allow themselves to be taken into custody alive. Both had military training and regularly trained with their firearms. Both of their wives died under suspicious circumstances.

The two were armed with semi-automatic and automatic weapons. They filled magazine upon magazine with ammunition prepared for a sustained gunfight. These men had committed a series of robberies on banks and armored cars along the South Dixie Highway in Miami. They brandished their weapons and did not hesitate to use them.

Even though Platt and Matix had no intention of being taken into custody alive, they were not suicidal. Rather, they were homicidal. They had but one rule of engagement when faced with arrest: kill or be killed.

The Investigation

The FBI knew a pair of heavily-armed bandits had been hitting banks and armored cars along the South Dixie Highway. These men had killed before, and the FBI had charged themselves with preventing these men from killing again.

On October 5, 1985, Platt and Matix murdered Emelio Briel while he was target shooting in a rock pit. They stole his car and dumped his body. It would be months before it was found and a year before it was identified. Since Briel was unable to report his car stolen, his vehicle became a safe ride to and from their robberies.

These two killers robbed often and proved themselves to be shooters. They seemed to enjoy using their weapons, and both possessed firearm skills beyond proficiency.

On March 12, 1986, Platt and Matix were training with their weapons once again in a rock pit outside Miami. They came across another hobby-shooter, Jose Collazo, and feigned friendliness. Suddenly, their real personalities emerged, and they gunned down the unsuspecting Collazo.

Platt and Matix abandoned Collazo after they shot him and stole his car. Killing the car owner to steal a car had proved successful once, so the two added the move to their modus operandi. If these two were not stopped, many citizens would die guilty of nothing except owning a car.

This time, however, the pair had made a mistake. Jose Collazo was not dead. He had been seriously wounded and played dead. After Platt and Matix left the area, Collazo lifted himself up and walked three miles back to civilization and reported his near-death experience to the police.

The Miami office of the FBI were certain this crime was committed by the bank robbing duo they were pursuing. An investigative decision was made to withhold the fact that Collazo had been shot and his car was stolen. They felt that if the killers believed the crime was undetected they would use the stolen car. Having the description of the vehicle Platt and Matix would use during their next robbery gave an invaluable edge to law enforcement. This proved to be the key piece of information leading to the demise of this modern day Butch and Sundance.

April 11, 1986: The Plan

After analyzing the patterns of the previous robberies, Special Agent Gordon McNeill was convinced the shooters would hit the South Dixie Highway area again, and they would do it on April 11, 1986. McNeill determined the two robbery suspects had become so comfortable with their continued success that they had slipped into a pattern of behavior making them predictable. McNeill could not be absolutely positive, but he was certain enough to request a moving surveillance on that date to cover the South Dixie Highway area. The request was approved.

A group of fourteen agents out of the Miami office were gathered for a briefing, and the plan was explained. There would be a loose, but coordinated, rolling surveillance of the banks along the South Dixie Highway. A description of Collazo's Monte Carlo and its plates were given out, but it was fully expected that the car would have different plates on it.

Some of the key agents at the briefing were veteran Ben Grogan, Richard Manauzzi, Gordon McNeill, Gilbert Orrantia, John Hanlon, Gerald Dove, Ron Risner, and Edmundo Mireles Jr.

The assignments were given with great seriousness, but the interaction among the group was sprinkled with the light banter of professional friends. Law enforcement officers involved in such hit and miss endeavors often experience a conflict of emotions. Part of them feels that these efforts are just another exercise in futility, while another part struggles to fight off apathy because this might be the day of days. After assignments were given, all units hit the South Dixie Highway and spread out as assigned.

Contact

At 9:30 AM the radio crackled to life as Ben Grogan and Gerald Dove spotted the stolen 1979 Monte Carlo with two suspects inside. The suspects had not even changed the plates.

Grogan and Dove began following the vehicle as they coordinated with the other agents to respond and assist them. After a short time, other units converged, and Platt and Matix realized they were being followed by law enforcement.

Before McNeil and Grogan could orchestrate a controlled Felony Stop, the suspects fled. The pursuit was short lived because a series of rams were almost immediately initiated by the FBI. Platt and Matix's vehicle crashed and was trapped. Manauzzi was to their left, McNeill was stopped just to the left of Manauzzi. Grogan and Dove's squad was to the rear of the Monte Carlo. To the right, a parked civilian's car blocked the killers' escape.

Almost as soon as the careening vehicles had come to a stop at 12201 82nd Avenue, Pinecrest, in Miami, Florida, Platt opened fire with his Mini-14. He aimed his opening volley at Agent Manauzzi directly to his left. Instantly seeing the threat, Manauzzi ducked as the rounds came at him. Manauzzi had removed his service revolver and placed it on the seat next to him before the crash, but the impact had caused his weapon to fly off the seat and land not only out of reach but out of sight. Manauzzi was unarmed throughout the rest of the gunfight. He was wounded, but he managed to exit his car quickly.

By this time, Gordon McNeill was out of his car engaging the bandits. He would later say, "I was the calmest I have been when I exited my vehicle. I saw everything clearly with my peripheral vision, I did some shooting, I got shot, I bore down and took two more shots. When I ran out of ammo and realized that it was still going on… then I got scared."

Agent John Hanlon also lost his service revolver when his squad crashed into a wall. He drew his five-shot snub-nose back-up revolver from his ankle holster. Hanlon gave up his position of relative cover and ran, while under fire, across the street to assist Dove and Grogan, who were both exchanging rounds with Platt and Matix.

Mireles separated from his partner, Hanlon, and ran toward Gordon McNeill because he appeared wounded. Even though McNeill was wounded, he was still heavily engaged. Mireles quickly covered the distance carrying his Remington model 870 shotgun. As he came running up to McNeill's position, a .223 round slammed into Mireles's forearm, severely wounding the special agent while knocking him to the pavement.

Due to the severity of the wound, Mireles was down and nearly out of the fight. He would later say in a presentation on the gunfight that he thought of death. He said, "Death was like a seductress." The dazed Mireles would struggle to maintain a tentative hold on consciousness.

Platt fired the wounding shot at Mireles. In fact, Platt did most of the damage in this gunfight with his Ruger Mini-14.

Ben Grogan stood his ground with his Smith and Wesson Model 459 9mm pistol. Matix, who was armed with a Smith and

Wesson model 3000 loaded with #6 buckshot had only managed to get off one shot with this weapon, hitting Grogan's car. As he extended the weapon out of the window of the Monte Carlo, Grogan hit him in the arm, preventing him from doing any more damage. At this moment Matix was also hit twice by McNeill, in the head and neck, effectively rendering him unconscious.

Due to the collision, Platt's car door could not be opened, so he decided it was time to evacuate the Monte Carlo. As Platt crawled out the passenger side window, Special Agent Dove fired his Smith and Wesson 459 9mm pistol at Platt. The round went through Platt's arm, into his chest, and collapsed his lung. Even if Platt could have had immediate surgical care, he would not have survived this wound. Sustaining a fatal wound, however, did not stop Platt from continuing the fight.

This is why officers are trained to shoot to stop, not shoot to kill. If Platt had not been hit another time during this gunfight, he still would have ultimately died. The round Dove fired technically "killed" Platt, but it did not "stop" Platt.

At the time of the crash, the Monte Carlo had come to a stop against a civilian's parked Oldsmobile Cutlass. After climbing out of the Monte Carlo, Platt slid himself across the hood of the Olds. It was during this movement he was hit two more times by Special Agent Dove. He struck Platt in the right thigh and left ankle.

Platt slid off the hood of the Cutlass, took cover by the fender, and began to fire with one of his .357 revolvers. He was armed with a Smith and Wesson model 586 as well as a Dan Wesson .357. From this location, he exposed himself and was hit by Special Agent Orrantia as well as Special Agent Risner. In spite of his multiple wounds, Platt continued shooting.

At this point during the gunfight, Agent McNeill, initially wounded in the hand, struggled to load two rounds into his Smith and Wesson model 19-3 .357 Magnum, from which he was firing 38 caliber +P rounds. Reloading was difficult to accomplish with a badly wounded hand while trying to put bullets into a revolver covered with gore from his own wounds. McNeill managed to unload the brass from the weapon, and during the pained process of reloading, McNeill decided he would be better able to continue the fight if he was armed with his shotgun.

Even though the agents knew they might be facing heavily armed criminals, McNeill and Mireles were the only two armed with shotguns. They were also the only two wearing vests. These vests were light body armor, which could only stop handgun rounds and shotgun pellets. No FBI special agent in this fight had access to a rifle. As luck would have it, the other six agents who carried the M-16 rifles and MP-5 submachine guns had not yet arrived when the gunfight began. They did not arrive at the scene in time to make a difference.

As McNeill turned to reach for his shotgun in the back of his squad, he was struck by Platt in the neck and instantly went down. McNeill would survive, but he was temporarily paralyzed. He was out of the fight.

Platt was now shooting using his left shoulder and uninjured left hand. He wounded Orrantia with shrapnel. He fired at Dove and managed to hit Dove's weapon, damaging it and creating a critical malfunction that disabled the weapon. Then Platt aimed at Hanlon, who had been firing at Platt but had paused to reload his snub-nose revolver. Platt's fire hit John Hanlon in the hand.

Platt, even though he had been shot repeatedly, advanced on the vehicle that three agents were using for cover. Hanlon was down with his wound. Grogan and Dove were using the car for cover, and both had their attention on Dove's inoperable weapon. None of them saw Platt's ominous approach.

As Platt rounded the back side of the FBI vehicle, he shot Grogan in the chest, shot Hanlon in the groin, and shot Dove twice in the head. Grogan and Dove died at the scene. Hanlon would survive.

Meanwhile, Mireles willfully won his fight against unconsciousness and realized that the gunfight was as yet undecided. He concluded, badly wounded or not, he had to do something. He propped himself up and reacquired his shotgun as Platt made his way toward driver's side of the Grogan/Dove vehicle. Platt's apparent plan was to make his getaway in the dead agents' vehicle.

With one arm totally disabled, Mireles managed to aim his Remington model 870 shotgun at the feet and ankles of the escaping gunman. He fired once and put buckshot into both of Platt's feet. Mireles turned, propped his shotgun between his legs, and operated the pump action with one hand, ejecting the fired round and charging a fresh round into the chamber.

As severely wounded as Platt was, he still managed to get into the squad at this point. Matix had regained consciousness and worked his way unseen from the Monte Carlo into the passenger side of the Grogan/Dove vehicle. With both killers in the FBI vehicle, Mireles fired and cycled four more shots at Platt and Matix using the 870. He did not hit either with any of these rounds.

Special Agent Edmundo Mireles Jr. could have succumbed to his wounds and let them drive away. No one would have faulted him. Instead, Mireles pulled himself to his feet and drew his .357 Magnum revolver, which was loaded with 38 caliber +P ammunition. He began a labored advance on the would-be getaway vehicle and aimed his revolver. He fired as he advanced, alternately aiming first at Platt, then Matix, and then at Platt again until his weapon was empty. Five of his six rounds found their mark. Finally, it was over. Platt and Matix were dead.

Aftermath

Ben Grogan, a fifty-three-year-old veteran, and his thirty-year-old partner Jerry Dove, who had been planning his upcoming marriage, were both killed in the line of duty.

Every one of the special agents on scene, with the exception of Special Agent Ron Risner, was hit. Platt fired 42 Mini-14 .223 rounds and three rounds from each of his .357 magnum revolvers.

People outside law enforcement wonder why modern law enforcement officers train, arm, and equip themselves as they do. This gunfight, where the officers were so outgunned, under-equipped, and at a distinct tactical disadvantage from the moment the first shots were fired, set the law enforcement community on the march toward what some call militarization.

Militarization is not only equipping police officers with vehicles and equipment that stop bullets, but also properly arming and training them to meet the Platt and Matix criminals of present times. Criminals in this category of hybrid killers seem to have increased both in number and viciousness.

Now they don't just attack banks; they attack schools, churches, malls, and theatres. Their motive is no longer just to acquire money. They kill for no reason other than to pile up victims.

The surviving agents helped the future of law enforcement by completing clear and accurate reports and even traveling around the country sharing their experience so law enforcement agencies could learn firsthand from the event. This incident clearly influenced law enforcement agencies to, once and for all, set aside the revolver and transition to the semi-automatic duty weapon nearly one hundred years after its development.

Special Agent Gordon McNeill used this occasion to address the "Monday Morning Quarterback" phenomenon which many Law Dogs have noticed throughout time. Often these quarterbacks are in a position to publicly comment on everything that transpired during an event without having experienced any of it. Agent McNeill closed a law enforcement training tape by reading the words of Theodore Roosevelt:

> It is not the critic who counts; not the man who points out how the strong man stumbles, or where the doer of deeds could have done them better. The credit belongs to the man who is actually in the arena, whose face is marred by dust and sweat and blood; who strives valiantly; who errs, who comes short again and again, because there is no effort without error and shortcoming; but does actually strive to do the deeds; who knows great enthusiasm, the great devotions; who spends himself in a worthy cause; who at the best knows in the end the triumph of high achievement and who at the worst, if he fails, at least fails while daring greatly, so that his place shall never be with those cold and timid souls, who neither know victory nor defeat.

What is amazing about McNeill and his compatriots' four and one-half minutes in the arena was that, in spite of the fact that they were obviously outgunned, these agents stood their ground. These brave men drew a line with supreme determination, which Platt and Matix desperately tried, but failed, to breach. These agents never took a step backward in their battle against these malevolent killers.

Through their courageous last stand, Grogan and Dove made sure Platt and Matix would not take one more life save their own. Dove did not even retreat when his weapon was hit and suffered a critical malfunction.

Standing firm beside them were McNeill, Manauzzi, Risner, Hanlon, Orrantia, and last, but certainly not least, Edmundo Mireles Jr. Each agent risked his life, and two gave their lives. These brave men suffered terribly but prevailed greatly.

CHAPTER 28

LAPD AT THE NORTH HOLLYWOOD BANK SHOOTOUT

The view that police are militarized ignores the fact that officers still patrol the streets of this country in sedans and SUVs emblazoned with the words "Protect and Serve." They patrol in boats, on foot, on bicycles, and occasionally on horses as smart as Hickok's Black Nell. These officers are armed with their sidearm, TASER, and might have soft body armor under their uniform shirt.

"Shots Fired! Shots Fired!"

After the FBI shootout in Miami, it became clear that officers needed to update their weaponry to at least match the criminals they were facing. Nationwide, agencies gradually began to arm their officers with semi-automatic sidearms. This transition was slow, and even ten years later it was not completely accomplished. On February 28, 1997, police administrators all around the nation were finally and absolutely awakened by the 2000 shots heard round the world.

On this date Larry Phillips and Emil Matasareanu walked into the North Hollywood Bank of America. These two seasoned robbery veterans had fashioned head-to-toe body armor and were armed with illegally modified, fully automatic Norinco Type 56 S-1, a Bushmaster XM15 Dissipator, and a HK rifle. They had high capacity drum magazines loaded with penetrating rounds that turned police body armor into expensive T-shirts.

By chance, an LAPD two-man patrol unit drove by and spotted Phillips and Matasareanu entering the bank. They called in the robbery in progress. By the time the two bank robbers exited the bank, it was surrounded by an ever-growing number of proud members of the LAPD. "Surely they will surrender," the officers on scene hoped.

The robbers saw what they were facing and almost nonchalantly opened up devastating fire on the police. The staccato of machine gun fire swept the area. The Los Angeles Police Department fought back courageously.

The suspects were hit by rounds fired from officers' shotguns, 9mm handguns, and even some revolvers. These hits did not stop the suspects. In fact, these rounds did not even cause a noticeable reaction from the criminals.

While the street officers tried to contain the bandits, one commander sent an officer to a gun store to commandeer some weapons they could use that would stop these suspects. The officer borrowed a shopping cart and accomplished commandeering a number of weapons and ammunition to wage battle with these men, but he would not return in time.

As a walking gun battle developed, officers desperately tried to maintain cover as Matasareanu and Phillips turned squads into scrap metal. The rounds cut through patrol cars like they were made of Chamois cloth.

One officer bravely careened through the gunfight to make rescues in his black and white squad. Another officer commandeered a private armored car to rescue the wounded.

Phillips' End

The two robbers eventually separated. Phillips literally tried to walk away on a sidewalk, shooting at every officer he saw. One officer's round finally hit Phillips' automatic weapon and rendered it inoperable. Phillips transitioned to a handgun as he continued to walk and fire. Finally, an officer took careful aim at an unprotected spot on Phillips' head and fired exactly at the moment that Philips decided to turn his weapon on himself. The two rounds struck at the same moment; Phillips was dead before he hit the pavement.

Matasareanu's End

Matasareanu continued his deadly, but meandering, flight toward freedom. He attempted to commandeer a truck when its driver exited on a run. When Matasareanu got into the truck, he realized the driver ran off with the keys.

As Matasareanu exited the truck, SWAT arrived. The officers, who had been involved in fitness training when the call came in, entered the fight wearing their Kevlar helmets and tactical vests. This contrasted sharply with their shorts and running shoes.

It was their weapons, not their clothes, that factored into the outcome. Finally, officers were present who were armed with weapons on an equal footing to the criminals' weapons.

The officers pulled up with weapons on full auto. It was the first time in the gunfight that Emil Matasareanu sought cover after two shots to the chest plate of his body armor stunned him. He curled up behind a vehicle and returned fire. The SWAT officers exited their squad firing on the move.

SWAT officers Don Anderson, Steve Gomez, and Richard Massa heavily engaged Matasareanu, hitting him repeatedly until Matasareanu capitulated.

The officers cautiously approached and handcuffed the bank robber. Matasareanu demanded that the officers shoot him in the head, but they would not oblige him. Even so Matasareanu would die in minutes, partially as a result of his own viciousness.

There just were not enough ambulances to care for all the wounded. Matasareanu would bleed to death in the street before emergency medical personnel could reach him. They had been overburdened by the carnage Matasareanu and Phillips created. They were the only two to die during this epic gunfight.

There were eleven police officers, seven citizens, and one dog wounded by these two bank robbers. Miraculously, all the wounded citizens, police officers, and even the dog would survive their wounds.

Bravery Recognized

There were many officers who showed great courage at the North Hollywood Bank of America. The following officers were recognized by earning the department's highest honor, the Medal of Valor.

SWAT Officer Don Anderson

Officer John Caprarelli

Officer Tracey Angeles

Detective Thomas Culotta

Detective Vincent Bancroft Jr.

Officer Edwin Dominguez

Officer Ed Brentlinger

SWAT Officer Steven Gomez

Officer Anthony Cabunoc

Detective Kevin Harley

SWAT Officer Richard Massa

Officer Conrado Torrez

Officer Israel Sonny Medina

Officer James Zboravan

Officer Charles Perriguey

Officer Richard Zielinski

Officer Todd Schmitz

These officers were recognized for engaging the suspects, even though they were outgunned, and for ultimately ending the gunfight. Some were recognized for risking their lives to successfully rescue wounded officers and citizens.

Militarization

The FBI shootout, the Bank of Hollywood shootout, and the tragedy of September 11 sent a dramatic message to law enforcement agencies that police officers need access to special weapons and tactics for criminals, terrorists, and killers that comprise twenty-first century threats. Members of the public decrying "police militarization" are not the ones who will be running toward the gunfire when it erupts. They should not be the ones to decide what the men and women running toward danger should be riding, wearing, and carrying.

What the Bank of Hollywood shootout had in common with the FBI Miami shootout besides the officers being outgunned was the fact that the officers involved courageously stayed in the fight and ultimately won. The Bank of Hollywood shootout was won with the blood, sweat, and courage of the LAPD.

PART NINE

NEVER OFF DUTY

CHAPTER 29

STACY LIM.
THE HEART OF A WARRIOR

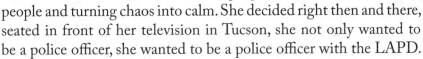

One night in 1990, a gangbanger armed with a .357 magnum found it was not so easy to quiet the heart of a warrior.

Stacy Lim grew up in Tucson, Arizona, and at the age of twelve realized her calling while watching *Adam Twelve*. This popular television program in the late 1960s depicted an older veteran showing a rookie the ropes with the Los Angeles Police Department.

She watched every episode as these officers went from call to call, helping people and turning chaos into calm. She decided right then and there, seated in front of her television in Tucson, she not only wanted to be a police officer, she wanted to be a police officer with the LAPD.

Her family eventually moved to Southern California where she started playing softball. While attending a college tournament, she witnessed the camaraderie of teammates of the California State Northridge College team. She decided she was going to attend college there and play softball on their team.

She was accepted at the college and had a walk-on tryout for the catcher's position and made the team as a freshman. In her first season, the starting catcher was injured and Stacy replaced her. She never relinquished the role after that. She developed a winning attitude at Cal State where her team placed second her first year and won the NCAA Division Two title her last three years in a row.

Stacy was known for her uncanny ability to calm pitchers into their best performances while she was behind the plate. While at the plate, she is remembered for her "big swing." Stacy was a long ball hitter.

She would need to apply that winning attitude established at Cal State in real life situations. After four years of college, Stacy was headed for the LAPD.

LAPD

At twenty-five Stacy joined the Los Angeles Police Department. She successfully completed the academy and then hit the streets in the iconic black and white squad of the LAPD. She was living her dream.

Stacy worked South Central Los Angeles and loved the life. She made probation and was on the department two years doing the "good works" of a police officer when, quite unintentionally, she became a legend... the hard way.

A Legend is Born

On June 9, 1990, Stacy Lim drove home from a post-softball-game get together, and she was tired. She had not been paying particular attention on the way home and did not notice she had been followed for thirty miles.

A vehicle with five members of a street gang called the Highland Park Crazies was behind her as she pulled up across the street from her home at 1:45 AM. As she stopped, a fifteen-year-old male exited the stalking vehicle and managed to approach unseen behind her. He intended to murder her and steal her car just to impress his fourteen-year-old girlfriend and fellow gang members.

Even though Stacy had slipped into an off-duty reverie, she followed a procedure she had practiced every night upon returning home. As she exited her vehicle, she took her pistol, which was tucked beneath her right thigh, and secured it under her left arm.

Officer Lim later described what happened next by saying, "As I stepped out I saw the barrel of .357 magnum. It looked like the size of a cannon."

Stacy still had grip of her weapon, so she drew it quickly and went into a two-hand hold firing position. She shouted, "Police Officer! Drop the gun!" While shouting, Stacy and her assailant fired almost simultaneously.

The suspect's first round hit her square in the left center of her chest. Stacy's round hit the suspect in the shoulder. Stunned, the Crazy turned and ran around the back end of Stacy's car.

The .357 round entered Stacy's chest, nicked her diaphragm, liver, intestine, shattered her spleen, and nicked the base of her heart after which it created a tennis ball size hole in her back as it exited. The impact caused her to take one step back, but somehow she maintained a good stance and proper grip of her weapon.

Stacy described the pain of that bullet traveling through her body in this manner, "If you take a javelin, heat it up about 1000 degrees, shove the thing through your chest, that's about what it feels like. A real burning sensation!"

In the moment she thought to herself, "No time for pain right now, I'll take time to feel it later."

She sensed the suspect had friends and she was still in danger, so she moved cautiously to the back corner of her car and leaned out a bit. She spotted the suspect with weapon in hand. He fired five more times at her, but the rounds flew over her right shoulder, high.

Stacy returned fire three more times, all of which hit the suspect. He was out of business. The gun battle inspired the other Highland Park Crazies to flee the scene.

It was at this moment Stacy realized she was seriously wounded. She began walking toward her home where she had a roommate. She was able to reach the bottom of her lighted driveway where she stopped. She said later she remembered thinking very clearly, "My blood feels warm. That's strange."

After thinking that thought, she rolled backward toward the ground but admitted, "I wasn't afraid, because I knew it was bad, but I knew I wasn't going to die." As she lay down on the ground she willingly placed her life, as always, "in God's hands."

When asked to put those thoughts into perspective she said, "It didn't feel like it was my time. I believe God will let me know when it is my time, and that was not it." She added, "I have always thought that it is important for police officers to realize people can die before it is their time if they give up. You can never give up."

Stacy's roommate heard the gunshots and looked outside. She dialed 911 and triggered another battle for Stacy's life that was just as desperate as the one Stacy had waged. The EMT's arrived quickly and placed shock pants on her immediately. They lost her pulse on the driveway but brought her back with the shock of a defibrillator.

Stacy was transported, and at the hospital Stacy said they had to "crack and spread" her ribs on two separate occasions and her heart stopped twice. On one occasion medical personnel had to manually massage her heart to keep it operating. Stacy would live to forget everything that happened to her for those seven days after she was shot.

Suspects

Officers at the scene found the suspect's fourteen-year-old girlfriend hiding in some bushes nearby. She identified the gang members who were in the car. She described how she even had picked out Stacy's car by saying, "That one would be nice." She said the others drove off when they saw Stacy come out fighting. All the accomplices were eventually taken into custody.

Back on Patrol

After surviving such a serious wound as this, many officers would be expected to leave law enforcement on a duty-related disability. This would be completely understandable. Stacy was determined she would resume her career and play softball again. She had to return to patrol for one reason, "The Lord put me on this Earth to be a cop."

Eight months after this deadly encounter, Stacy returned to duty without restrictions. By choice, she went back to patrolling the same tough streets she patrolled before she was shot. She felt it was important to go right back to what she was doing because she said, "I did not want to lose touch with what I got into it for."

Training becomes a Passion

In the mid-90s, well-known police trainer Frank Mika saw Officer Stacy Lim speak to a group and realized Stacy had incredible skills as a trainer. She was offered an opportunity to join the Los Angeles Police Department Training Team. She has been telling officers to "prepare your mind for where your body may have to go."

There are three reasons she is so very effective as a police trainer:

1. The message she delivers.
2. The way she delivers it.
3. She does not just talk the talk; she has walked the walk.

The message she delivers is positive, professional, and truly inspiring. Stacy explains that when you ask cops—and citizens—to describe the worst moment of their life, in a blink they can come up with an answer, but they usually struggle to define the best moment of their life.

Now Sergeant Stacy Lim says, "We concentrate too much on the negative. I choose to look at the positive and teach others to do the same." Stacy recognizes that not everyone she teaches accepts her message. Even so, she gives her all in every class because, "I speak for the one! The one person in class who takes that one thing away from class that somewhere down the line saves them. If I can inspire one person not to give up, then I have done my job."

Sergeant Lim teaches full time tactics for survival to the Los Angeles Police Department. She says, "Police officers have to prepare for the worst and hope for the best. Even if the worst never happens, we have to be ready for it when it does... A police officer's job is to protect people who can't protect themselves. Shame on us if we are not prepared for that."

In a violent flash, Sergeant Stacy Lim's life almost ended. Friedrich Nietzsche once said, "What does not kill me, makes me stronger." The Highland Park Crazies tried to kill Officer Lim, but all that .357 magnum bullet succeeded in doing was make Stacy Lim and everyone she teaches stronger.

As remarkable as her story is, Stacy insists, "For me all I did was what I had to. I did what I was trained to do. There was nothing heroic about it." From the outside looking in, it is difficult not to conclude that heroism played a part in Stacy's successful outcome. Stacy Lim is a humble heroine and a gentle spirit, who also happens to be in possession of an indomitable warrior's heart. Law enforcement is blessed to have her.

One may believe that God put Sergeant Lim on Earth not only to be a cop but also to be a cop trainer. God blessed you, Sergeant Lim. Carry on.

CHAPTER 30

DEPUTY FRANK POBJECKY. THE COP AND THE PIZZA MAN

In a recent run for sheriff in Winnebago County, Illinois, Deputy Frank Pobjecky was asked, "How can a thirty-one-year-old man such as yourself be ready for the great responsibilities of being sheriff?"

Frank answered truthfully, "I have had experiences that have matured me beyond my years."

This story may be the last story in *Law Dogs,* but it is certainly not the least.

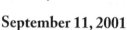

September 11, 2001

Frank Pobjecky was a teenager when he watched the World Trade Center Towers go down. He was so moved by the events of September 11, 2001, he, along with many in his generation, enlisted in the United Sates Army. Frank explained, "I wanted to give back to the country that gave so much to us."

At twenty years of age, Frank took part in the push to Bagdad in 2003, supporting the Third Infantry Division. As Frank, whose specialty was transport, recalled the historic advance, he said, "When they shot at me, it was my job to hunker down and keep on driving and that's what I did."

Frank did a second one-year combat tour in Iraq serving at the rank of a sergeant in 2005-2006. He survived the Improvised Explosive Devices, the ambushes, and everything else the war threw at him and eventually rotated back to the states.

A Terrible Crime Helped Frank Choose a Career

After two combat tours, Frank joined the Illinois National Guard. Upon returning home, like most vets, he had a decision to make. "What next?" His decision was partially influenced by a family tradition of law enforcement; however, there was another motivating factor involved.

On June 15, 2007, while pumping gas, Frank noticed officers around the home of his cousin, Nick Halsted. To his horror, the officers began hanging bright yellow crime scene tape around Nick's home. Frank left his car at the pump and crossed the street to find out what had happened.

Frank's mind swirled, imagining the worst. He did not have to imagine long. When the officer at the scene discovered Frank's relationship to Nick, he gave him the terrible news. His cousin Nick had been murdered.

Nick had been asleep in his home when at least three members of the Satan's Disciples Street Gang entered. These gangsters knew Nick worked at the post office and wrongly believed that anyone who had a steady job, as Nick did, must have large quantities of cash lying about the house. They wanted to steal some cash to bond out one of their gang members who had just been arrested.

The members of the gang entered the home and discovered Nick asleep. Without any regard for Nick's humanity, one of the gangbangers shot Nick below the right eye with a .357. Nick died instantly.

The Disciples of Satan fled empty handed. Three were eventually arrested for the crime. Two were convicted, and one was acquitted by a jury of his peers.

Frank was so moved by this senseless crime that he decided he was going to make a difference in his community. In 2008 he became a night shift patrol officer for the Winnebago County Sheriff's Department.

Frank went to work trying to make a difference one call at a time. He discovered he loved being a police officer.

All He Wanted To Do Was Pick Up a Pizza

On October 1, 2011, Frank Pobjecky was off duty. He decided pick up pizza for his family at his favorite pizza place, Marie's Pizza, known for its traditional Italian pizza. Frank liked to go in and order the pizza then hang about the counter talking to owner Vincenzo Tarara as he worked.

As Vincenzo began taking Frank's order, four thugs entered and loudly proclaimed that the place was being robbed. They demanded cash and cooperation and, in their own street vernacular, promised imminent death to anyone who resisted. To Frank, these violent young men seemed to be perfectly capable of murder. Frank thought it best to cooperate since he had left the house unarmed. He put up his hands up and began processing the descriptions of the robbers, hoping to be a good witness later. He thought this was the best course of action.

One of the armed robbers was not satisfied with compliance from Frank. He shoved the .357 magnum into Frank's face and made Frank believe his own death was imminent. Frank thought, "The bullet is going to enter right below my eye and kill me just like Cousin Nick."

Frank's opportunity to take action came in an instant when the gangbanger moved the muzzle from Frank's face to Vincenzo's. Instinctively, Vincenzo grabbed the hand of the robber, and an intense struggle was on between Vincenzo and the armed robber.

As the pizza shop owner and the armed robber grappled over the gun, Frank sprang into action. He knew that Vincenzo carried a gun concealed in a holster on his person.

Frank moved quickly behind Vincenzo and ripped Vincenzo's Glock 27 from his concealed holster and engaged the four robbery suspects in a gunfight. In seconds, Frank fired all nine rounds in the weapon.

Frank's shots were fast and accurate. He hit all four of the suspects with those nine shots. Three of the suspects were wounded and incapacitated by their wounds. They would live to be convicted of their crimes. The fourth suspect was hit, staggered outside, fell, and died in the parking lot.

Aftermath

This incident was extremely unique in that Frank engaged four suspects while off duty and personally unarmed. In spite of this handicap, Frank, by being aware of his surroundings, was able to acquire a gun owned by someone else. His decisions and actions were vindicated, and the suspects were tried and convicted.

His department, family, and community stood by him throughout the entire ordeal. Frank was ultimately awarded the Police Medal of Honor for his courage and decisiveness.

Since that incident, Frank joined the SWAT team and plans on continuing his life mission, to pursue criminals in his home county. Frank believes the criminal gangs that prey on the good citizens of his community are "homegrown terrorists."

Frank predicted his style of policing, "…will be popular with the community, but unpopular with criminals, drug dealers, and gang members. They are the problem, and we will be on their doorsteps attacking the problem."

Conclusion

When Frank was asked about his incredible actions inside Marie's Pizza, he answered in a manner similar to what so many other heroic people say after they doing something beyond the call of duty.

Frank replied, "I did what anyone else would do."

Frank's career is a current work in progress. He represents the thousands of law enforcement officers that continue to hit the beat 24/7, 365 days a year in this nation.

Frank and the rest of these officers start each shift by entering the unknown. Each officer has a story worthy of the telling. They police the streets of New York and New Ulm. They roll up and down the interstates and prowl the back roads, alleys, and county trunks across the country.

These men and women know, because they have chosen to wear the uniform and badge of law enforcement, some of the people they serve will admire and respect them for it. Others will malign, misrepresent, physically assault, and even try to kill them, just because they are wearing that badge.

Whether people respect the badge or hate the badge, they all have something in common. When the wolf is at their door, they will dial 9-1-1. Then they will pray for the speedy arrival of the people who have been driving the wolf from the door for over 200 years in this country. These are the men and women who have sworn an oath to serve and protect their communities possibly even unto their own death. Who are these men and women?

The Law Dogs.

EPILOGUE

This book began with a dedication to the 100,000 officers whose names were etched upon the walls at the Law Enforcement Memorial in Washington D.C.

As this book goes into publication in 2015, one such officer took part in the attempt to apprehend an armed fugitive. There was a gunfight, and at its conclusion the criminal was killed but not before he was able to shoot Officer Kerrie Orozco of the Omaha, Nebraska, Police Department. Kerrie succumbed to her wounds. Her name will be added to the wall in 2016.

In life Officer Kerrie Orozco was an officer who aggressively pursued criminals as a member of the gang task force. She was also an officer who compassionately reached out to her community by coaching kids and interpreting for the Spanish speaking public she served.

She had recently given birth to a daughter, Olivia, who was hospitalized after she was born prematurely. Kerrie had held off taking her maternity leave after the birth so she could use it to spend time with her daughter when Olivia was strong enough to leave the hospital.

Tragically, Kerrie was scheduled to begin her maternity leave the day after she was killed in the line duty. That was to be the day her newborn daughter was deemed strong enough to leave the hospital.

I would like to end this book with a poem I wrote originally for Police Memorial Day a number of years ago, which was previously published by policeone.com. At the end is a sentiment from one of Kerrie's fellow officers for all officers, family members, and community members, who have lost a brother, sister, mother, father, neighbor, or friend killed in the line of duty.

Messages from a Fallen Officer
by Lt. Dan Marcou

To My Partner
You did all you could; I fell and you stood.
You know sadness was never my style.
Those were the cards we drew, nothing more to say or do,
Except remember me, friend, with a smile.

To My Spouse
Don't think me gone, but away, I wish I could stay.
I'm not there, but our love did not end.
We had faith, we had love, sure as God is above,
I feel your love from here that you send.

To My Children
I know for you it is hard to be alone in the yard,
In that place, where we laughed and we played.
My girl, my boy, you know you still give me joy,
Live your life as I did, unafraid.

To Officers Left Behind
Each day you hit the street to cover your beat,
Prepare for the dangers you face.
Train hard, wear your vest, you'll be put to the test,
Each day with your family embrace.

To the Criminals
Now that I'm here and God's plan is so clear,
To you there is but one thing to say.
You steal, rape, and kill and abuse your free will.
Your time will come, when there's Hell to pay.

To All
I seem gone from you now, but I know that somehow,
We will reunite in another place.
For "The good they die young," is a song often sung,
But this verse is flawed on its face.

You see the good don't die young, but instead they live on,
In memories and many a heart.
The good that you do does not die when you do,
For the good, death's not an end but a start.

To all of you, good readers, "Kerrie on."

REFERENCES

This book would not have been possible without the following learned sources:

Section One - The Wild West

Chapter 1: John 'Jack' Coffee Hays - Texas Ranger

Kyle, Chris and William Doyle. *American Gun: A History of the U.S. in Ten Firearms.* New York: William Morrow, 58–60.

Weiss, Jr.,Harold J., "HAYS, JOHN COFFEE," *Handbook of Texas Online* (http://www.tshaonline.org/handbook/online/articles/fhabq). Uploaded on August 31, 2010. Modified on June 1, 2015. Published by the Texas State Historical Association.

Wilkins, Frederick A., "Texas Rangers: Birth of a Legend." *Wild West Magazine,* August 1998.

"Tribute to John Coffee 'Jack' Hays" (http://www.texasranger.org/halloffame/ Hays_John.htm). Texas Ranger Hall of Fame Museum.

"California and the Indian Wars: The Paiute War." (http:// californiamilitaryhistory.org/PyramidLake.html). California Sate Military Department. California Sate Military Museum.

Chapter 2: Samuel Walker. The Real Walker Texas Ranger

Adler, Dennis, *Colt 175 Years: The History of America's Premier Gunmaker.*

Kyle, Chris, and William Doyle. *American Gun: A History of the U.S. in Ten Firearms.* New York: William Morrow.

Nieman, Robert, "Sam Walker." *Texas Ranger Dispatch,* Issue 9 March 2002 (http://www.texasranger.org/dispatch/Backissues/Dispatch_Issue_09. pdf).

Robenalt, Jeffrey, "Sam Walker and the Texas Rangers and the Walker Colt." *Texas Escapes* (http://www.texasescapes.com/JefferyRobenalt/Sam-Walker-Texas-Ranger-and-the-Walker-Colt.htm).

"John Coffee 'Jack' Hays" (http://www.texasranger.org/halloffame/Hays_John. htm). Texas Ranger Hall of Fame Museum.

Chapter 3: James Butler 'Wild Bill' Hickok

History.com Staff, "Sheriff Wild Bill Hickok proves too wild for Kansas," *This Day in History: September 27, 1869,* (http://www.history.com/this-day-in-history/sheriff-wild-bill-hickok-proves-too-wild-for-kansas). Published by A+E Networks: 2009.

Hough, Emerson, "Wild Bill Hickok," (http://www.legendsofamerica.com/we-billhickok-hough-2.html). *Compiled* and edited by Kathy Weiser. Legends of America, Updated April 2015.

Richards, John P., "Chronology on Life of James Butler (Wild Bill) HICKOK," (http://www.kansasheritage.org/gunfighters/JBH.html). Kansas Heritage online.

Rosa, Joseph G., *They Called Him Wild Bill, the Life and Adventures of James Butler Hickok.* University of Oklahoma Press, 1974.

Weiser-Alexander, Kathy, "Old West Legends: Phil Coe - Gunfighter and Gambler," (http://www.legendsofamerica.com/we-philcoe.html). Legends of America, November 2011.

Wexler, Bruce, *John Wayne's Wild West, An Illustrated History of Cowboys Gunfighters, Weapons and Equipment.* Skyhorse Publishing, 2010.

"Benjamin McCollough," (http://en.wikipedia.org/wiki/Benjamin_McCulloch). Wikipedia.

Chapter 4: Deputy U.S. Marshal Bass Reeves "A Real Lone Ranger"

Burton, Art T., *Black Gun, Silver Star: The Life and Legend of Frontier Marshal Bass Reeves.* Bison Books, 2008.

Burton, Art T., articles on Bass Reeves.

Tzu, Sun, *The Art of War*, Translated by Samuel B. Griffith.

Chapter 5: Deputy U.S. Marshal Grant T. Johnson. The Best Law Dog You Never Heard Of

Burton, Art T., "Was Grant T. Johnson the Real Tonto?"

Burton, Art T., "The 'Tonto' of Indian Territory," History.Net (http://www.historynet.com/the-tonto-of-indian-territory.htm).

State of Wisconsin, *Domestic Violence Training Student Handbook.*

Weiser-Alexander, Kathy, "Grant T. Johnson," (http://www.legendsofamerica.com/wc lawmenlist j k.html). Legends of America.

Wigington, Patti, "The Legend of John Barleycorn," (http://paganwiccan.about.com/od/lammas/a/Barleycorn.htm).

Chapter 6: The Earps of Tombstone

"Wyatt Earp," (http://www.biography.com/people/wyatt-earp-9283338). Bio. A&E Television Networks, 2015.

Kyle, Chris and William Doyle. *American Gun: A History of the U.S. in Ten Firearms.* New York: William Morrow.

Tefertiller, Casey, *Wyatt Earp: The Life Behind the Legend.* Wiley, 1999.

Trachtman, Paul, *The Gunfighters,* Edited by Time-Life Books. Time Life Books, 1981.

Warren, Harry, "Wyatt Earp Theme Song," (https://www.youtube.com/watch?v=2HrY2Ynn4Jo).

Chapter 7: Bill Tilghman - The Best of Us All

Curly of BadHombres.com, "Bill Doolin." (http://www.badhombres.com).

Laughead, George, "W. B. "Bat" Masterson Dodge City Lawman Ford County Sheriff," (http://www.kansashistory.us/fordco/batmasterson.html). Ford County Historical Society, 2006.

Masterson, W. R. (Bat), "Old West Legends: Bill Tilghman - Thirty Years a Lawman," (http://www.legendsofamerica.com/we-billtilghman.html). Compiled and edited by Kathy Weiser, Legends of America, 1907.

Nash, Jay Robert, *Encyclopedia of Western Lawmen & Outlaws.* Da Capo Press, 1989.

O'Neal, Bill, "Bill Tilghman," (http://digital.library.okstate.edu/encyclopedia/entries/T/TI002.html). Oklahoma Historical Society.

Shirley, Glenn, *Guardian of the Law: The Life and Times of William Matthew Tilghman, 1854-1924.* Austin, Tex: Eakin Press, 1988.

Tilghman, Zoe Agnes Stratton, *Marshal Of The Last Frontier: Life And Services Of William Matthew Bill, Tilghman, For Fifty Years One Of The Greatest Peace Officers Of The West.* Glendale, Calif.: Arthur H. Clark Co., 1949.

"Bill Tilghman, Killed in the Line of Duty," (http://www.odmp.org/officer/15642-city-marshal-william-matthew-tilghman). Officer Down Memorial Page.

"The Three Guardsman," (http://www.jcs-group.com/oldwest/good/guardsmen.html). The Spell of the West.

Chapter 8: Deputy U.S. Marshal 'Heck' Thomas. 'True Grit'

Trachtman, Paul, *The Gunfighters,* Edited by Time-Life Books. Time Life Books, 1981.

Weiser-Alexander, Kathy, "Old West Legends: Heck Thomas - Tough Law in Indian Territory," (http://www.legendsofamerica.com/we-heckthomas.html). Legends of America, 2012.

Section Two - The Gangster Era

Chapter 9: The Legendary Captain Frank Hamer

Cushman, Russell, "Navasota Current on Frank Hamer," (http://russellcushman.blogspot.com/p/frank-hamer.html).

Nieman, Robert, *Interview With Bud Hamer, Bobbie Hamer and Harrison Hamer Texas Rangers Descendants,* (http://www.texasranger.org/E-Books/Oral%20History%20-%20Hamer%20Family.pdf). Waco, Texas: Texas Ranger Hall of Fame & Museum, 2006.

"Francis Augustus Hamer: 'Frank,'" (http://www.texasranger.org/halloffame/Hamer_Frank.htm). Texas Ranger Hall of Fame.

"Hamer, Francis Agustus," (https://www.tshaonline.org/handbook/online/articles/fha32). Texas State Historical Society.

"Red Lopez," (http://en.wikipedia.org/wiki/Red_Lopez). Wikipedia.

Auction of Clyde Barrow's Thompson Machine Gun on Youtube.com, (https://www.youtube.com/watch?v=RGpvn9UZAyk).

Chapter 10: The 'G Man'

Cowley, Jr., Samuel P., "My Father, Samuel P. Cowley," *The Keepapitchinin*, September 5, 2011, (http://www.keepapitchinin.org/2011/09/05/guest-post-my-father-fbi-special-agent-samuel-p-cowley/).

May, Allan and Marilyn Bardsley, "John Dillinger," (http://www.crimelibrary.com/gangsters_outlaws/outlaws/dillinger/1.html). In Crime Library, 2015.

Wack, Larry E., "Charles Winstead," (http://historicalgmen.squarespace.com/fbi-application-of-charles-b-w/). Faded Glory: Dusty Roads of an FBI Era, 2010.

Wack, Larry E., "Little Bohemia: Remembering Constable Carl C. Christensen," (http://historicalgmen.squarespace.com/little-bohemia-remembering-car/). Faded Glory: Dusty Roads of an FBI Era, 2014.

"Biography Baby Face Nelson," (http://www.biography.com/people/baby-face-nelson-9542636). The Biography.com, 2015.

"Machine Gun Kelly," (http://www.biography.com/people/machine-gun-kelly-507610). The Biography.com, 2015.

"John Dillinger," (http://www.fbi.gov/about-us/history/famous-cases/john-dillinger). FBI Famous Cases and Criminals.

"Samuel P. Cowley," (http://www.fbi.gov/about-us/history/hallhonor/cowley). FBI Hall of Honor.

"W. Carter Baum," (http://www.fbi.gov/about-us/history/hallhonor/baum). FBI Hall of Honor.

The Famous Little Bohemia Lodge Web Page, (http://www.littlebohemialodge.com/index.php/history).

Chapter 11: Delf A. 'Jelly' Bryce: The Fastest Gun-Fighter Ever

Chaffin, K.B., "Jelly Bryce: The FBI's Legendary Sharpshooter," (http://www.gutterfighting.org/jellybryce.html). Gutterfighting.

Conti, Mike, *Jelly Bryce, The Legend Begins,* Saber Press, 2014.

Owen, Ron, *Legendary Lawman: The Story of Quick Draw Jelly Bryce,* Turner, 2010.

Wack, Larry E., "The G-Men of the 1930's," (http://historicalgmen.squarespace.com/agents-of-the-30s-biographie/). Faded Glory: Dusty Roads of an FBI Era, 2010.

Wilson, Linda D. , "Bryce, Jacob Adolphus," (http://www.okhistory.org/publications/enc/entry.php?entry=BR030). Encyclopedia of Oklahoma History and Culture, 2009.

National Law Enforcement Officers Memorial Fund, *To Serve and Protect, A Tribute to American Law Enforcement.* Turner Publishing Company, 1995.

Chapter 12: The Most Difficult Shots Ever Made In Law Enforcement History?

Marcou, Dan, *The History of the La Crosse Police Department 1870-1989.*

Marcou, Dan, personal interview with Captain Clarence Koblitz (retired) while he was at St. Francis Hospital.

La Crosse Tribune archives

Section Three - Presidential Security

Chapter 13: Theodore Roosevelt of the NYPD

Klein, Christopher, "Shot in the Chest 100 Years Ago, Teddy Just Kept Talking," (http://www.history.com/news/shot-in-the-chest-100-years-ago-teddy-roosevelt-kept-on-talking). History in the Headlines, 2012.

Remey, Oliver E., Henry F. Cochems, and Wheeler F. Bloodgood, *The Attempted Assassination Of Ex-President Theodore Roosevelt*, (http://www.theodore-roosevelt.com/images/research/scholars/trattemptedassassinationbook.pdf). Milwaukee, Wisconsin: The Progressive Publishing Company, 1912.

Roosevelt, Theodore, Quotes, (http://www.brainyquote.com/quotes/authors/t/theodore_roosevelt.html), Brainy Quotes.

"Theodore Roosevelt Assassination Attempt," (http://www.shapell.org/manuscript/theodore-roosevelt-assassination-attempt-hearty-as-a-bull-moose). Shapell Manuscript Foundation.

Chapter 14: The Officers Who Saved President Truman

History.com Staff, "An Assassination Attempt Threatens President Harry S. Truman," (http://www.history.com/this-day-in-history/an-assassination-attempt-threatens-president-harry-s-truman). This Day in History, November 1, 1950, Produced by History Channel, A+E Networks, 2009.

"The Truman Assassination Attempt," (http://www.whitehousehistory.org/whha_tours/citizens_soapbox/protest_03-truman.html). White House History.

"Attempted assassination of Harry S. Truman," (http://en.wikipedia.org/wiki/Truman_assassination_attempt). Wikipedia.

Chapter 15: J.D. Tippit the Forgotten Hero of Day Everyone Remembers

Appleton, Roy, article on Tippit. *Dallas News,* November 2, 2013.

O'Reilly, Bill and Martin Dugard, *Killing Kennedy.* Henry Holt and Co., 2012.

"Officer J.D. Tippit Killed in the Line of Duty," (http://www.odmp.org/officer/13338-officer-j-d-tippit). Officer Down Memorial Page.

"J.D. Tippit: an Ordinary Life, 1924-1963," (http://www.jdtippit.com/).Oak Cliff Press.

Section Four - Doing the Right Thing

Chapter 16: Frank Serpico - Uncompromising Integrity and Courage

Kilgannon, Corey, "Frank Serpico." *New York Times*, January 22, 210.

Marcou, Dan, personal conversation with Frank "Paco" Serpico, 2006.

Maas, Peter, *Serpico.* Viking, 1973.

Serpico, Frank, "Police Are Still Out of Control. I Should Know." *Politico*, 10-23-2014.

"Serpico," Biography on A & E Channel.

Chapter 17: John Dodson and Brian Terry - Fast and Furious

Atkinson, Cheryl, interview with John Dodson, (https://www.youtube.com/watch?v=N23_I720Qi8).

Dodson, John, *The Unarmed Truth, My Fight to Blow the Whistle and Expose Fast and Furious.* Threshold Editions 2013.

Dodson, John, Testimony to Congress, (https://www.youtube.com/watch?v=--kOSO1o6uY).

Marcou, Dan, personal interviews with John Dodson.

Marcou, Dan, personal interviews Brian Terry's cousin

Marcou, Dan, personal interviews Brian Terry's sister

Section Five - Great Prevailing

Chapter 18: Officer Katie Conway,and the Night Unlike Any Other

"Kate Conway: Courage Under Fire," (http://www.enquirer.com/conway/). The Cincinnati Enquirer, 1998-1999.

"The Iron Will to Survive," Line of Duty Tape, Volume 5 Program 9, (http://www.youtube.com/watch?v=UIcJC68m9X4)

Chapter 19: Officer Marcus Young Meets the Devil

Marcou, Dan, personal conversations with Marcus Young.

Remsberg, Charles, *Blood Lessons: What Cops Learn From Life-or-Death Encounters.* Calibre Press, 2008.

Young, Marcus, "Good Versus Evil A Story of Officer Survival." *Law Officer Magazine.*

"Thank You Sergeant Marcus Young," (http://ukiahpolice.com/news/hot-topics/thank-you-sergeant-young/).

Chapter 20: Gunfight at the Sikh Temple

Marcou, Dan, Notes from an oral presentation given by Lt. Brian Murphy, International Law Enforcement Educators and Trainers Conference.

Marcou, Dan, Notes from an oral presentation given by Sam Lenda.

Chapter 21: That Day in September

The Memory of a Nation

The Fallen of September 11, 2001, (http://www.odmp.org/search/incident/september-11-terrorist-attack). The Officer Down Memorial Page.

Chapter 22: Officer Justin Garner, the Standing Hero of Carthage

Marcou, Dan, personal interview with Justin Garner.

Section Six - Great Detectives

Chapter 23: James Hume, Wild West Sherlock Holmes

Dillon, Richard H., *Wells, Fargo Detective: A Biography of James Hume.* The Write Thought, 2012.

Hart, Will, "Rebel Robbery at Boullion Bend," *Wild West Magazine* February 1996.

Hoeper, George, *Black Bart: Boulevardier Bandit.* Word Dancer Press, 1995.

McLaughlin, Mark, "Breakout at Nevada State Pen," (http://thetahoeweekly. com/2013/10/breakout-at-nevada-state-pen/). *Tahoe Weekly,* December 20, 2014.

Reader, Phil, "Copperheads—Part 2," (http://www.santacruzpl.org/history/ articles/71/). Santa Cruz County History - Crime & Public Safety.

Riggs, Charles, "James Hume, Wells Fargo Law Man," (http://blogs. wellsfargo.com/guidedbyhistory/2006/11/james-hume-wells-fargo- lawman/). Guided by History, November 3, 2006.

Waddell, James, "James Hume—Wells Fargo Detective," (http://blog. westernpowders.com/2014/07/james-hume-wells-fargo-detective/). Western Powders, July 11, 2014.

"Black Bart (Outlaw)," (https://en.wikipedia.org/wiki/Black_Bart_(outlaw)). Wikipedia.

"John Hicks Adams," (https://en.wikipedia.org/wiki/John_Hicks_Adams). Wikipedia.

"Sheriff James Hume," (https://www.edcgov.us/Living/Stories/Sheriff_James_ Hume.aspx). County of El Dorado, California.

Chapter 24: Detective Pierce Brooks Most Influential Detective of Our Times

Bonar, Samantha, "Criminal Mindset," (http://www.oxy.edu/magazine/ summer-2012/criminal-mindset). Occidental College Magazine, Summer 2012.

Brooks, Pierce, *"... Officer Down. Code Three."* Motorola Teleprograms Inc, 1976.

Marcou, Dan, "The Dirty Dozen: Updating the '10 Deadly Errors' of Policing," (http://www.policeone.com/police-trainers/articles/6900255-The-Dirty- Dozen-Updating-the-10-Deadly-Errors-of-policing/). Police One, Feb 24, 2014.

Marcou, Dan, personal interview with Lt. Dan Brooks West Covina P.D. (Retired).

Rule, Ann, *Kiss Me, Kill Me,* Pocket Books, 2004.

Wambaugh, Joseph, *The Onion Field.* Delacorte Press, 1973.

Dragnet episode designed after Pierce Brooks' Lonely Hearts Club Killer, (https://www.youtube.com/watch?v=61Wr5Vh-c8o).

Pierce Brooks Obituary, (http://www.sfgate.com/news/article/OBITUARY- Pierce-Brooks-3011469.php). *San Francisco Gate,* March 4, 1998.

"1959: Harvey Glatman, signature killer," (http://www.executedtoday.com/tag/ pierce-brooks/). Executed Today, September 18, 2012.

"Harvey Glatman," (http://murderpedia.org/male.G/g/glatman-harvey.htm). Murderpedia.

Section Seven - Real Community Policing

Chapter 25: Doc Holliday

Traywick, Ben, "Doc Holliday." *Wild West Magazine*, 1997.

Trachtman, Paul, *The Gunfighters*, Edited by Time-Life Books. Time Life Books, 1981.

Tefertiller, Casey, *Wyatt Earp: The Life Behind the Legend*. Wiley, 1999.

Weiser-Alexander, Kathy, "Old West Legends: Doc Holliday— Deadly Doctor of the West," (http://www.legendsofamerica.com/we-docholliday. html). Legends of America, updated 2015.

"Wyatt Earp," (http://www.biography.com/people/wyatt-earp-9283338). Bio. A&E Television Networks, 2015.

"Gunfight at OK Corral," (http://en.wikipedia.org/wiki/Gunfight_at_ the_O.K._Corral). Wikipedia.

Chapter 26: The Citizens of Northfield and Madelia - Minnesota

Davis, William C. *Spies Scouts and Raiders, Irregular Operations*, Time-Life Books, 1986.

Marcou, Dan, notes from Northfield Museum Tour

Marcou, Dan, notes from James Farm/Museum Tour

Trachtman, Paul, *The Gunfighters*, Edited by Time-Life Books. Time Life Books, 1981.

Younger, Cole, *Story of Cole Younger: By Himself*. Minnesota Historical Society Press, 2000.

"Jesse James. The Defeat of the James Gang at Northfield." *True West*, August/ September 2002 Issue Collector's Edition.

"Civil War Diseases," (http://www.civilwaracademy.com/civil-war-diseases. html). CivilWarAcademy.com

"The Retreat and the Battle of Hanska Slough," (http://www.angelfire.com/ mi2/jamesyoungergang/hanska.html).

Section Eight - Militarization of Criminals

Chapter 27: The FBI Miami Shootout

Anderson, Dr. W. French, "Forensic Analysis of the April 11th, 1986 FBI Fire-fight," (http://www.firearmstactical.com/briefs7.htm).

Marcou, Dan, notes from a presentation by Edmundo Mirales, Milwaukee American Society of Law Enforcement Trainers Conference.

Reed, Robert, "A Look at the 1986 FBI Miami Shootout 27 Years Later," (http://www.examiner.com/article/a-look-at-the-1986-fbi-miami- shootout-27-years-later). Examiner.com, April 11, 2013.

Roosevelt, Theodore, quotes, (http://www.goodreads.com/quotes/7-it-is-not- the-critic-who-counts-not-the-man). Goodreads Quotes.

"FBI Shootout," (http://en.wikipedia.org/wiki/1986_FBI_Miami_shootout). Wikipedia.

Chapter 28: Los Angeles Police Officers at the North Hollywood Bank Shootout

Marcou, Dan, notes from a presentation at the American Law Enforcement Trainers Conference in Los Angeles by Acting Chief of the Los Angeles Police Department on the North Hollywood Shootout.

Orloff, Rick, "North Hollywood Shootout," *Los Angeles Daily News.*

"The Hollywood Shootout," ABC News.

Los Angeles Police Department Medal of Valor recipients List, (http://www.lapdonline.org/inside_the_lapd/content_basic_view/27320).

Section Nine - Never Off Duty

Chapter 29: Stacy Lim - The Heart of a Warrior

Leech, Paige A. , "From Catcher to Police Officer, Lim a Legend Under the Gun," (http://articles.latimes.com/1996-07-13/sports/sp-24826_1_police-officer). *Los Angeles Times,* July 13, 1996.

Marcou, Dan, personal interview with Stacy Lim.

Marcou, Dan, notes from a presentation by Stacy Lim at the American Society of Law Enforcement Trainers.

LAPD—Life on the Beat, (https://www.youtube.com/watch?v=UhSACg_QWz4).

Chapter 30: The Cop and the Pizza Man - Deputy Frank Pobjecky

Marcou, Dan, personal interviews with Deputy Frank Pobjecky.

Marcou, Dan, notes from articles in contemporary news coverage as researched for policeone.com.

IMAGES

Chapter 1
Hays, John "Jack" Coffee: Public Domain

Chapter 2
Walker, Samuel: Public Domain

Chapter 3
Hickok, James Butler "Wild Bill": Courtesy of Kansas State Historical Society
Smith, Marshal Tom: Courtesy of Kansas State Historical Society
Thatcher-Lake, Agnes: Courtesy of Kansas State Historical Society

Chapter 4
Reeves, Bass: Public Domain

Chapter 6
Earp, Wyatt: Courtesy of the Kansas Historical Society

Chapter 7
Tilghman, Bill: Courtesy of the Oklahoma State Historical Society

Chapter 8
Doolin, Bill: Public Domain
Thomas, Henry Andrew "Heck": Public Domain

Chapter 9
Hamer, Frank: Courtesy of Texas Ranger Hall of Fame

Chapter 10
Baum, W. Carter: Courtesy of Faded Glory: Dusty Roads of an FBI Era
Cowley, Samuel P.: Courtesy of Faded Glory: Dusty Roads of an FBI Era
Hollis, Herman E.: Courtesy of Faded Glory: Dusty Roads of an FBI Era
Hoover, J. Edgar: Courtesy of Faded Glory: Dusty Roads of an FBI Era
Little Bohemia: Photo by Lt. Dan Marcou
Winstead, Charles: Courtesy of Faded Glory: Dusty Roads of an FBI Era

Chapter 11
Bryce, Delf A. "Jelly": Courtesy of Barclay Gibson

Chapter 13
Roosevelt, Theodore: Public Domain

Chapter 14
Coffelt, William Leslie: Public Domain

Chapter 15
   Tippit, J.D.: Public Domain, Courtesy of Dale Meyer From Warren Commission, Carlin (Bruce Ray) Exhibit 1, National Archives College Park, Maryland
Chapter 17
   Terry, Brian: Photo Courtesy of the Terry family
Chapter 18
   Conway, Kathleen "Katie": Academy Photo Courtesy of Cincinnati Police Department
Chapter 19
   Beckman, Neal: Courtesy of Marcus Young
   Young, Marcus: Courtesy of Marcus Young
   Young, Marcus with President Bush: Courtesy of Marcus Young
Chapter 20
   Lenda, Sam: Courtesy of the Oak Creek Police Department
   Murphy, Brian: Courtesy of the Oak Creek Police Department
Chapter 21
   That day in September: Photo by Lt. Dan Marcou
Chapter 22
   Garner, Justin: Courtesy of Justin Garner of the Carthage North Carolina Police Department
Chapter 23
   Boles, Charles "Black Bart": Public Domain
   Hume, James: Courtesy of Wells Fargo Archives
Chapter 25
   Holliday, John "Doc": Courtesy of Kansas State Historical Society
Chapter 28
   Medal of Valor Recipients: Courtesy of the Los Angeles Police Department
Chapter 29
   Lim, Stacy: Courtesy of the Los Angeles Police Department
Chapter 30
   Pobjecky, Frank: Courtesy of Frank Pojecky Winnebago County Illinois Police Department

INDEX

ABOUT THE AUTHOR

Lt. Dan Marcou, retired from the La Crosse, Wisconsin, Police Department as a highly decorated police officer with thirty-three years' experience. At various times throughout his career, he was officially recognized for his performance on the street. He was awarded Police Officer of the Year, SWAT Officer of the Year, Humanitarian of the Year, and Domestic Violence Officer of the Year. Marcou is an internationally recognized police trainer in many police disciplines.

Since retirement, Marcou has authored four novels. Due to his knowledge and experience, Marcou has been able to breathe realism into all of his stories. Three titles comprise a completed trilogy: *The Calling: The Making of a Veteran Cop, S.W.A.T. Blue Knights in Black Armor,* and *Nobody's Heroes.* In October 2013 he released his fourth novel, *Destiny of Heroes,* the story of a modern day warrior who is a soldier/police officer in relentless pursuit of an international terrorist.

"Lt. Dan" is a featured columnist for the largest online police magazine in the nation, policeone.com. Additionally, he was recently a contributor to the very successful Old West historical series on Fox News, *Legend and Lies.*

Dan hopes you enjoy this introduction to some of the best cops you never heard of past and present... *the Law Dogs.*